THE GOD OF
THE DEAF ADOLESCENT

The God Of The Deaf Adolescent

An Inside View

by

Rev. Anthony Russo, C.Ss.R.

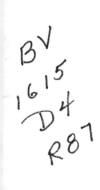

PAULIST PRESS
New York / Paramus / Toronto

IMPRIMI POTEST
Very Reverend Joseph L. Kerins, C.Ss. R.
Provincial, Baltimore Province
November 20, 1974

NIHIL OBSTAT
James McGrath
Censor Librorum
December 6, 1974

IMPRIMATUR
✢ John Cardinal Krol
Archbishop of Philadelphia
December 9, 1974

Library of Congress
Catalog Card Number: 74-27902

ISBN: 0-8091-1868-8

Published by Paulist Press
Editorial Office: 1865 Broadway, N.Y., N.Y. 10023
Business Office: 400 Sette Drive, Paramus, N.J. 07652

Printed and bound in the
United States of America

Contents

This volume is dedicated to the

GREATER HONOR
AND
GLORY OF GOD

and to the memory of

CARL MOORE (†)

a deaf adolescent

Preface

"Is God a man or a woman?" asks a seventeen-year-old deaf youngster. As the teacher steadies himself to answer, he becomes aware that communicating religious truth to deaf youth presents a special challenge. This book is a partial response to that challenge. It is the finished product of research begun four years ago because of a desire to upgrade the religious education of deaf adolescents.

Those unfamiliar with deaf people tend to restrict the handicap to a loss of physical hearing, nothing more. Yet deafness makes a profound impact on other areas, one of which is language comprehension, a point which is examined in the appendix and which will become abundantly clear as this study progresses.

Accordingly, those (especially theologians) who are inexperienced with deaf people should realize that the formulation and content of the questions and drawings were dictated more by the human condition of deafness than by theological correctness. To cite two examples: (1) the arrangements and contents of the drawings sometimes employ the proven principle of teaching the deaf by comparison and contrast; (2) terms like "proof," "heaven as a place" and "body and soul" emerge from the deaf youth themselves and they are retained for investigative purposes even though modern theology discards them. To single out the question on "proof," obviously we have no scientifically demonstrable "proof" for what we hold by faith. But the question, although badly posed and theologically unacceptable, was inserted because it is a live issue on the minds of deaf youth, as was discovered in the pre-testing. Our goal here is not to begin with theological correctness but to end with that theological correctness which comes from listening to what deaf youngsters tell us, a procedure that can lead to a catechesis designed specifically for the deaf. The information about to be laid out before the reader supplies, it is hoped, raw material for the future construction of such a catechesis.

An observation about prose style should be made. Early in the book, the reader will notice several genres: empirical scientific, religious hortatory, theological expository, and pedagogical. Normally, the presence of several genres in one volume violates the rules of rhetoric. Editing, however, has marked them off and kept them apart. It is hoped that the reader will find compensating merit in the function the genres perform, the function of cutting the vast tangle of religion down to size and still preserving a multifaceted presentation. It was felt, for example, that if we carry religious information from the deaf teenagers to the reader (empirical scientific), we owe the reader an explanation of what this information means (theological expository) and, once the meaning is clear, what can be done about it (religious hortatory and pedagogical).

I owe affectionate gratitude to others without whom this volume would not exist. They know who they are and they know that my hearty "thank you" extends to them. I would like, however, to single out several to whom I owe special gratitude: Mr. and Mrs. Arthur M. Blanche, Jr., whose initial encouragement helped launch this project; Dr. Eugene Albrecht of Villanova University, whose guidance in statistical analysis was invaluable; Rev. Eugene McAlee, C.SS.R., whose scriptural suggestions added insight to the manuscript; Sister Mary Immaculate, S.S.J., whose assumption of some of my pastoral work released me to devote more time to this project; Rev. Gerard S. Sloyan, Dr. McCay Vernon, and Joseph P. Youngs, Jr., all of whom read the first draft of the manuscript and offered suggestions for the final draft.

I thank the deaf young people and their hearing peers of the control group: their frank and friendly cooperation made the interviews a pleasurable experience for me. For allowing me to conduct interviews at their schools, my gratitude extends to the following school superintendents and their staffs:

William N. Craig
Western Pennsylvania School for the Deaf

David M. Denton
Maryland School for the Deaf

Lloyd V. Funchess
Louisiana State School for the Deaf

Ralph L. Hoag
Rochester School for the Deaf

Charles M. Jochem
Marie H. Katzenbach School for the Deaf

Rev. Paul Klenke
St. Rita School for the Deaf

Sister Nora Letourneau
St. Mary's School for the Deaf

Kenneth R. Mangan
Illinois School for the Deaf

Roy M. Stelle
New York School for the Deaf

Joseph P. Youngs, Jr.
Governor Baxter State School for the Deaf

Finances always support projects of this size. Therefore my deepest gratitude reaches out to the Raskob Foundation for Catholic Activities and to His Eminence, John Cardinal Krol, Archbishop of Philadelphia. Their generous grant is responsible for seeing this volume through to the light of day.

Seven years have passed since my initial interest in the religious formation of deaf youth was aroused. It was at the outset, as a member of the Catechetical Committee of the International Catholic Deaf Association, that I became alerted to the religious needs of the deaf. To the I.C.D.A., whose endorsement was so important for the launching of this project, I owe lasting gratitude.

St. Boniface Rectory
Philadelphia, Penna.

Rev. Anthony Russo, C.Ss.R.
M. Rel. Ed., M. Div.
Chaplain to the Deaf
Archdiocese of Philadelphia

LIST OF ABBREVIATIONS

CAT   — California Achievement Test

CMMS — Columbia Mental Maturity Scale

CNE   — Chicago Non-Verbal Examination

MAT   — Metropolitan Achievement Test

MP   — Merril Palmer Test

NCE   — New Catholic Encyclopedia

RBE   — Revised Beta Examination

WAIS — Wechsler Adult Intelligence Scale

WISC — Wechsler Intelligence Scale for Children

GLOSSARY OF TERMS

Deaf: in this study the term "deaf" is used as a noun and sometimes as an adjective. It refers to the condition of those individuals to whom spoken human language remains unintelligible regardless of the speaker's volume or clarity and regardless of whether the recipient is wearing a hearing aid. The Committee on Nomenclature of the Conference of Executives of American Schools for the Deaf defined the deaf as "those in whom the sense of hearing is non-functional for the ordinary purposes of life" (cf. American Annals of the Deaf, 83, 1, 1938). A clinical definition refers to the deaf as those with an organic peripheral hearing loss of 70 decibels or more for the frequencies of 500, 1000, and 2000 cycles per second.

Congenital Deafness: refers to those who were born deaf.

Pre-Lingual Deafness: designates those who became deaf before the acquisition of language. With the exception of the control group, all the respondents in this study are congenitally or pre-lingually deaf.

Siglish (Signed English): Fant in the Foreword to his *Ameslan* describes Siglish as sign language that follows English syntax. Siglish, he says, is "signing in proper English order," "grammatical sign language" or "schoolroom signing."

Total Communication: is Siglish and fingerspelling with a simultaneous speech accompaniment.

Verbalism: The empty parroting of a word or phrase without an understanding of its meaning.

John 16 WISC106 A (or V): "16" is the chronological age. "WISC106" is the abbreviated name of the aptitude test and score. "A" designates that the student is enrolled in the academic program, and "V" indicates that the student is in the vocational program. "AV" appears where the school does not have separate academic and vocational programs. This information allows the reader to estimate whether the deaf youth is "low verbal," average or bright.

Joseph 17___ A (or V): indicates that the school had no evaluative information about the student.

Strict Oralism: is that educational and communicative approach which avoids sign language and fingerspelling and relies solely upon speech and speechreading.

Fingerspelling: refers to the motions of the hand as it visually spells words by finger movements which correspond to the English alphabet. It is actually spelling in the air.

Sign Language: a generic term to denote visual gestures used to convey an idea or concept or the meaning of a word. It is sometimes referred to by the shorter term "sign" or "signs."

Ameslan (American Sign Language): synonyms for this term are "real deaf sign language," and "street signing." In the Foreword to his *Ameslan,* Louie J. Fant, Jr. gives these synonyms and describes Ameslan as a language wholly different from English syntax. English intrudes upon the sign-vocabulary, but not the sign-order. The gestures of Ameslan uniquely re-create in the air the event narrated or described. One might refer to it as visual picture painting.

GLOSSARY OF RELIGIOUS TERMS

Anthropomorphism: refers to conceiving God in human shape and with human attributes. An example of assigning human characteristics to God would be, for instance, to think of God as literally eating, drinking or walking. Since God is pure spirit, however, he has no body and therefore does not eat, drink, or walk. The human mind, nevertheless, often reaches for anthropomorphism when it struggles to express the purely spiritual.

Atonement: indicates a reunion or bringing together of two parties who had been estranged. A reconciliation takes place between the offender (man) and the offended (God). Because of his mercy, God initiates a reunion with his people whose sins had offended him.

Catechesis: that branch of the Church's pastoral ministry which concerns itself with the transmission of the Christian message and which seeks pedagogical techniques to clarify the contents of that message. In missionary catechesis, the term "catechesis proper" presumes two preceding stages: pre-evangelization and evangelization.

Classical Theism: while acknowledging and using biblical revelation, classical theism prefers to construct a philosophically based theology that reasons toward the existence and nature of God. The result is one God—eternal, free, immanent, omnipotent, omniscient, personal, simple, transcendent, and infinitely perfect and worthy of unlimited worship (NCE, Vol. 14, p. 10). A chief source for classical theism is the *Summa Theologica* of St. Thomas Aquinas.

C.C.D. (Confraternity of Christian Doctrine): the Catholic Church's official organization charged with the work of religious education. Equated in the popular mind with "Sunday school," the CCD in the United States reaches primarily for those Catholic youngsters enrolled outside the Catholic school system.

Christology: a systematic study of the person of Christ which focuses upon Jesus' identity and which describes him as indivisibly one and as simultaneously fully human and fully divine. The central problem of Christology is how to coalesce these two affirmations, humanity and divinity, without distorting or minimizing the one or the other.

Council of Chalcedon: distressed by previous divergences about the identity of Christ, Church authorities convened the council on October 8, 451. It settled the question by combining previous traditions containing Greek philosophy and defined one Christ, perfect God and man, consubstantial with the Father and with man, one sole being in two natures, without division or separation and without confusion or change (NCE, Vol. 3, p. 425). In short, the definition is the classical two-natures-in-one-person Christology that we find in the creed today.

Eschatology: eschatology is the study of the mysteries that surround man's end, his death, his particular judgment, heaven, hell, and purgatory. In a collective sense, eschatology treats of the end of the world, the second coming of Christ, the resurrection of the dead, and the general judgment.

Evangelization: the second stage of missionary catechesis, evangelization uncovers and elaborates the goodness in the "good news" of our salvation in Christ. It presents the person of Christ and his basic message in a way that moves and challenges the listener to a decision, evidences of which are (1) repentence, (2) earnest searching for Christ, (3) intensified prayer, and (4) a desire to live the Christian way of life. Recently the term has been expanded to include believers who remain blind to some aspect of the Gospel or who have lapsed into a spiritual coma and need resuscitation.

Existential: in this work the adjective "existential" derives from the noun "existentialism," the Christian branch of which has been elaborated by Gabriel Marcel. "Existential" indicates that an objective truth (or historical event) is brought to bear upon the deaf adolescent in his own concrete life situation. The deaf youth would view such a truth not as a spectator but as a participator. If we say, for instance, that a particular religious truth is existential for the deaf, we mean that (1) it spreads outward from the intellect throughout the psyche of the person, and (2) its insights are made alive again. It is immediate, not remote. And, if put to work, it affects the individual personally. All of this contradicts the limited view which narrows Christianity to a doctrine to be learned speculatively.

Hellenism: as used in this work, Hellenism refers mainly to that system of Christological thought introduced by Greek thinkers toward the close of the second century. They sought to develop New Testament Christology by mixing it with Greek philosophy, thus laying the seeds for Christological debates which raged from the 3rd to the 7th centuries.

Hermeneutics (here restricted to biblical hermeneutics): the science of interpreting or explaining the books of the Bible.

Pre-Evangelization: the first stage of missionary catechesis, pre-evangelization prepares the ground for the second stage, evangelization. Pre-evangelization, therefore, addresses itself to preliminaries such as divesting the individual of his spirit of self-sufficiency, awakening a realization that this is not the final world, performing acts of charity, or removing obstacles that block a true understanding of the Christian message.

Soteriology: a section of theology limited to the field of the redemptive work of Christ. It continually seeks insights into the process by which the incarnation, death and resurrection of Christ deliver man from evil and unite him to God.

Natural Theology (Theodicy): refers to knowledge of God that men can attain from philosophical reasoning about creation, working from the seen to the unseen. In popular terms, natural theology searches for the fingerprints of God in nature.

Theophany: an appearance of God to man. A famous example is the Mount Sinai theophany involving Moses and the burning bush (Ex. 3:1-10). The terms hierophany and epiphany are of similar meaning.

Yahweh: a Hebrew personal name of the God of Israel as handed down in one Hebrew tradition. Although God is known by other names, all Hebrew traditions unanimously affirm one and the same God.

I
Introduction and Methodology

1
Objectives of the Study

Like anyone else, the heart of the deaf person is restless until it rests in God (St. Augustine). Uniting the heart of the deaf person, therefore, to the heart of the divine is a major aim of religious formation. Sometimes, however, inadequate religious education falls short of this goal and dooms the deaf individual to the pursuit of an illusory or caricatured god.

Sometimes the teacher beginning apostolic work with the deaf feels that he or she can completely overcome the challenge of deafness by mastering a communication technique, whether it be strict oralism, total communication, the Rochester Method, or some other. Very little time passes, however, before the newcomer becomes aware that he faces more than the mastery of a communication technique, for the repercussions of physical deafness affect the innermost recesses of the human person—psyche and emotions.

Later, the more enlightened teacher concludes that the deeper issue of language deficiency is what needs most attention. All that has to be done, then, is to use the best communication technique to shore up the deaf student's weak vocabulary, teach syntax, and nurture the deaf to manage more effectively abstract concepts of immaterial things. Consequently the teacher, now a capable communicator with deaf persons and knowledgeable about their language deficiencies, searches the market for catechetical materials printed for children and adolescents with normal hearing* and adapts them to the deaf.

After initiating this process, however, feelings of uncertainty may envelop the teacher as he senses inaccuracies and begins to pour religious content haphazardly into the mind of the deaf, hoping that, like cement, it will coalesce. To anyone in such a predicament, teaching religion to the deaf is as elusive as shoveling smoke.

A coherent religious education program, complete with materials, texts, and curricula custom-made for the deaf, will lessen or eliminate smoke shoveling. Some such materials do exist, but many more are needed and much more work must be done in this area.

An Oriental proverb reads: "With one flower, spring does not come." Spring is that day when a comprehensive religious education program will impart new life to the deaf, for Jesus says to them and hearing people alike: "I came that you may have life and have it more abundantly" (Jn. 10:10). This study makes no pretense of masquerading as spring. Instead, it hopes to be one flower, a beginning. While one flower does not bring spring, it may perhaps germinate other flowers

---

*For the sake of brevity, hereafter the phrase "adolescents with normal hearing" will be shortened to "hearing adolescents" or "hearing group" and the like.

and thereby fulfill the ultimate hope of this study—the development of more effective religious education for the deaf, the arrival of spring.

This study deals directly with the deaf themselves. It is written primarily for religion teachers of the deaf and those in pastoral ministry, although others in the education of the deaf may benefit from parallel insights. It therefore presumes a basic knowledge of Scripture and theology. The writing style is simple and clear, without being elementary or condescending. Abstruse theological language is held to a minimum.

The religious thinking of the deaf is the concern of this book. It would be foolhardy, however, to attempt to cover the entire area of religious thought; the area had to be narrowed. The decision to focus upon fundamental or basic Christianity was made after consultation with several deaf adults. More precisely, it was decided to explore the question of God, the most basic of all; for all other issues such as revelation, grace, sacraments, covenant, Church, and eternal life become mere fabrications if there be no God. Salvation history, kerygma, and religious experience are some catechetical perspectives that have been stressed in recent years; but regardless of perspective, God is the unifying principle running through each. And it is the character and nature of the deaf person's God that will engrave a distinctive stamp on his entire religion. The objectives of this book, which consist of a primary objective and two lesser objectives, therefore center on God.

The primary objective is to obtain an inside view from deaf adolescents of their conception of God, to allow them to express themselves freely and thereby "paint a portrait" of their God. Hence, this is not a test, properly so called, but a diagnostic inventory in which no hypotheses are made. This study is being launched with no presuppositions. It seeks insights by allowing them to flow freely from the mind of the deaf, and proceeds with the conviction that an ambiguity well diagnosed is an ambiguity half clarified. The principal offering of this work, then, is the responses of the interviewed deaf adolescents, responses which are not empty words but a refreshing and honest revelation which imparts sure knowledge of the religious thought of the deaf adolescent.

Since the study finds particular significance in the responses, the raw data were first carefully recorded. Then the entire body of responses was studied and compared with the control group for each of the interview questions in order to formulate a statistical analysis, discern patterns and trends for each question, and present illustrative quotations from the respondents. The control group strengthens the study, since added insights are gained when the hearing responses are compared with those of the deaf. The responses of the hearing group bring the responses of the deaf into sharper focus and, on a given question, make possible an evaluation as to whether and to what extent the deaf share the thinking of their hearing peers. Two Catholic schools for the deaf (35 pupils) are included in the survey so that the findings on their pupils may be compared to those of the selected Catholic students in secular schools for the deaf. When noticeable divergences between the two groups appear on a particular question, they can be seen in the statistical analysis. If, however, the Catholic school students' exhibit a better comprehension of a given question, this indicates that perhaps the more frequent drill of the Catholic school may be responsible and there may be no need to look elsewhere for contributing factors. Conversely, if little or no divergence appears where one would expect to find a large one, this may indicate that the Catholic school instruction was to no special advantage. The primary objective encompasses all of this and is co-extensive with the inventory proper, the accumulation and presentation of the statistics, patterns, and quotes.

In addition, there are two lesser objectives which go beyond the boundaries of the inventory proper. Often the writing draws no clear line between the inventory proper and the lesser objectives. But the content will make obvious to the reader that he has left the responses and moved over into the lesser objectives. The first is a theological evaluation of the meaning of the responses. This usually takes the form of a theological commentary and a relating of the responses to what is already known from revelation and tradition. The value of such discourse derives from the light it throws upon the responses and therefore leads the teacher to a clarified view of the thinking of the deaf youth. The discussion, of course, is directed at the intellect, the sole exception being the treatise on conversion, where the writing reaches for the will and emotions as well as intellect. Faith affects the whole man. If it is absent there must be a change of heart before religious discourse can go forward. Correct conceptualizing remains essential to the on-going nourishment of personal faith and therefore the intellectual endeavors of theology can never be relinquished.

The second lesser objective is to draw parallels between the thinking of the deaf and the thinking found elsewhere. Brief suggestions will be presented that should illumine the faith of the deaf. The parallels became apparent after the responses had been analyzed and the study neared completion. Later these parallels will be elaborated; for now it is sufficient to say that they may be an interpretative key which, if considered in conjunction with contemporary language and experience, may open the door to a higher level of deaf understanding.

As for the suggestions, there are two exceptions to brevity: conversion and the Eucharist. Here, expanded treatments are given because at whatever age conversion is experienced and however it is conceived (i.e., as emotional and sudden or quiet and gradual), it is necessary for personal faith. The Eucharist, God continually with us, is at the center of Christian worship and is therefore of extreme significance.

From what has been said, it becomes clear that this book works from the views of the deaf adolescents through its objectives toward the future formulation of more effective religious education for the deaf. Along the way it can help individual teachers seeking guidance on specific religious questions.

As mentioned previously, the material covered in the inventory proper centers on God and is divided into three broad categories: belief in God, identification of God and relationship with God. The first two categories bear further comment. The initial inventory question, "Is God real?", along with follow-up questions, was designed to probe belief. Of the 140 deaf adolescents thus questioned,* 36 were apparently sincere in their non-belief although they had been baptized and reared in the Roman Catholic faith. After elaborating the reasoning behind their non-belief, the 36 adolescents were not questioned further. Consequently the remainder of the data is contributed by the 104 deaf young people professing belief in God. The control group was subjected to the same procedures, which revealed 4 non-believers out of a total of 24.

The second category concerns identifying the divine. Allowing for some deviation, the method used was the traditional list of attributes. The break-up of God into attributes is, needless to say, for study purposes only, since in reality God's attributes are unified. It must be emphasized at the outset that dividing God in this way has nothing in common with attempts to de-personalize him. An existentialist who was reading these lines might perhaps assume that the discourse which follows threatens to convert God into an object, a thing. But this assumption, as Owen points out, rests on a confusion of epistemology with ontology.[1] The desire of the existentialist to see God almost exclusively in terms of personal relationships deserves high praise, but it must be remembered that God merits adoration for his own sake, independently of the believer's personal relationship with him.[2]

Daily experience further confirms that we "talk about," "think about" and "formulate concepts of" people whom we dearly love, and our talking, thinking, and conceptualizing does not de-personalize them or make them any less persons. In fact, our thoughts about each other often result in mutual enrichment and deepened love. The hope is that the religion teacher, as a result of this work, may present a more personal and loving God to the deaf than before.

Long-standing and deep-seated differences of opinion as to the most appropriate method of communication for the education of deaf children have plagued the deaf and those whose lives are dedicated to them. This study refrains from entering the controversy. At the same

---

*At one residential school a mechanical error in statistical procedure necessitated the removal of 15 deaf students from the statistical analysis. Thus, the total number dropped from 155 to 140.

time, it chooses a course of action. The entire survey was conducted by personal interviews and required swift, easy and comfortable communication to and from the deaf adolescent. This was essential to the success of this work; hence, the method of total communication was chosen, with the sole exception of the Rochester Method which was used at the Rochester School for the Deaf. The use of total communication, of course, had the prior approval of the schools visited. The investigator presented essential English on his hands, using signs (with the occasional intrusion of fingerspelling) and following the order of English syntax with a simultaneous voice accompaniment.

During the interviews, communication ambiguities appeared infrequently because the questions themselves were simple and clear and most often accompanied with a drawing. However, when doubts arose, the investigator shifted into Ameslan to insure clarity. This happened, for example, in Question 10, the Eucharist, and Question 14, listing the persons most wonderful to the deaf and comparing them with God.

That the expressive and receptive language proper to this method of communication was consistently and accurately understood and recorded will be substantiated later in our treatment of "content validity."

2
Choosing a Research Method Suitable for Use with the Deaf

How does one test what is happening religiously in the minds of deaf teenagers? Their linguistic difficulties warn the investigator to shy away from group approaches that depend on written responses. For one thing, the jargon of the deaf (coined "deafisms"), so common in their written language, is likely to prevent accurate feedback. Even multiple choice or true-false tests could be suspect, since it is impossible to determine if the deaf person has understood a question clearly. Although pretesting can alleviate this somewhat, prudence dictates that linguistic complexities be virtually eliminated.

The questionnaire method is also limited in value because the written answers of the deaf may not accurately reflect their thoughts even if the questions are clearly understood. Furthermore, the answers evoked by this technique even with hearing people are usually brief, and they force the investigator to content himself with their limited scope without means of further exploration.

To minimize these problems and insure greater accuracy, we chose the personal interview method. This technique frees the investigator to clear up immediately any misinterpretations, to reject stock answers, to ask follow-up questions when necessary, and to use the total communication approach. It has the further advantage of permitting the investigator to build a friendly rapport with the one tested, thereby helping the investigator to evoke interest and insure honesty.

A technique was developed and applied individually to 155 Catholic deaf adolescents in the United States. Twenty-four youngsters with normal hearing in this same age bracket were chosen as a control group. An explanation of how this investigation was conceived, pre-tested, finalized and administered is given below.

3
Conceiving and Pre-Testing the Personal Interviews

Religion can be concerned with such matters as creed, code and cult, a scope so wide that anyone attempting to investigate it would do well to limit himself. Religion is also more than an intellectual exercise; it is belief flowing into behavior and therefore reaching into the deepest recesses of the human person. It involves love, values, attitudes, emotions, prejudices and mysteries. This study takes due notice of these aspects, but focuses mainly on understanding.

The *Survey Form for the School*,[3] a background paper filled out by school authorities for each pupil tested, contains questions on the pupil's emotional adjustment and family background. The influence of these factors on religious thinking is widely recognized and notations have been made on these areas for each pupil tested. To the extent that they have affected a given individual's response, they will be made known to the reader.

Our investigation focuses on the intellect while fully acknowledging that religious truth demonstrated by logic is not very compelling to youth, whether deaf or hearing. Nevertheless, a knowledge of the intellectual operations and abilities of the deaf is invaluable for the catechist. One must not make the mistake of downgrading the intellect, since God's work within the deaf person involves both illuminating and inspiring it.

4
Initial Design of the Interview

An inventory was devised to explore, in as much depth as possible, religion from the viewpoint of understanding. Although some questions were asked in sign language (total communication) alone, consideration was given at the beginning to the idea of having the teenagers draw pictures on given topics. Pictures would be vehicles leading to an understanding of their religious thinking. We rejected this idea, however, after learning that some investigators for hearing children discovered this method to be highly subjective, ambiguous and, above all, time-consuming.

But this rejected idea suggested another preliminary procedure which was adopted. A series of drawings was commissioned which would serve as projection devices. It was decided that in part of the first section on Belief in God, questions with no accompanying pictures would be asked in Siglish or Ameslan, while the investigator accurately recorded student responses on the *Interview Form*. A fourth question which required the student to draw a picture of God was eliminated for the reasons given in the previous paragraph. After the fifth question which is accompanied by a Nativity drawing, almost all subsequent questions have an accompanying drawing or group of drawings.

Careful attention was paid to the phraseology of each question; the search for a satisfactory way to ask each question proved no easy matter. To shape a question in Siglish, one must keep in mind a variety of pitfalls: the morphological[4] deficiencies of the deaf, verbal difficulties, ambiguities, local sign language differences, and finally the temptation on the part of the investigator to ask leading questions. Although there is a category of "natural" signs which are universally understood by the deaf, there is an area of "arbitrary" signs which may not be universally understood. In addition, colloquialisms abound in the language of signs; for example, New York City's deaf population has an entirely different sign for the word "be" than Philadelphia's deaf. These idiosyncrasies had to be considered in framing the questions.

After the pre-testing was completed, the questions were systemized. Flexibility, however, was still needed.

To contend with these sign language differences, the test was first scrutinized by an official competent in sign language in each school. The official then taught any necessary colloquialisms to the investigator who, in turn, was able to use them in the interviews This procedure of standardization with variation helped to reduce testee misunderstanding and also minimized the recording of inaccurate feedback by the investigator.

To allow the greatest possible freedom of expression, the pupils did none of the writing. After a friendly rapport was established, the testee was encouraged to sign as much as he or she wished in answering each question. The investigator then carefully recorded the response on the *Interview Form*, maintaining always an attitude of friendly neutrality, never evaluating anything in the student's response or attitude. It must be added that immediately after the deaf signed or responded with total communication, the investigator recast these into correct grammatical English, at the same time being very careful to preserve the entire meaning of each response. Thus, as far as syntax is concerned, the responses will appear in this book as though they were spoken. This was done for purposes of clarification and to continue the flow of the text.

The Personal Interview Technique means, of course, that deaf pupils were interviewed singly. The same procedure was used with the control group of 24 hearing teenagers. The schools provided a private room with a table and two chairs. In this way no interruptions were experienced and a continual flow of communication was possible.

All school personnel were instructed in advance not to inform the students that the investigator was a priest. This was necessary for several reasons. First, it was feared that the adolescents would feel inhibited in the presence of an official representative of organized religion, thus detracting from the truth and sincerity of their responses. All their energies would be diverted to telling this representative what he obviously wished to hear, saying nothing derogatory about religion and making him feel happy and satisfied. Second, rapport had to be established quickly since time was limited, and this informal climate was easier to establish with a layman rather than with a priest. Third, for the purposes of this test it was important to forge a horizontal relationship rather than a vertical one. Again, we reasoned that this could be done more quickly and more easily by a layman. A criticism could be made that the deaf are so honest that a bishop in formal attire could be a valid administrator of the test. This may be true, but we were convinced that the "incognito" approach seemed the less risky of the two.

5
Deaf Adults Study Basic Questions

The first stage in the construction of the test was a series of preliminary discussions with seven deaf adults; from these talks evolved a tentative picture and sign language interview. The adults were first interested in the content of the test and the investigator brought up with them the following questions: Should the inventory deal with the deaf at the human level or the level of faith? Should it treat of God more than of the deaf themselves? Should it concern itself with modern catechetical ideals such as the developing of a reverence for life, freedom, Christian social concern, seeing the signs of God's continuing revelation in everyday events, etc.? Should it stay with very basic Christianity? Should it include Christian morality?

It was the judgment of the deaf adults that current catechetical trends would not be suitable subject matter to probe since the deaf would have had only a limited exposure to them. Therefore, it was decided to test the deaf for knowledge of basic Christianity.

The inclusion of morality was primarily rejected on the grounds that faith would be a more vital area to explore. The premise is that if a person has faith, morality would follow. Jesus' moral demands, in other words, originate from his religious message, to which the Christian adheres. Conversely, however, Christian morality without faith makes no sense. For example, if a deaf person is to grow in love of neighbor, this should be the result of his growth in the knowledge and love of God who is acting in our society. A second reason for eliminating the inquiry into morality was the time factor. It took one hour to explore the area of faith, and it was felt that anything beyond this would fatigue the students.

The next question that occupied the discussion with the adults was: "What is basic Christianity?" The investigator wished to find out whether the term "basic Christianity" included grace, the sacraments, the parables of Jesus, the ten commandments, or the Church's infallibility, or, if none of these topics, which? The deaf adults consulted agreed that while these points may be important, there remains something still more basic which needs to be recognized by the deaf. This led to an even more fundamental diagnosis.

A consensus revealed that this study should seek a more precise insight into the minds of Catholic deaf adolescents regarding their belief in the divine, their identification of the divine, and their personal relationship with the divine. The following more specific questions were developed to explore the adolescent's foundation for belief: Why does (or doesn't) he believe in God? How does he identify God: as real or fantasy? as a person or non-person? as Jesus exclusively? Does he put any limitations on God? If so, what is the nature of these restrictions? To illustrate: Is God weak? helpless? aloof? strong? helpful? caring? Does the deaf adolescent have a sense of belonging to God? Can the deaf teenager enter into a personal relationship with God through prayer? How is this done? Does God respond?

This series of questions explores underlying belief: faith is the response of the human person to a personal God, "a meeting of two persons"[5] wherein the whole man is involved. If this personal act of faith never took place, the person is not truly oriented toward God, and Christianity has remained external to him. Thus, the basic subject matter chosen for our test was belief, identification and relationship.

6
Age Level of the Sample

Before the tentative draft of the inventory was embarked upon, a decision had to be made regarding the age level of the students to be tested. We asked ourselves if the child's religious needs and capacities would best be learned by testing at various age levels, if his religious growth went through stages of development.

We are indebted to the monumental studies of child psychologist Jean Piaget who showed that the child indeed goes through stages of thought development. Mythological artificialism, he said, characterizes a child's religious thought from roughly 4 to 7 years of age. This is a tendency on the part of the child to regard things as a product of human creation, a tendency which means that the child sees God as a powerful man and man as a powerful God—all-powerful and all-knowing.[6] Artificialism is shed later as the older child purifies his concepts through concrete and formal operational thinking. It would be most interesting to compare the process of the deaf child with his hearing peers as they move from the sensory-motor and pre-operational stages into concrete operational and finally formal operational thinking (12 to 15 years). Such an ambitious undertaking, however, is beyond the scope of this research.

Instead, we decided to work exclusively with deaf adolescents 16 years of age and older—the "wrap-up" stage in catechetics when they are on the threshold of adulthood with most of their formal religious instruction behind them. It was found that many of the deaf teenagers had not yet reached Piaget's final stage of formal operational thinking, an observation which will be elaborated later.

7
Size of the Sample

Having decided on age, we moved on to consider the size of the sample which would be representative of the national Catholic deaf teenage population. Working to eliminate as many variables and biases as possible, we decided that a random sampling of approximately 150 Catholic adolescents would be interviewed. Time and finances available also helped to dictate the size of the sample.

Fifteen pupils were selected from each of 10 schools for the deaf in the United States: 8 state residential schools and 2 Catholic residential schools.[7] All 15 pupils selected from each school had the following qualifications: they were congenitally or pre-lingually deaf, they were of the Roman Catholic faith, they had received some systematic religious instruction in a CCD or similar program, and they were of a minimum age of 16 (except in the control group where a few 15-year-olds were tested); if the residential school had the two-track system of academic and vocational programs, 4 or 5 testees were chosen from the academic department, and the rest from the vocational area; lastly, 7 boys and 8 girls or vice versa made up the total.

A control group of 24 teenagers with normal hearing was chosen from CCD programs in the Philadelphia area. These had spent little or no time in parochial schools. This selection was made in order to parallel their instruction more closely with that of the deaf youths.

Relevant background information pertaining to intelligence, the communication technique used at the school, and the emotions of each pupil is contained on the form, *Survey Form for School*, which school authorities completed. A copy of this form is included in the Appendix, as well as the *Survey for the Religion Teacher* which provides background information on the religion teachers of the testees.

8
Belief in God

With the above prefacing material agreed upon, we began to design a tentative draft of the test. Part I, Belief in God, was drawn up with the assumption that many deaf and hearing people are "conventional Christians," that is, their religious orientation is an accident of birth, and true faith has never touched their heart or influenced their actions. This portion of the test seeks to learn whether the deaf student is a real Christian, a conventional Christian, or no Christian at all.

After some hesitation about pre-testing phraseology, a straightforward first question "Do you believe in God?" was adopted, to be followed by "Can you explain why you do or do not believe?" To accommodate the low-verbal deaf, a parallel question was offered: "Is God real?" with the follow-up: "How do you know?"

In teaching religion at the Pennsylvania School for the Deaf and in pastoral work with the adult deaf community, the investigator encountered an occasional demand for some "proof" about God. This request for tangible evidence occurred often enough to convince him to include the word "proof" in Question 2. If the deaf person answered that he is a true believer, the investigator asked: "Do you have proof?" and if so: "What proof?"* If, on the other hand, the person responded that he does not believe, the question became: "Do you want proof?" If so: "What proof?" This writer cannot forget a liturgical wake service in which the homily concerned Jesus' raising several dead people to life. A deaf adult in the audience rose to his feet and demanded that Jesus raise the deceased deaf person to life. Nor can we forget three deaf teenagers who periodically asked for photographs—not paintings—of Jesus.

To conclude this test unit, the youngsters were asked if they wanted to see, meet or touch God.

On the assumption that there was some kind of belief, Question 3 addressed itself to the object of that belief. Instead of the questioner asking specifically for this object of belief, a different approach was designed that would require the deaf person to give this information without any leads from the questioner. The question became simply "Who is God?"—the answer revealing the object of faith. This simple query leaves much room for maneuvering. For example, the questioner can pursue an initial response: if the youngster answers that Jesus is God, a follow-up question might be: "Are any more persons God?" If the response is "Yes, Joseph and Mary are God," the confusion surfaces

---

*Obviously there is no scientifically demonstrable "proof" for what the Christian believes. The inclusion of "proof" in Question 2 is in keeping with our primary objective: to utilize information offered by the deaf youth to further explore their thought and thereby ultimately arrive at theological correctness.

and it becomes obvious that the teenager has no knowledge of the Father and the Holy Spirit.

Question 4 originally required the deaf teenager to draw a picture of God. After the pre-testing revealed this to be too time-consuming and impractical for other reasons previously mentioned, it was eventually dropped. Before it was, however, the teens at the Pennsylvania School for the Deaf had completed the drawings with results interesting enough to be shared. Nearly all of them had God as a bearded, long-haired male adult dressed in either a religious habit or robe or something resembling ancient Near Eastern clothing. Here are some examples.

Dennis exposed God's heart and commented simply that God is a "man with a good heart." Charles, on the other hand, drew God as a stern figure sitting on top of the entrance gate of heaven. Charles drew the gate meticulously, included a lock, and explained that it was now locked so that only God can open it—which he does not often do. Linda portrayed God as a remote king sitting on his throne in the clouds, entertained by trumpet-playing angels. Thomas drew God as a long-haired man dressed in a religious habit, including a rosary hanging from the waist. "Jesus and God," he explained, "are the same; but God has white hair." The pre-test sampling here, of course, is too small to justify deeper comment. The catechist may, however, wish to try this experiment with his own local group.

The next three questions—5, 6 and 7—are actually drawings which the adolescent is asked to identify. The Nativity Scene (Question 5) has the accompanying question: "Who is this baby?" If the reply is "Jesus," then the question which follows is: "Is Jesus God?" (a check on Question 3). The two follow-up questions which come with the Nativity picture are: "Is the baby God or did Jesus grow up and then become God?" and "Who is the father of the baby?" It is obvious that the questions are designed to shed light on the deaf person's understanding of the incarnation and divinity of Christ and the virginity of Mary.

A first impression of the casual observer might be that these questions are beneath any deaf teenager. Religious teaching experience with the deaf, however, warns one not to presume anything. The hesitant responses in the pre-testing reinforced the investigator's initial suspicions that these simple questions should be asked.

While they led to a wide variation among individual answers, the three identification pictures (Nativity, Jesus, Mary) still posed problems for the pre-testees. Seventeen-year-old Nancy, for instance, was not sure if the baby in the Nativity scene was indeed Jesus. Even after being assured of it, she simply did not know if the Infant Jesus was God.

When asked to identify the Jesus portrait (Question 6), Dennis said, "That is God, but I don't know (his) name." Gerald correctly identified the portrait but was confused by the relationship between Jesus and

God. When pressed further with the question "Are Jesus and God the same?" he responded, "I don't know . . . (that is a) hard question."

The challenge that these questions posed, coupled with the approval of an advisory group of deaf adults, led us to retain them for testing.

The identification of the Blessed Virgin (Question 7) serves to check Question 3 where many of the deaf had said that Mary is God. Although there was no problem in identifying the picture as Mary, the follow-up "(Are) Mary and God (the) same?" did dispel the confusion which may have cropped up in the earlier query.

In the pre-test discussions one deaf adult insisted emphatically that the deaf are "afraid of the cross," a concept which puzzled us because we had never encountered such fears in five years of pastoral experience with the deaf. Nonetheless, we decided to include this in the pre-testing. Due to the importance of the crucifixion, we ultimately retained the question on the final draft although no fear of the cross was manifested in the pre-test.

The aim of this unit is to ascertain what degree of insight the deaf adolescent has regarding Jesus' death as a substitution or as a ransom for sin, and whether his death has any contemporary value for humanity as a whole or for the adolescents' own personal life. The interpretations that the deaf young people put upon the death of Christ turned out to be revealing and will be discussed further.

To assess the pupils' comprehension of the sacrificial and vicarious nature of Christ's death, proper language for the framing of the question had to be chosen. Samples of formulations experimented with in the pre-testing included: "Did the Father want Jesus to die?" "Did the Father ask Jesus to die?" "Did Jesus want to die?" "Was Jesus happy to die?" "Why did the soldiers crucify Jesus?"

Larry answers the question "Why did the soldiers crucify Jesus?" with "Because the soldiers did not believe in God." Thomas, commenting on the same question, says: "The king told the soldiers to crucify Jesus." Gerald responds in cruder terms: "I don't know. Jesus talked back to the soldiers. Jesus was fresh to the soldiers. The soldiers were cruel to Jesus because Jesus did something wrong." These responses exposed the difficulties of literalism, difficulties which the questions on the final draft set out to explore more fully.

The questions which seemed to do this most reliably in a language (signed or spoken) understandable to the deaf are simply: "Why did Jesus die?" with the follow-up "Whose fault is this?" and "Anyone else's?" In those responses which revealed the most literalistic mode of thought, one last check was added: "Did Jesus die to forgive the sins of people?" or "Did Jesus die to open heaven for you?"

There was no intention to emphasize the crucifixion over the resurrection, the subject matter of the next question. Yet if the deaf pupils cannot put a transferred meaning on the death of Christ, the resurrection will mean little more to them than a magic act hardly signifying the beginnings of a universal resurrection of the dead (Col. 1:18), hardly signifying the ultimate confirmation on his identity and authority. Rather than formulate questions designed to probe their understanding of the significance of the resurrection, it was decided simply to ask if they believe in the resurrection, if Jesus arose in body and soul or only in the spirit, and if Jesus is still alive. As a check on the contemporary Jesus Christ, a question on God's living presence (Question 18) is asked later in the interview.

Still pursuing the paschal cycle, the next topic for scrutiny is the Holy Eucharist (Question 10 and the accompanying drawing). The illustration shows the large host raised by the priest at the elevation immediately after the consecration. Where the respondent showed bewilderment, an additional detached drawing of the host was shown. One can hardly underestimate the centrality of the Eucharist in Christian life and worship, since it enthrones the work of Christ and dethrones Satan, sin, and death. "He who eats my flesh and drinks my blood has life everlasting—and I will raise him up on the last day" (Jn. 6:55-56). Because of this primacy and its "supreme efficacy in building up the Church,"[8] it was decided to probe the mind of the deaf in this area.

We used the following technique. The investigator points to the drawing and asks simply "What is this?" If the teenager says or signs "communion," then the issue is pursued by asking (signing) "What is communion?" If the youngster answers that communion is bread or holy bread, the investigator pantomimes (or signs) the consecration and elevation and asks, "In the church, can the priest say words to change the bread and wine?" Another way of formulating the question in Ameslan is: "(Are) the host (pointing to the picture) and Jesus (the) same?"

Life after death, characteristics of such a life and God's activity in the after-life are matters of concern to the deaf (Question 11). The drawing is the tombstone of a man who died in 1971. (A curious sidelight of this illustration: some deaf youngsters asked who died and insisted on reading the deliberately obscured name on the stone.) The accompanying questions were easily comprehended by the teenagers. In addition to asking "Is this the end?" the investigator (pointing to the grave) sometimes asked: "Is his life finished or is there more life?"

Subsequent parts of Question 11 pertain to the reality and location of heaven and hell, God's activity in heaven, and his knowledge of what is happening on earth. To speak of heaven or hell as a geographical "location" may be far from theological correctness. Yet the goal of the question would best be served if "location" were pursued, since the deaf youth already think in these terms.

This terminates the first section of the Belief in God part of the test. As was stated earlier, this section purposely deals more with the intellectual process which gives light to the heart than with the probe of the heart itself to discover whether a personal act of trust or personal acceptance of Christ was ever made. Nevertheless, this personal acceptance and trust, often called living faith, is vitally important. It will come up again later.

9
Identification of God

It has been said that we have remolded God to our own image, become disgusted with the product, dismantled it and declared boldly: God is dead.

The research of Piaget and others show that the child, as a general rule, does not think of God as the adult does. The religious phase of the child's thinking, according to this authority, goes through stages culminating at the level of what Piaget calls "formal operational thinking." This last stage, usually occurring between the twelfth and fifteenth year, is the one which enables the adolescent to reflect upon his own thoughts, use analogies, raise and purify many of his concepts, and shape deep convictions about the future, the meaning of life, etc. It is at this stage that the adolescent sheds his materialistic notions of God and his previous need to "parentalize the diety." For the first time he can think more maturely about God.

Yet, it is known that some high school and college students adhere to caricatures of God. It sometimes seems as if every other area of their intellectual life grew, while the growth of the religious aspect was stunted. Such distortions emerge as: God acts arbitrarily—so be careful; God is someone whose feelings are easily hurt; or perhaps God belongs to remote history after having left a "deposit of faith" which the Church passes on to each generation.

It is surely obvious that the formation of the correct image of God pertains to the essence of Christianity. Therefore, it was decided to explore carefully the minds of the deaf adolescents in this important area. The Belief in God part of our test contains 11 basic questions on God, followed by questions dealing with God's attributes and how the teenagers conceptualize him.

10
Pantheistic Trends

Due to the monumental work of Teilhard de Chardin, there is an awareness of the participation of creation in the redemption. God is everywhere, but God is not everything. The latter view—that everything is God—is usually referred to as pantheism. If there are pantheistic trends in the minds of the deaf, Question 12 should discover them. The question seeks to discover whether God is equated with a tree, a city, children, an angel, the Blessed Virgin or Jesus—with an appropriate drawing accompanying each.

The investigator pointed to the drawing and asked, using total communication, "The tree is God. Is that true?" or "(Are the) tree and God (the) same?" Notice the progression in the drawings from nature (the tree), to man-made objects and people (the city), to human beings (the children), to a supernatural being (the angel), to the Blessed Virgin, to God. The progression of drawings was chosen because the pre-testing revealed that deaf youngsters answered that the tree and the city are not God, but that children, the angel, the Blessed Virgin and Jesus are God. The divine intermingled at the human level and upward. (This question is also a check on Question 3, seeking God's identity.)

The series of drawings which comprise Question 13 was difficult to assemble and the questions were difficult to formulate. The aim here is to ascertain whether the deaf adolescent is still at the fairy-tale stage of religion. Since the whole realm of the spiritual is not deduced from direct sensory perception, will the pupil relegate it to the realm of unreality or fantasy? Is the invisible necessarily unreal to the deaf? Are the deaf more limited in forming an understanding of the spiritual as compared with the hearing because of their limited sensory intake? This is a most difficult area to assess, and it is hoped that some insights may be offered as a result of this study.

A preliminary set of drawings used for pre-testing was prepared: Donald Duck, Superman, the Flying Nun, a bishop, and Jesus. The adolescents were shown these pictures and asked, "Is God like this?" The response was negative for all drawings with the exception of the bishop and Jesus. The wording of this question, however, was rejected as unsatisfactory because it is open to several interpretations. For example, God may not be like Donald Duck, not because the one is real and the other isn't, but because Donald Duck is an animal and God is not. To improve upon this situation, the question was revised to ask, "When you see this picture, do you think of God?" After some experimentation, this, too, was found unacceptable on the grounds that some of the pretested adolescents did not clearly understand the syntax of the complex sentence.

Finally, after further trial, it was found that the deaf adolescents clearly understood the following sign-language phraseology: the investigator pointed to the picture and asked in total communication "(Are) God and duck (the) same?" This became the technique adopted for this question. The picture of Donald Duck was replaced with a group of Disney fantasy characters. The drawings of Superman, the Flying Nun, the bishop and Jesus were retained. The progression now proceeds from pure fantasy (the Disney characters), to fantasy mixed with the human (Superman), to fantasy and human and holiness (the Flying Nun), to holiness and humanity (the bishop), to the reality (Jesus). With the control group, this progression was unnecessary. The hearing teenagers were shown the drawing of the Disney characters and simply asked: "Do you consider God as a part of the world of reality or fantasy?"

11
God's Personality

The next group of questions (14) concern the quality of God's character. Is it positive, negative or arbitrary in the mind of the deaf adolescent? Is God concerned about men? Fair in his dealings with men? A punisher? Aloof?

To obtain from them the degree of intensity of God's love, a specific comparison was supplied to the youngsters. They were asked to list five persons who have been most wonderful and loving to them, beginning with the best and ranking them in order down to number five. "Who loves you the best?" asked the investigator, adding, "Give that person number 1." Another way this question was asked in total communication was by making use of the spatial relations of sign language. Number 1 was signed high, above the head, accompanied by the sign "best person." Number 2 was signed under it, with 3, 4, and 5 in descending order. The investigator handed the pen to the respondent who proceeded to write the five names in order.

Upon completion of the ranking, the investigator compared God with each name on the list, beginning with number 5: "Does God love you more than ___name___ (#5) loves you, less than ___name___ (#5) loves you, or equal?" The same mode of questioning is used for each number until the love of God is identified with or shown to surpass the love of a person on the list. This comparison technique, understood well in the preliminary stages, was adopted for the final version of the test. In the tentative version, Nancy, quickly grasping the meaning of the question, wrote "(1) Uncle Tony, (2) mother, (3) sister Patty, (4) cousin Davy."

However, when the investigator began the comparison of each person with God, Nancy insisted that God loves *all* people. When probed about God's *personal* love for her, Nancy said that she did not know if God loved *her*. Such doubting of God's personal love for the individual is an interesting phenomenon. In the testing, numerous able pupils answered as Nancy did. The repercussions this will have on the deaf youngster's view of Christianity is of utmost significance and will be pursued later. A partial check on this is provided in Question 15, where the testee is asked if God knows *him, his* name and *his* address. This question will also be studied in connection with Question 26 (Does God love the deaf or hearing people more?).

Pursuing the same thought concerning the qualities of God's personality, the young person is assured that he is a fine person and then asked if God is a better person than he is. More than a few adults conceive of God as stern. "Jesus never smiled," they say. God, they would have us think, is perennially unhappy. To what degree do the deaf youth share in this? To find out, a drawing of an angry man was made.

Various modes of presenting the question were experimented with in the tentative stage—e.g., "Is it easy to hurt God's feelings?" In the final version it was decided to simply ask: "Is God angry like this man?" followed by, "If so, is he always angry or sometimes angry, and why?"

Initially, it was pondered that perhaps an investigation into the thought of the deaf on God's justice might be fruitful. A series of drawings was made showing a boy stealing a specified number of apples each week from a market, his friend stealing some from him, and God punishing them both. The drawings and questions were geared to see if the deaf could distinguish between retributive and distributive justice. This approach was rejected because of both a time and complexity factor. We posed instead the following more basic questions without accompanying illustrations: "Does God punish people?" "Often or sometimes?" "Now or later?" "Who told you that God punished people?" "Are you afraid of God?" "If so, when?"

At the conclusion of this package of questions a judgment is made on the adolescent's classification of God's character as positive, negative or arbitrary.

12
God's Knowledge

The next block of drawings, for Question 15, concerns God's knowledge. The import of this is relevant especially in relationship to God's love, for if the divine knowledge is restricted, then he may be unaware of the existence of the individual deaf person. Divine knowledge is also a significant dimension in the pupil's overall view of God as a person and the limitations, if any, which the deaf adolescent may place upon the deity. It also may have an effect upon communication with God, since—if his knowledge or intellectual acumen were limited—he may not be aware that the deaf person is praying to him, may not understand sign-language, and may not know what is happening within the mind of the deaf. Therefore, trying to contact him may be futile.

To examine this area a package of 5 drawings with accompanying questions and 3 additional questions without pictures was devised. The first drawing is of simple arithmetic: $2 + 2 = 4$. The investigator points to the picture and asks: "Does God know more than $2 + 2 = 4$?" In the preliminary experimentation, two low-verbal deaf youngsters responded to this in the negative, saying that "God did not go to school." This relegation of God to straight history was disturbing. Because of this, we included a follow-up question in the final version: "Does God know the new math?" Where the deaf adolescent showed no familiarity with the new math, the question was dropped. The second drawing, demanding more knowledge of God, is of a chemistry teacher explaining a lesson. The question is: "Does God know more than this teacher?" The third picture steps up to a higher plane of knowledge. It shows President Nixon who, along with any other president, would personify vast knowledge to the deaf teenager. (Although this may not be as true nowadays as formerly, it was judged to be valid enough for test purposes at that time, which was pre-Watergate.) The fourth drawing in the package is a boy with a balloon caption containing a bat and baseball. The investigator points to the boy and asks, "What is the boy dreaming about?" After receiving the correct answer, a second question is asked: "Does God know that the boy is dreaming about baseball?"

Finally, a print stating that God knows the most is presented to the adolescent, and he is asked to comment on whether this statement is true.

To bring divine knowledge down to the personal level in order to see if it has any bearing on the private life of the teenager, three additional questions (15 f, g, h) without drawings were asked: "Does God know *you*?" "Does God know *your* name?" "Does God know *your* address?" Our search here is centered on whether the deaf adolescent reduces divine knowledge to human dimensions and if God's intellectual abilities and operations are linked to his own personal life.

13
God's Power

Divine power is the subject of the next question (16) and corresponding picture series (also related to Question 11 on God's activity). Is God's power unlimited or reducible to human proportions? A restricted or weakened God could hardly establish the laws of nature, govern the universe absolutely, or, more meaningfully, influence or help the deaf adolescent in distress. If there is a limit to God's strength, he may not be *able* to establish a relationship with the deaf even if he wished to —a major reason why this question is considered significant in the testee's overall view of God.

In the preliminary version, five detached pictures were devised showing a progression of increasing strength: a boy pulling a wagon, to a weightlifter, then, beyond the human, to a train, a rocket, and God. (Instead of drawing a picture of Jesus it was decided to print the word God, which would give a neutral appearance and thereby be more reliable for test purposes.) The respondent was then asked to arrange the pictures in order from the weakest to the strongest.

Another approach was also tried. The investigator took each picture, held the "God" card next to it, and asked, "Who is stronger?" These approaches were good and evoked a valid response from the deaf. Yet they consumed too much time. To conserve time, a third approach was used in the final version. The adolescent was shown the pictures in succession of increasing strength and was asked, "Is God stronger than this boy?" "Is God stronger than the weightlifter?" "Is the train more powerful than God?" "Is the rocket more powerful than God?"

14
God's Eternity

Are the deaf youth aware that God has no beginning or end, or is there a possibility that God can die and that God was born? Does God fall within our concept of time? Can God age? These questions, all pertaining to God's eternity, are the concern of Question 17. A previous study[10] showed this idea of God and time or God's eternity to be poorly apprehended by many deaf pupils. Since almost as many did not understand the idea as those who did, it became apparent that this area would be most difficult to test. Many changes were made between the first and final draft in the interest of presenting this clearly to the deaf. First, a succession of drawings were made, beginning with the shortest life and ending with the longest life: an infant, a child, a middle-aged man and an elderly man. Added to this were the Roman Colosseum, a relic from the Stone Age, and a card containing the word "God." These were all detached. The pupil was asked to examine and arrange them in order, starting with the youngest and ending with the oldest. The "God" card placed after the Stone Age relic would indicate that God existed before the Stone Age.

As follow-up questions, we decided to ask if God *always* existed and if God always *will* exist. When tried out with the pre-test group, this process proved cumbersome. Interruptions were experienced as the deaf stopped to ask the meaning of the Colosseum and the relic. After receiving satisfaction from the investigator's explanation, the pupils grappled with picture-sorting. Unfortunately, however, too great a time-lag developed and the procedure had to be streamlined: The Colosseum and relic were omitted, the age progression from youngest to oldest was reversed and the respondent was not required to arrange the drawings.

The following procedure was devised. The drawing of an old man was shown first with a comment that he may die in two or three years. The deaf youth was then asked, "Will God die in two or three years?" The middle-aged man was shown second with the remark that he may die in 20 or 30 years and the question asking if God may die in 20 or 30 years. The same process was used with the remaining drawings with a variable of a longer time span. For example, the infant may die in 70 or 80 years; will God die in 70 or 80 years? Finally, a calendar was presented with a pantomime depicting the passing of the years and accompanied by the questions: "Does God get older and older?" "How old is Jesus?" Soon into the actual interviews, the deaf students quickly dissipated the investigator's initial hypothesis that this would be a difficult point for the deaf. Numerous boys and girls interrupted the process to say simply, "God will never die." The investigator then dispensed with this process with bright pupils and asked two questions: "Will God die?"

"Was God born?" He also offered explanations and asked follow-up questions to clarify ambiguities or misconceptions. Further discussion would reveal that the deaf are certain that God will not die, but there was considerable confusion regarding divine beginnings.

In the Christmas liturgy, one hears the cry "Emmanuel"—God with us. Do deaf adolescents think that God (or Jesus) is still with us? Is God a contemporary living figure or has he merely passed into history like Caesar, Alexander the Great, and all mortals? Question 18 purports to find out while also checking Question 9 on the resurrection. The method chosen to test this was a matching technique. The artist was instructed to make a total of six drawings: two rows of three drawings each. Row A consists of three deceased historical personages well known to these students; Row B consists of three famous living persons.

George Washington, Abraham Lincoln and John F. Kennedy were selected for Row A. Row B was more difficult to decide upon, since three living figures whom the pupil would recognize had to be found. President Nixon and John Wayne were accepted, but deaf adults who were consulted could not agree on the third. After some discussion, it was agreed to use Mickey Mantle—with a short explanation where necessary. The investigator confronted the adolescent with the two line-ups, assuring him that Row A is deceased and Row B is living. The testee received a portrait of Christ and was asked if he would line up Christ with Row A, Row B, or both. If the pupil put Christ in Row A, he would likely conceive of Christ as a mere historical character, unresurrected, and of limited consequences for our society or the student's life.

15
God's Location

One of the most intriguing parts of this study concerns the deaf person's conception of the location of the divine. Is God everywhere? Is he circumscribed in space? *How* is God everywhere? Is he aloof in a separate world? Is he part of our world? A package of drawings for Question 19 was designed to uncover the viewpoint of the deaf.

The adolescent is shown the first drawing of deep space and asked, "Is God out here in the stars?" The second picture, a farm, is presented with the question, "Is God here on the farm?" A city is the content of the third drawing and has an accompanying question following the same pattern: "Is God in the city?" The illustration of an empty living room carries the question, "Is God in the room?" The head of a man was first used for the fifth drawing, but for the sake of greater clarity a full figure was adopted for the final version. The teenager is asked if God is in the man. Finally, a drawing of a church is presented with the question, "Is God in the church?" Assuming an affirmative answer, two follow-up questions were designed: "Is God in all churches or some churches?" If he is in some churches, then "What churches?" If he is in all churches, then "Is God in all churches at the same time or at different times?"

An additional step was taken in the tentative version of the inventory. If the respondent showed no discriminations, freely acknowledging that God is present in each of the six locales, the adolescent was asked if he thought there is a place where God is not. If so, he was asked to draw a picture of that place. This last request was prompted by a social conversation the investigator had with Richard. When asked to explain the poor performance of his school's varsity football team, Richard, himself a player, responded by signing, "The coach is soft." This use of a figure of speech illustrates Richard's capacity for abstract thought. Yet Richard's materialistic conception of God prevented him from applying this capacity to religion. According to Richard, God has a powerful pair of physical eyes, but even he cannot see everywhere. "Can God see you if you are swimming under water?" inquired the investigator. "Yes," Richard volunteered, "but not if the water is dirty." Startling responses like Richard's led to the inclusion of the request to draw a picture of where God is absent. Unfortunately once again the art work was taking up too much time and had to be eliminated on the final draft.

Is there any link between the life of the adolescent and God? Did God give the deaf person life? Does God give the person life? Is God continually supporting the life of the deaf person? Question 20 seeks to determine insights into this.

A sequence of drawings was prepared to show the origin and development of life at the vegetable, animal and human level. The investigator, pointing to the tree and the seeds on the ground under the tree, explains that the seeds give life to the tree. He then passes on to the second drawing saying that the cat gives life to the kittens. The same is done with the third drawing, where it is pointed out that the mother gives life to the infant. The last of the series, a sketch resembling Michelangelo's creation masterpiece, depicts God giving life to Adam. After the entire sequence is briefly described, the adolescent is asked if God gave him life, if God gives him life now, and if God is always supporting his life.

In the pre-testing it was found that not every pupil needed the entire process from tree to "Michelangelo," so in the actual administration of the test it was used only with the slower deaf pupils. To save time, this question was eliminated on the final version, but it remains clear from the pre-testing that the idea of God-the-Life-Giver makes little sense to numerous deaf youth.* Numerous pupils answered that God gave them life at birth and may even support their life now, but their attitude was so nonchalant that it is doubtful if the deaf adolescents tested had ever given much thought to this matter previously.

---

*Although it was decided to omit Question 20, the accompanying drawings are retained for use by teachers who may wish to give further thought to the question.

16
Relationship with God: Group and Individual

Do the deaf, as members of the Church, achieve a group relationship with God? Does the deaf individual achieve a personal relationship with God through private prayer? The exploration of these topics brings us to two broad areas: the Church and prayer.

Let us consider the Church first. It has been said that deaf people will go to any church—wherever the action is. "Action" here refers to the signing ability of the minister or priest, the presence of the person's deaf friends, and the vigor of the social program following the worship service. It has also been commented that the handicap itself is the single predominant factor in gathering a deaf community together.

While acknowledging the value of these factors—especially the importance of social functions for the deaf—one must explore the deeper issues at stake here. In the mind of a deaf adolescent, is the Church equated with a building of brick and mortar and nothing more? Are such vital truths as the Church as an extension of Christ into our world or the Church as the people of God (the inner nature of the Church) lost to the deaf? Is the deaf adolescent condemned to a shallow understanding of the Church?

Question 21 was constructed to illumine this area, clarifying for us what "Church" ideas are present in the mind of the deaf adolescent. First, a drawing of a church building is shown to the deaf person and he is asked "Is this (building) the Church?" To get a deeper aspect of the Church, a second drawing was made: a group of people with a priest holding up the Eucharist. The people are saying "We belong to Jesus" and a mystical presence of Christ permeates the scene. The investigator remarks that the people say, "We belong to Jesus." The adolescent is then asked, "Do *you* belong to Jesus?" The remaining questions in Question 21 do not have drawings. The pupil is simply asked, "Do you go to church?" "With whom?" "How often?" The question "With whom?" was inserted to obtain the degree of family influence. To learn whether the deaf person mingles with a congregation of hearing people or goes to a church exclusively for the deaf, he is asked "Do you go to a hearing church or deaf church?" If he answers "deaf church," he is asked "Is the deaf church Catholic?" The question is constructed to unearth in the deaf student an inkling of the inner reasons or motivations which bring hearing people to church.

The question left open for discussion is: "Why do hearing people go to church?" The response is, of course, recorded verbatim. With brighter pupils an additional question is here inserted: "What does the Mass mean to you?" As a check on the extent of family influence, the adolescent is asked if he is forced to go to church. If so, he is queried as to whether he would still go if he were not forced and whether he will go at a later age when parental pressure is removed. Some of the respondents were confused by the next question, "Does going to church help you?" or simply, "Does (or can) church help you?" Where confusion persisted, the question was rephrased, "Can church help you on Monday, Tuesday, etc.?"

To probe whatever predominates their inner activity while in church, the adolescents were asked to describe what they think about in church. This was thought to be a more efficient question than a tentative previous one requesting a list of items they liked most and disliked most about church. Their description of their thoughts is meant to provide clues as to whether they are absorbed with stained glass windows or with a display of the latest fashions, whether they are bored, or whether any understanding of worship or prayer is operative within them.

The last two questions are a check on the Eucharist and the eucharistic presence in church, and whether the fact that the church is "God's house" is linked to God's living there in a sacramental sense in the Eucharist. The two questions are: "Who lives in church?" and "Why do people genuflect in church?"

17
Probing Prayer

Question 22 grapples with prayer, a supremely significant aspect of anyone's religious life. The first drawing contains two adults with a child and a caption with the words "Our Father"—indicating that they are praying aloud. To assess the deaf adolescents' understanding of the one to whom this prayer is addressed, he is asked quite simply "To whom are these people talking?" (Here, as in other parts of the test, the question is always rephrased in simpler terms whenever the youngster does not understand the question.) To expose the student's views on the content of the prayer, he is asked to explain why these people are praying. As the prayer of the people progresses, is God aware that he is being prayed to? (If not, prayer for the adolescent would be pointless.)

To gather information on the respondent's thinking about this, he is asked, "Does God know what they are saying?" If he does, then, "How does God know?"

The next question, 22e, is deliberately worded incorrectly for the deaf. It was feared (and subsequent testing confirmed this fear) that the adolescent would place too narrow an interpretation on the word "answer," believing that the investigator is really asking if God would give a direct, vocal response. The question was retained to test the validity of this suspicion, reinforced, however, by two supplementary questions: "Can God help people?" and "Can God give these people what they are asking for?"

To explore the possibility that God indeed communicates to the deaf in a physical, auditory way, Question 22g asks: "Does God answer with his voice?" If yes, "Would you ever know the answer, since you are deaf?" Question 22h pursues the same point: "Does God talk only to hearing people?" If not, "How does God talk to the deaf?" A criticism of Question 22g could be made that its phrasing is too heavily weighted in favor of a materialistic answer, since there is a presupposition that God has a voice. While the criticism is merited, it is felt that Question 22g taken in the wider context of the block of questions will yield a true reflection of the thought of the deaf on the mechanics of divine communication.

Question 23 moves into the area of private prayer. It is accompanied by a drawing of a boy kneeling down with hands folded on his chest in an attitude of prayer. The boy's face was to have appeared indifferent to evoke a more valid response from the deaf as to why this boy was praying. Unfortunately for test purposes, numerous teenagers thought the boy appeared sad and therefore was praying because he sought relief from a problem. The original aim was to ascertain whether the deaf would attribute altruistic or joyful motives to the boy's prayer.

It is felt now that to some extent this aim was inhibited by the bias in the picture. Perhaps it would have been better to give a rear-view of the boy.

Question 23 tries to determine whether the deaf person as an individual is aware of a divine "Thou" with whom he can communicate. Assuming an awareness of God's presence and that communication happens, what is the nature of this communication? Is it monologue or dialogue? Is the deaf person cognizant that one can talk interiorly to God? Is sign-language a barrier for God? Does God respond?

18
Relationship with One Another and with God

A vacationing missionary told of several South American infants who died because they lacked a relationship to any human being. This confirms philosophical and psychological teachings which propose that the idea of an isolated person is self-contradictory. Relationship is essential in forming human beings, and the most profound and beautiful of all relationships is love. Without attempting to define love, the remainder of the interview explores some specific areas of this virtue which is the essence of Christianity. The adolescent is asked if he loves his mother and father, if they love him, and, shifting to the school (assuming the pupil is in a residential school), if he has any love for his house parents. We justified this question on parental love because of our awareness that in families of hearing parents with deaf children there is sometimes an appalling lack of communication which can lead to an absence of love.

Question 25 investigates feelings toward the black man. The testee is asked if he loves black people, if they love him, and if God loves the blacks.

19
Forgiveness

Forgiveness, insisted upon so strongly by Christ, is the concern of Question 26a. The drawing depicts an automobile accident in which the front driver, who is deaf, has stopped for a red light. His vehicle is damaged in the rear by a careless driver, obviously at fault. This is explained to the adolescent, who is then asked if he can forgive the driver.

Question 26 goes further and asks the testee if he loves hearing strangers and if God loves hearing strangers.

The next picture shows a young man and woman embracing each other. It is remarked that they obviously love each other, and the adolescent is then asked if God loves him like this (a check on Question 15). Furthermore, the investigator explores whether or not the deaf student thinks that God loves deaf or hearing people more.

The last question, on compassion, is the result of some reactions which the investigator encountered while taking a census of deaf adults, several of whom had withdrawn from socializing with other deaf people on the grounds that the deaf population at large lacks compassion. When the investigator asked for specific reasons, these adults replied that the deaf in general have "hard hearts." To explore the possibility of hardness of heart and at what age it began, Question 27 was included. A package of five drawings was compiled: a kitten in distress, an accident victim, a student doing homework, two boys fighting, and an elderly lady attempting to cross the street. The adolescent is simply asked if he would offer help in each instance.

II
Statistical Procedure

20
The Nature of a Diagnostic Inventory

It is here important to restate the primary objective of this treatise: to obtain an inside view from the deaf adolescents of their conception of God, specifically with regard to belief, identification and relationship. The two lesser objectives fall outside the statistical analysis and therefore are unrelated to this discussion. Those who adhered to no belief were queried no further after the completion of the initial questions on beliefs. These numbered a total of 36 (as well as 4 control group members) and they are excluded from further statistical analysis.

To achieve the primary objective, a method of collecting information (including explanatory information and reasoning) had to be devised, since existing tests or questionnaires are not quite appropriate for this purpose. The result is the *Interview Form*—or questionnaire, if you will—administered by personal interview as described earlier. Even though this device employs sets of drawings, it is not a "test" in the sense that it yields some cumulative score, or in the sense that there are correct and incorrect answers, or that the responses of one person might be compared with those of some normative group, etc. Instead, each item on the *Interview Form* yields a specific facet of the religious beliefs of the respondent. The function of the drawings is to smoothen and quicken communication and elicit responses of individuals.

Because the inventory is so constructed, certain questions which might be posed about a test are here inappropriate. Each interview item represents a particular facet of the individual's beliefs. This is true even though, in trying to achieve an overall view of beliefs, answers to one item may be related to those of other items. Accordingly, the traditional testing concepts of reliability and validity are inappropriate.

In one sense, reliability means internal consistency. The subject (or testee), in other words, responds in substantially the same manner to one part of the test as to another. This is unsuitable here. In another sense, reliability means that one form of the test yields the same results as another form. This, too, is inappropriate for our purposes since there are no alternate forms. In a third sense, it means that the test yields the same results on different occasions—the testee, in other words, achieves substantially the same score on two occasions—or that the information derived from the test is stable from one point in time to another. Again, this ill suits our purpose, since the interview was administered only once to a given individual.

21
Content Validity

Similarly, questions of validity which may be treated statistically are unsuitable. "Concurrent validity" means that the test yields the same results as another device. But this does not fit our purposes here since no other device was available, and therefore this one was formulated.[1] "Predictive validity" means that the information obtained is related to subsequent behavior, but it, too, is unsuitable, since no claim is even made that such a relationship exists. "Construct validity" means that the device yields information about a general construct or concept (not observable) or some generalized state of the organism. The closest approximation here might be "religiosity," but even that seems inappropriate. The only type of validity which can legitimately be claimed is "content validity," where the items appear to really be sampling an area of beliefs which they are intended to do.

Although all of these traditional "test" concepts might be either dismissed or evaluated subjectively—a questionnaire is personally judged as adequate or inadequate to the task it was designed to perform —it is possible to pose a critical question which can be scrutinized objectively. Does an individual questionnaire (or, in our case, *Interview Form*) item yield consistent results from one group of subjects to another group where those groups may be presumed to constitute comparable samples of a larger population? If not, then the individual item must be judged ambiguous, or the examiner is interpreting the responses incorrectly or inconsistently; in short, a major error is somehow intruding.

To illustrate: if 100 persons are randomly divided into two groups and therefore presumed to be relatively comparable, and if they are asked a question, and if 5 of 50 in one group answer yes and 45 of 50 in the other group also answer yes, there is good reason to believe that "something is wrong." It is possible, of course, that the 45 yes-people just happened to fall into a 5 and 45 distribution (and, indeed, the statistically computed "significance of difference" is an estimate of the probability of such an event). Because the probability of such a distribution is so remote, however, it is more prudent to assume that the "something wrong" is to be found in the question asked or its treatment. In effect, if such results were obtained with a pair of samples presumed to be comparable and then with two samples which one was seeking to learn more about—that is, whether or not they did represent a common population —it would be indefensible to say of the first that "the difference is a matter of sampling error" and of the second that "the two groups represent different populations." It is for this reason that the statistical analysis was performed separately on each item listed in the *Interview Form*.

As noted previously, the items are not cumulative in the sense of yielding a score or set of scores—at least not as they are treated in this study.

In accordance with this general rationale, half of each of the subgroups of subjects (Catholic students in secular schools, Catholic students in Catholic schools, and control group) was assigned to one group, the other half to a second group. The frequencies of responses to an individual *Interview Form* item were then compared statistically. This procedure was repeated for virtually every item in the entire *Interview Form* with a few exceptions to be explained shortly.

That the interview procedure is successful or scientifically acceptable is shown by the results of the separate analysis of 107 items: only 4 even approached the criterion of "statistical significance." Of these, two fell between the .05 and .02 level, one between the .10 and .05, and one approached the .10 level (Questions 16, 19h, 19g and 22g). It should be noted that these deviations possibly represent some inadequacy of the separate items or they might represent simple sampling error. Indeed, with more than 100 separate statistical tests, it is likely that some would achieve "statistical significance." Nevertheless, because such variable frequencies were detected in these 4 questions, their responses must be evaluated with caution. Conversely, where significant differences between various subject groups such as secular (i.e., the Catholic students in secular schools) and Catholic are found and, at the same time, no differences between the random groups, it is unlikely that the obtained secular-Catholic difference arose from the item itself—i.e., from its ambiguity, subjective recording errors made by the examiner, etc. (This does not mean that the obtained statistical significance assumes greater value, but simply that one possible source of that difference may reasonably be rejected.)

22
Chi-Square and Yates Correction Factor

The method of statistical analysis bears comment. In both the evaluation of the *Interview Form* questions (or items) and in the comparison of the subject groups (secular—Catholic—control) the statistical device employed was Chi-square.[2] In this, the observed frequencies of samples are compared. (In discussing the obtained results, the use of percentages is most informative, but actual frequencies, not percentages, are used in the statistical analysis.) Where the combined observed frequency of a response is small, serious distortion of the results of a Chi-square analysis can arise from the use of small numbers. To make such an analysis it is often necessary to combine two or more responses into a single category. For example, where three responses are recorded—yes, no, and don't know—with an inadequate observed frequency of "don't know," that response must be combined with one of the others. Thus, the comparison of the research groups is: Do they represent samples of a single population in terms of "yes" and "other than yes." This procedure was necessarily employed in many of the statistical analyses of this study.

In four of the *Interview Form* items, it is impractical to combine responses into two or three categories since the responses are sufficiently discrete. In Question 22b, for example, concerning types of prayer, the recorded categories of responses were petition, contrition, love, don't know, and other. Consequently, there is no statistical analysis and Question 22b will be handled cautiously in the forthcoming discussion of results.

Similarly, besides the 107 items statistically analyzed and the 4 just mentioned, one item was not statistically analyzed because the number of respondents was too small.

One final note is in order. In many instances the expected frequency computed within Chi-square was between 5 and 10 cases (as determined by the actually observed frequencies). In such cases, the "Yates correction factor" was incorporated into the computation of Chi-square so as to reduce the statistical distortion which otherwise would result from small frequencies.[3]

Question 21c, "Do you go to church?", was selected at random to illustrate the statistical computations—the number of respondents, percentages, break-up into groups a and b and the Chi-square and Yates correction factor.

Number 21c   Question: Do you go to church?

Answer	Catholic N	%	Secular N	%	
Yes	16	64.0	42	53.2	N
Sometimes	3	12.0	23	29.1	O T SIGNIFICANT
No	6	24.0	14	17.7	

	Deaf N	%	Control N	%	
Yes	58	55.8	18	94.7	Yes vs. not yes
Sometimes	26	25.0	1	5.3	Significant
No	20	19.2	0	0	beyond .01

	Group a N	%	Group b N	%	
Yes	40	64.5	36	59.0	O.K.
Sometimes	11	17.7	16	26.2	No significant
No	11	17.7	9	14.8	difference

Question #21c

Groups compared:

( ) Catholic and Secular

(√) Deaf and Control

( ) Secular and Control

( ) a and b

<table>
<tr><td></td><td colspan="3">Data</td></tr>
<tr><td></td><td>Response
Yes
Sometimes</td><td>No</td><td>Totals</td></tr>
<tr><td>Group</td><td></td><td></td><td></td></tr>
<tr><td>deaf</td><td>84 A</td><td>20 B</td><td>104</td></tr>
<tr><td>control</td><td>19 C</td><td>0 D</td><td>19</td></tr>
<tr><td>Totals</td><td>103</td><td>20</td><td>123</td></tr>
</table>

(√) Yates correction factor used because smallest frequency   3.089

( ) Yates correction factor not used

FORMULA: $x^2 = \dfrac{N(|AD - BC| - N/2)^2}{(A+B)(C+D)(A+C)(B+D)}$

COMPUTATION: $x^2 = \dfrac{12 \quad 477 \quad 396.75}{4 \quad 070 \quad 560}$

$x^2 = 3.065$

Interpretation:

( ) Observed difference is NOT statistically significant.

( ) Difference is statistically significant at _____.

With 1 degree of freedom,

$x^2_{.20} = 1.64$ $x^2_{.05} = 3.84$ $x^2_{.01} = 6.64$

$x^2_{.10} = 2.71$ $x^2_{.02} = 5.41$ $x^2_{.001} = 10.83$

Question #21c

Groups compared: Data

( ) Catholic and Secular   Response
                                                        not
(✓) Deaf and Control   Group   Yes   Yes   Totals

( ) Secular and Control   deaf | 58 A | 46 B | 104

( ) a and b   control | 18 C | 1 D | 19

                                Totals   76   47   123

(✓) Yates correction factor used because smallest frequency 7.26

( ) Yates corrrection factor not used

FORMULA: $\chi^2 = \dfrac{N(|AD - BC| - N/2)^2}{(A+B)(C+D)(A+C)(B+D)}$

COMPUTATION: $\chi^2 = \dfrac{61\ 742\ 586.75}{7\ 058\ 272}$

$\chi^2 = \quad 8.747$

Interpretation:

( ) Observed difference is NOT statistically significant.

(✓) Difference is statistically significant at <u>beyond .01</u>.

    With 1 degree of freedom,

$\chi^2_{.20} = 1.64$ $\chi^2_{.05} = 3.84$ $\chi^2_{.01} = 6.64$

$\chi^2_{.10} = 2.71$ $\chi^2_{.02} = 5.41$ $\chi^2_{.001} = 10.83$

III
Examining and Discussing
the Responses

A few other words should be said here about the comparisons among the groups: Catholic deaf adolescents in secular schools (called the secular school group), Catholic deaf adolescents in the Catholic schools (called the Catholic school group), and the control group. As stated before, the primary objective of this study is to discover more precise insights from the minds of all the deaf adolescents tested and therefore holds as a lesser priority the comparison of the groups with each other. Adolescents were deliberately selected from the secular—Catholic —control category to add precision and approach more closely the roots of the thinking of the deaf. Ordinarily the statistical analysis allowed a combination of the two groups. It must be emphasized that the two groups were statistically compared; but where no noteworthy difference was found, they were joined together as a single group and thus compared with the control group. Where noteworthy or significant differences were uncovered, the secular school and Catholic school groups were kept apart. It was agreed to surmise that where the two groups, secular school and Catholic school, exhibit a notable divergence (at a given level of statistical probability) they should be combined and thus compared with the control group. Therefore, wherever secular— Catholic school significant differences are found, each group is compared separately with the control group.

23
Belief in God

As mentioned earlier, our study gets underway with a probe into belief. Is the deaf adolescent's faith real, apparent, or non-existent? A total of 71% of the Catholic school pupils answered the question "Is God real?" affirmatively, whereas 3% of the Catholic school pupils responded negatively. Some 26% of the Catholic school pupils doubted. This is similar to the answers given by the adolescents in the secular schools: 75% affirmative, 5% negative, and 20% doubtful. A full 84% of the control group said that God is real, none denied his reality, and 16% doubted God's reality. Most of the responses were a simple "yes," "no" or "I don't know" without further elaboration.

Moving over to Question 1b, the sum of 60% of the secular school pupils gave creation and revelation as the basis of their faith. Ann 19CMMS128V says that she believes "because God made ideas and the world." Similarly Judith 17CMMS99V comments that "God made light, everybody." Joan 19MAT Adv.4.7A likewise explains her faith: "It is safer to believe because God made everything. Where did I come from?" Henry 19MAT Adv.4.2V wonders about origins as he remarks: "How did the earth start? It could be that a person made it. God made people—all the things on the earth." As these quotes make clear, "creation," according to the deaf, simply means God's getting things started in the beginning. It is a concrete manifestation of God's activity which can bring the deaf to an attitude of faith.

Yet the deaf youngsters would do better to connect creation with providence, a connection without which deaf and hearing people alike may logically ask: "If I am going to suffer, grow old and die, why was I made in the first place?" If God's creation is not connected to his providence, it will be connected to aging, neglect, dissolution and death. Hence, the deaf must be taught that God creates and cares afterward, and in his providence he will not allow corruption to prevail over a creature finally.[1]

Another basis for the deaf person's faith is revelation. Here the deaf show a partial grasp of the historical revelation of the Old Testament and the later revelation in Christ.

John 19WAIS114A, when asked to explain his belief says, "Yes, I read in the Bible about the apple—started trouble—about Jesus on the cross." Some revelation is present in Patrick's 18CMMS74V answer, "I know stories from church about Jesus." Phyllis 16MAT Adv.3.8V likewise says, "I believe because of the true stories about Jesus in the Bible."[2]

The deaf youngsters' understanding of revelation can be strengthened by stressing several important biblical themes, among which is the Old Testament theme of God visiting his people. In order to make and restore relationships with himself, God visits Adam in the garden, Noah preparing for the flood, Abraham preparing to kill Isaac, Joseph in prison, Moses to give him the mission of leading the Israelites out of Egypt and again on Mount Horeb, Isaiah praying in the Temple, Samuel to instruct him on which of Jesse's sons to choose, Amos pasturing his herds, and others.[3] These revelatory visits culminate with the visit of Jesus Christ. "When the designated time had come, God sent forth his Son born of a woman" (Gal. 4:4). Revelation can be taught effectively to the deaf in the context of these visits. God came because he had words to say, agreements to make, and work to do. The concrete, colorful literary form of these visits is apt for teaching the deaf. One may add that these visits still happen between an invisible God and the psyche of the deaf person.

When we say that 40% of the secular school students responded that human authority, natural reason (or other) underpins their faith, we mean mainly that they have leaned heavily on the word of their catechist, or the example of people, or that they somehow saw God in nature. Wayne 19WAIS98A says he believes: "The priest explained it to me. He explained about Jesus and about God." The prayerful activity of people is the basis for the faith of Frank 19WAIS90V, who remarks,

"Priests and sisters pray all the time. People pray, so I believe." Joseph 17WISC118__ shows a simple acceptance, "Priests and nuns explain a story to me that Jesus was born many years ago." Karen 16WISC81A believes "because many, many people go to church on Sunday." The actions of her mother and father shape the faith of Mary Lou 18WISC89_: "I believe in God because my mother and father send me to church. And they go to church with me." Edith 18WISC97__ says simply that she believes because "Mr. Mullin taught me about God." Reflecting the same basis, Michael 18WAIS112V remarks, "The priest talks about God. The sisters talk about God. And I read in the Bible that Jesus was born a long time ago." Steven 18_A believes "because we have a church, priests, holy days during the year. It must be true." Judy 19WISC110A says: "My grandmother is a very strong Catholic. She showed me a lot. Also, when I do something wrong, I feel it. I believe." This sampling, taken with the others in the 40%, shows a heavy dependence upon the authority, or word, of a teacher or parent. The emphasis, therefore, that is placed upon the witness value of the catechist seems to be doubly important for the catechist of the deaf.

Only a few of the adolescents are able to see the finger of God in nature. One of these is Larry 17_A, an exceptionally bright young man who sees God as the author of all living creatures. "God," repeated Larry, "is wonderful, wonderful. I feel that he is wonderful because of the gift of life. Maybe God is looking for another world; he can make new life—anything." Larry was impressed with the goodness of God diffusing itself into this world. Having expended itself here, that goodness now searches other areas in space hoping to find room to create more life. Perhaps he shares the precious insight of the philosopher Plato who expresses the Christian view of the created world in these words: "Let me tell you then why the creator made this world of generation. He was good, and the good can never have any jealousy of anything. And being free from jealousy, he desired that all things should be as like himself as they could be. This is in the truest sense the origin of creation and of the world: God desired that all things should be good and nothing bad, so far as this was attainable."[4]

A few of the deaf also based their belief on the possession of observable evidence of some kind. Elizabeth 17__A, for instance, associates her faith with Veronica's towel. Asked why she believes in God, she said: "Because a long time ago soldiers crucified him. A woman washed his face and wiped his face with a towel. And a picture of Jesus' face stayed on the towel." Barbara 16WISC93_ also pins her faith on the observable: "A long time ago Jesus died. I saw it on TV." Robert 19_A wanted more evidence about Jesus. When asked what kind, he responded: "I want to see his face and what he has been doing. In Texas, about two years ago, people saw Jesus' face on a big door screen. They took the door screen down to wash it, but the face was still there after wash-ing." Lack of this type of evidence confused Jean 20WAIS94_: "No. No. I can't see God. I believe in Jesus, yes. But sister told me that draw-ings of Jesus are not Jesus' real face. Is that true? I'm confused."

A small minority of individuals equated their faith with their feel-ings. Thus does Thelma 17WISC131A express herself: "I believe some. I believe that God is watching me . . . that God can forgive my sins. But when I pray, God doesn't answer me. Sometimes I feel nothing and I don't believe." Guilt feelings appear in the comments of Alyce 18CAT13.4A: "Yes, I believe in God. When I do something wrong, I feel hurt. Maybe that is a punishment from God. So I believe in God."

The responses of the Catholic school pupils deserve mention, since, percentagewise, they differ noticeably from the secular. A total of 75% —an increase of 15% over the secular schools—of these adolescents con-sider creation and revelation as the basis of their faith. Yet, these 75% express their thoughts similarly to the 60% from the secular schools. "How did the earth start?" asks Christopher 20RBE104_. "Someone had to make it. It is so beautiful. And sometimes I feel faith myself." "How can things be without God," "God put many people here," and "God started Adam and Eve and they spread all over" are more sample creation responses.

Thinking similar to the secular school thinking on revelation sur-faces in the comments of the Catholic school pupils. They had read parts of the Bible, remembered some stories and formulated some con-clusions under the guidance of their teachers.

Sameness is also evident in the answers from human authority and natural reason of the Catholic school pupils. The human authority is the catechist, whose word is accepted without question. Natural reason, again, is intuitive, arguing to God from his fingerprints in the natural world. The percentage drop from 40% in the secular school to 25% in the Catholic school is significant. The drop indicates that the Catholic school students depend less on the word of their teachers. They also tend to evaluate more critically what the teacher says.

Moving to the control group, one again observes a marked devia-tion in percentages. Only 27.3% base their faith on creation and revela-tion. Kathleen, 16, says, "All the nice things in the world. I think some-body had to create it—even the bad things too." Joseph, 17, applies natural reason to creation: "There's gotta be a reason why everything is on earth. There's gotta be something after we die; otherwise, life would not make much sense." Another Joseph, 16, reflects, "Even rationally, just thinking about it, you'd have to believe in God, because who made everything? You look around and you ask how did all this get here?" Rev-elation shows in the answer of Patti, 16: "All the things the apostles wrote and all the miracles they did on the people—it's gotta be true."

Although these hearing adolescents were more sophisticated and more linguistically competent than the deaf, they showed little interest in reading Scripture. Sample responses are: "I don't read the Bible," "I read Scripture once every few months," "I don't read the Bible now, but I did in Catholic school," "The Bible doesn't interest me. It is a code of living for everyone to live under." In general, it is fair to say that these young people have the ability to explore the sources of revelation, yet apparently they seldom choose to do so.

A surprising 72.7% of the control group gave human authority, natural reason, or personal religious experience as the basis of their faith. Sarah, 16, supplies personal religious experience: "Each time I pray, I always get what I ask for; for instance, in my piano lessons. It's like having a big brother you can depend on. I really don't see how anyone can get along without him." Steven, 17, neglecting revelation and preferring his own reasoning, has been wrestling with the question for a considerable time: "I believe in a being. I know there is something up there —a spirit or something like that. I go to one person, but I don't know much about this person or if it is a person. It could be like a rock or something." Cheryle, 16, confirms her reasoning as her guide: "I believe in God depending on how God is defined. I believe God is a force, not a man. God is our explanation for things we don't understand. God is the motivating force behind creation. Everything has a basis and God is the basis." Gerard, 18, an alert young man who admitted that he never reads Scripture, gives this explanation: "Yes, I believe in God. I suppose he really exists. It is nicer, more convenient, to believe in God. If you start thinking that there is no God, this causes problems. I don't worry about religion. It is not a thing that bothers me." Answers like these, which form the bulk of the 72.7%, show a serious consideration given, and an active intelligence applied, to the question of God's reality.

These hearing young people exuded confidence that their unaided powers of reason and feelings would eventually either affirm or deny the divine. Such confidence in themselves, born of the empirical scientific method, and in accord with adolescent psychology, coupled with a naturalistic outlook on man, has reduced revelation to background importance.

We now begin our investigation of unbelief and doubt as exhibited first by the deaf, then by the hearing control group. Our discussion here concerns only the 5% of secular school deaf youth who deny the existence of God and the 20% who have severe doubts in this area. Along with this will be considered the 3% of the Catholic school pupils who deny God and the 26% who waver. Finally, we will remark on the 16% of the doubters among the hearing adolescents.

We may begin by dividing the whole into two fairly well-defined groups: those who reject or doubt God because they see a conflict between religion and positive science, are confused by the teachings of different religions, or are confused by the idea of God; and those who demand tangible evidence that he still performs miracles as he did in scriptural times.

Part of the problem with positive science is biological evolution. In at least one school the religious educators were apparently unaware that the deaf had acquired an understanding of evolution from biology class, compared this with the Adam and Eve story, and were troubled by the resulting conflict. Holly 17CMMS125A, for instance, is a non-believer because "man comes from the apes." When asked if perhaps God made the earth, Holly was quick to say: "No. The earth broke off from the sun." John 17WAIS96A, echoing the same thought, says: "No. I don't believe—because God did not give people things. God did not make the earth. Science is different from God." Ruth 17WISC131A, a bright girl with an excellent command of English, remarks, "Science and God are enemies. Scientists don't believe in God. And God does not bother with science."

Attempts, perhaps undertaken in an ecumenical spirit, to enlighten the deaf on the teachings of different religions has resulted in doubt and bewilderment, at least for some deaf. This appears in the remark of Linda 18RBE109_: "Sometimes I believe in God, not always. There are many different religions in the world. Which one is right? I want to know the difference between religions. It is mixed up." Dora 16WISC104A expresses her confusion this way, "Sometimes I believe. Some people believe in God and some don't. It is hard to know who is right. People believe different things. Who is right? It is hard to find proof about God." Pamela 18CMMS107A seemed sincere in her unbelief as she advanced this reason, "Catholic, Protestant, and Jewish churches teach different things about Jesus. They give conflicting stories and it is hard to find the truth—where they agree. I want one Church with the same teaching for the world."

In the second group of non-believers and doubters are those who insist upon some tangible evidence of God. The deaf desired a wide range of evidence: photographs of Jesus, the exact burial place of Christ, a wish to see Jesus, to meet and shake hands with him, some indication of contemporary miracles. It is this group which used the word "proof" so often and at the beginning of the interview, before any use of this word by the investigator. "I want some proof about God," "There is no proof," "Some people say that God is here, but I never see him," and "I want to meet God" are some samples of the thinking of this group. Some deaf youth were disappointed at never having seen or met God. To seek a better understanding of the reasoning in these responses, three relevant factors deserve consideration: (1) positivism, (2) the relationship between faith and the senses of sight and hearing, and (3) an appreciation of adolescent psychology.

1. In rejecting belief in a reality beyond what the senses can perceive, this group of deaf and hearing adolescents resembles those who use the philosophy of positivism to disprove the claims of religion. Although positivism is a diminishing problem in society, it deserves further mention here.

Equipped with the observational language and instruments and categories of science, positivism seeks to scientifically describe and explain, via the empirical method, all behavior, experience, and reality. Positivism says that any behavior, experience or reality is unreal if it fails to fit into the empirical method. Such principles and premises enable us to conquer outer space, but they hardly help us conquer ourselves. For the human person loses his autonomy, dignity, self-mastery, responsibility and freedom once positivism is applied to him. Thus it is not only God who is dead: man is also.

Vague acceptance of the empirico-scientific method and the application of it to the person of God has gripped the imagination of some deaf. Although the adolescents interviewed had no explicit knowledge of positivism and its principles and lacked the language refinement for sophisticated expression, nevertheless what they said is positivistic. Consider these reactions. Paul 17WISC103V, when asked if God is real, responded, "I don't know. I can't see anything." "The priest told me stories about God, but there is no proof. I read in books about science. Scientists don't believe in God. God didn't make the earth," says Lorraine 17WISC121A. The response of Kimberly 16CAT6.9A reveals the reason for her uncertainty: "I don't know about God, because I can't see God. People die. Where do they go? I don't know. I can't see." Diane 19CAT7.0A is adamant: "No. I don't believe. I can't see a spirit, so I don't believe. Some of the other boys and girls feel the same way."[5]

A few of the deaf link their belief to their desire to witness a contemporary miracle. Such is Arthur 17_A who says, "I don't know if I believe or not. Why can't God give sight to the blind? Why can't God make the deaf hear? I want to hear now."

Although, as we saw from the statistics, the majority of the deaf are believers, still we must acknowledge that scientific method has eroded the faith of some deaf youngsters. The religion teacher can ignore this issue only at the risk of allowing more deaf to lose their faith. We pause here to comment about the reaction of the control group and to examine what can be done to alleviate this problem.

First of all, the problem of the apparent conflict of science and religious belief extends far beyond the deaf and reaches into much of modern life. Indeed, it has been called a characteristic of our time.[6] A total of 16% of the control group of hearing teenagers share the doubt and unbelief of the deaf. They can provide some specific insights. Kevin, 17, explains that so many accretions have accumulated around Jesus that it is hard to decipher the situation. Ancient religious certainties are no longer certainties. Says Kevin, "I still believe in him; but I don't believe he exists now. When Jesus was here, all sorts of things, miracles, happened. I don't see anything like that happening now." David, 16, believes because "it is the way I was brought up and taught in the CCD." If someone challenged David's faith, he would merely say: "You are entitled to your own opinion and I am entitled to mine." Shallowness shows in the reply of Christina, 16: "I suppose so. I was taught about God. My religion believes that, so I guess I do." Several others acknowledged that they benignly ignore religion and religion benignly ignores them. A dispensable generality evoking little awe, God becomes but a small asset to daily life. Thoughts such as these call for further insight into positivism.

To begin, positivism is devoid of everything which escapes the observations of science. Positivism insists that the scientific method can decipher *all* reality and can answer *any* legitimate question raised by the mind of man.[7] Much can be said for positivism, especially its contribution to the birth and growth of sociology. Our purpose here, however, is to see it in relation to religion. Its greatest fault is its failure to recognize the validity of other modes of knowledge. Only some, not all, experience is measurable, definable, responsive to instruments and capable of fitting into logically organized categories or catalogues. What positivism says is valid for the world of things, less valid for the world of persons and least valid for the world of God. A positivistic observer, for instance, fails to detect the mysteries of nature or the uniqueness of the human person. But that does not prove that these do not exist. The situation of the positivist and those, including the deaf, who have been hurt by the positivist position can be compared to the situation of an unmusical scientist.

Imagine a completely unmusical scientist. If a tune was played for him on the piano and he was asked to interpret and define scientifically what had just taken place, he would, if he was a first rate physicist, express it in a precise scientific formula. Because he was only a physicist and quite unmusical, he would feel that he had thoroughly explained what had happened. If it was objected that he had overlooked something, and that something was the heart of the matter, he would smile incredulously. Because he was quite unmusical, he would lack the faculty to observe the tune itself. The tune could not be detected by methods available to him, with the faculty with which he comprehended reality and believed himself able to comprehend it thoroughly. Yet it does exist.[8]

Similarly, there is mystery, behavior, experience and reality that no amount of discursive reasoning or scientific method can identify. For some of this, a religious faculty is required.

2. The rationale for the "proofs" required by the adolescents may well be the positivistic mentality we have just finished describing; nevertheless, another factor should be placed alongside positivism to more fully account for the adolescents' need for evidence. The factor that appears often in the responses is the sense of sight. And this raises the disturbing question of what a heavy reliance on sight joined with deafness can do to the virtue of faith. Immediately, St. Paul's famous passage to the Romans comes to mind, a passage which he might have changed had he lived after the inventions of printing and photography. At any rate, here is what he says: "But how shall they call on him in whom they have not believed? And how can they believe unless they have heard of him? And how can they hear unless there is someone to preach? And how can men preach unless they are sent? Scripture says, How beautiful are the feet of those who announce the good news!" (Rom. 10:14-15)

Does this mean that faith is acquired only when it is based upon a divine revelation which Paul perceives as a spoken and therefore heard revelation? An affirmative answer supposes that God would have to see to it that everyone can physically hear, since he efficaciously wills the salvation of *all* men. Yet some men cannot hear and God still includes them in his salvific will. Therefore God reaches them through the other senses.

The fourth Gospel presents a clue as to how this is done. Divine revelation, John implies, sufficiently reaches someone through the sense of sight. John speaks often of light and darkness, seeing and believing (cf. Jn. 1:5, 14, 17; 3:11-12, 19ff.; 8:47; 9:39; 12:45; 14:9, 17; 20:29). Beginning with physical sight and ending with spiritual sight, the fourth Gospel's simple combination of seeing and believing can thus be summed up:

seeing, and yet not believing;
not seeing, and therefore not believing;
seeing, and therefore believing;
not seeing, yet believing;
believing, and therefore seeing.

To lead to belief is the purpose of the fourth Gospel's signs, a purpose fully achieved in the great act of believing: to see the sign of Jesus' exaltation. What is physically seen is the cross—the elevation of Jesus between heaven and earth. What is spiritually seen is his going to the Father. Bearing all this in mind, it seems safe to conjecture that John would encourage the religious educator of the deaf to begin with the visual and prepare the deaf to leap beyond what is seen to what is unseen.

Would it also be safe to conjecture that John perhaps would allow the photograph or drawing to carry the Word of God or function as the Word of God?

3. Lastly, a factor that asserts itself into the adolescent-God relationship is adolescent psychology, a field so vast that we can here do no more than point to it. For the first time in his life, the adolescent feels his uniqueness, which sometimes plunges him into his well-known dilemmas of rebellion versus authority, subjective judgments versus objective reality, dependency versus autonomy, reasoned judgments versus runaway emotions, peers versus adults and the like. As they struggle to free themselves from childhood and remake their personality, it seems that their greatest need is not to be needed, as Dr. Haim Ginott has remarked. Parents and religion teachers alike recognize this as a developmental phase and react, hopefully, with empathy and genuineness.

Eager to put his new-found mental abilities to work (especially his propositional and hypothetical thinking of Piaget's Formal Operational Stage), the adolescent begins to analyze the person of God. Therefore the teacher should expect requests for evidence, an onrush of questions and probings, and a lowering of God to the level of their own experience. In his work with hearing teenagers, Pierre Babin explains that the God they have constructed resembles more the God of theodicy (natural theology) than the God of revelation. Revelation is closely associated with authority, and the adolescent prefers to rely upon his own reasoning rather than accept something imposed from above, from a tradition, or from adults. Attitudes mix with judgments and so their God often fits their needs, their natural experiences and their personalities.[9] Evidence up to here, and evidence soon to reveal itself, indicates that in this regard numerous deaf adolescents are similar to their hearing peers, although there are some differences—e.g., evidence shows that a proportionately greater number of deaf are willing to accept the word of authority. Later in the study we will have an observation about the position of the deaf in Piaget's sequence of thought stages that are related to age.

We are now in a better position to understand those deaf who ask for photographs of Jesus, a personal meeting, a handshake with Jesus and other "proof." But it should be pointed out to them that although our faith is reasonable and based on historical revelation, it depends not on the tangibility of the evidence but on the credibility of the person. Perhaps the key to the right approach is not in memorizing doctrines, although knowledge is necessary, but in experiencing God at a deeper level. Perhaps we have neglected the heart (the psyche or center of personality) and concentrated too much on the intellect, as if this were a detached and independent mental faculty. A mere intellectual change of ideas affects little of the inner religious life of men.

Interconnected with his intellect is a spiritual side of man that is more profound than his intellect and his verbal (or sign language) communication of the contents of that intellect. Words (or signs), sentences and formulas are a symbolic attempt to pass on an experience that is beyond words, and the deaf are as receptive to this experience as anyone else. The religion teacher, then, should appeal to the heart of the deaf, to their most intimate life, to their conscious and unconscious psychic life where attitudes, convictions and values are constantly being formed and revised and where the sense of the sacred is awakened and the God within is discovered and believed in. Paul Ramsey beautifully expressed the relationship between love and reason: "One's loves are always deeper than his reason: and reason is always in the employment of some love."[10]

Clearly, theoretical knowledge in catechetics is insufficient. After all, the person who knows the most about God is the devil. Knowledge can never be devalued, but it cannot be the *only* thing communicated, since it gives the deaf (and hearing) the means of deciding the truth, but the individual remains free not to make use of it. Catechetical knowledge is like combustible material thrown on a fire already burning. Material thrown on an unlit heap will never ignite. To get the fire burning should be a major aim of adolescent catechesis for both the deaf and hearing.

The fire, of course, is living faith, and living faith is the genuine affirmative answer to the great question: "What do you think of Christ?" This question leaves no alternative other than to accept or reject Jesus, for indifference results in dead faith. Loving acceptance places Christ in the psyche, stirs an inner transformation, and living faith grips the person. "On that day you will know that I am in my Father and you in me, and I in you" (Jn. 14:20). When this happens the deaf person will be aware of his deep bond with the divine and will say along with the boy Jesus, "Did you not know that I had to be in my Father's house?" (Lk. 2:49). And unless this happens, the person must stand outside the New Testament as an observer, with an understanding that remains external and therefore dead.

Alfonso Nebreda, Heinrich Fries, Jean Mouroux, Carlos Cirne-Lima and others have given close attention to living faith in their writings.[11] The terminology changes to "personal" faith, but it is basically the same as "living" faith. A summary of their thoughts would add to the warmth and efficiency of any religious education program for the deaf. Their basic point is that faith is totalitarian: it affects the whole person and it is a full response of the human person to the personal God. God makes himself known to the person's psyche, which receives but does not cause the divine communication or experience. Not only is God the transmitter, but also the final guarantee of the experience.

If the person accepts the experience and puts his confidence and loyalty in it, a change of consciousness ensues and his new attitude enables him to say to Jesus: "I believe in you; therefore, I believe what you say." This "I trust you" attitude is the beginning of the whole life of faith. On the human level an example of this kind of faith is the loving wife who believes in the innocence of her husband even after he has been convicted of theft. True faith is directed primarily to the person along with his assertions and not to his assertions alone.[12] Hence, without trust or faith in the person of God, one acquires no faith in his assertions and indeed no faith at all, just as one who fails to trust the water never learns to swim, regardless of the number of swimming lessons studied.

Since faith is personal, to explain it in non-personal or positivistic terms is impossible. The personal approach of God toward the human being and vice versa is not a method, technique, or formula. It is analogous to what happens when one human being wishes to meet another.

If I approach you and wish to strike up a friendship with you, I depend on you to reveal yourself to me. Therefore the relationship is only partially up to me. You reveal yourself to me; then I have the option of believing or disbelieving you. If I believe, a new relationship is born. God has already expressed his desire to meet and disclose himself to the human person; he has already shown his belief in us. Furthermore, he enables this disclosure to be received. It is the high honor of the religion teacher to elucidate this and hope that the recipient will respond and thus give birth to a personal faith.

As a result of this special nature of Christianity, the teaching of it should not be regarded as just another branch of education. Instead, the teaching and learning roles are altered because of the special nature of the content. "All teachers are learners, too, of course, whatever their subject matter, but in most formal education it is helpful to keep the roles of teaching and learning distinct; in the teaching of Christianity, however, the actual mark of success is to surrender the teaching role to the content. To do this requires a trust of both the content and the learners beyond that ordinarily expected of teachers, and in this case made possible by the content itself."[13] What is new about this situation is that the content, far from being inert subject matter, is active along with the teacher and pupils.[14] Quoting St. Thomas' De Veritate (q. 11, a. 1), Jungmann puts it this way: "In the educational process the teacher has the same role as that of a doctor toward his patient; the patient is cured chiefly by nature which knows how to take care of itself. The doctor is only a servant of nature; he is called in to lend his assistance to nature. It is, however, nature which is active and effects the cure."[15]

The purpose of this teaching, then, is not coercion but conversion, an idea touched upon before but so important that it warrants a closer examination. Explaining how the mechanics of faith operate on the deaf (or hearing) adolescent or adult is a complex venture. What follows is only a brief attempt.[16]

At the outset, one must realize that conversion does not mean arriving at God as the conclusion of a syllogism or discovering him scientifically, but *recognizing* God. Although this recognition may happen quickly, there is usually a gradual prelude to it. The deaf adolescent may become acquainted with Christ through his parents, friends or catechist. Perhaps in the weekly religion class at the state school for the deaf the catechist may familiarize him with fragments of information on the life of Christ. From visual aids, banners, drama, sermons, hymns and other techniques, the adolescent (or adult) recalls Christ healing the sick, raising Lazarus, and arguing with the Pharisees. The teacher explains that Christ rose from the dead and sent his disciples on a mission to spread belief. He learns that many of these disciples died violent deaths defending what Christ stood for. If someone dies for a belief, he muses, there must be something to it. The infant Church springs from this belief, and with her saints, sinners, persecutors and popes comes down to us through the centuries.

At first, all of this remains submerged as scattered, irrelevant knowledge, some of which is understood clearly and some minimally. Then, as time passes and circumstances change, the deaf person may meet a devout friend or fiancée, or a good sermon may impress him or suffering may enter his life. A priest may take him on a weekend of religious experience, a cursillo, or retreat. The evolving circumstances and divine grace working within raise the submerged knowledge to the surface. The person ponders the information, and gradually it begins to make sense; it becomes more and more relevant. Previously scattered and sterile, concepts and judgments now coalesce and ignite into a single, large intuition in which the person *sees* the beauty, goodness and holiness of God and contrasts this to his own spiritual impoverishment—much like the prodigal son (Lk. 15).

The intuition is such that a decision is called for. If a true conversion takes place, the person repents of his sins, embraces God and parallels Thomas with the sentiments: "You are *my* Lord and *my* God and I surrender unconditionally to you. You are *my* way, *my* truth and *my* life." The person has made a decision and a deep change has occurred. He has discovered treasure hidden on someone else's property (Mt. 13:44): he has found God. Now nothing can stop him from selling everything he has to buy that property; he reorders his priorities and offers his services to the Lord, as did St. Paul after his striking conversion. This is the climax; this is conversion; this is the personal act of faith.[17] It must be a major goal of any religious education program. With this beginning, correct information about God will take hold on the person; he begins to think as a Christian and behave as a Christian, and the liturgy sustains his new faith.

At this point, it is helpful to make three brief comments about some aspects of conversion, or the personal act of faith: first, its relationship to the language deficiency of the deaf; second, its relationship to baptism; third, its relationship to psychology.

The language limitations of the deaf need not be a roadblock to achieving conversion. This process, as we have seen, is as much a matter of the heart as of the mind. Pascal's four degrees of rationality, beginning with instinct on the lowest level, then progressing through reason to the more profound areas of the heart and faith, show that there is much more to a person than cerebral activity and discursive reasoning. The great human experiences are beyond the verbal and the conceptual. They belong, in Pascal's hierarchy, in the realm of the heart and faith. Words, for instance, whether they are spoken, written or signed, become inadequate in times of great joy or sorrow—not because there is nothing to say, but because there is too much to say. Thus the person keeps quiet or goes into non-verbal communication. The deaf may experience conversion like anyone else, but lack the words to express it—a deficiency common to everyone. It can truthfully be said, then, that in the area of conversion, the deaf are at no disadvantage.[18]

The second comment concerns the relationship of personal faith to baptism. What follows is not an attempt to criticize infant baptism, since sound theological reasons support it. These are the elimination of the guilt of original sin, the incorporation of the infant into the body of Christ, and the initiative of divine grace which begins operating within the child. Strong as these reasons are, they weaken if the religion teacher presumes too heavily upon them. The presumption, for instance, that baptism performs a personal act of faith for the child is inadequate. The sponsor first spoke for the child, and in the early years the influences of the sacrament do not come to the conscious notice of the child. A day must come when the recipient speaks for himself and the unconscious influences of the sacrament become conscious. Only a process of religious education and exposure to the belief and practices of the Christian community can place the person in a position to respond. It is hoped, but cannot be presumed, that this will culminate in a personal act of faith which, in turn, gives the fullest efficacy to the sacrament.

The third comment concerns the relationship of conversion to psychology. Heeding the advice of M. Rokeach[19] may help effect conversion. Urban T. Holmes summarizes this procedure: "Rokeach has demonstrated that a very effective way to change certain values within a person is to ask him to rank his values, and then to bring him to a point of considerable anxiety by proving the incompatibility of those values."[20]

Psychology sheds more light on conversion as it tells us of the forces that shape people into becoming what they are. A famous professor once startled his colleagues at a convention of educators with this challenge: "If all the books on the art of moving human beings to action were condensed into one brief statement, what would that statement be?" This is the statement they finally agreed upon:

What the mind attends to, it considers.
What it does not attend to, it dismisses.
What the mind attends to continually, it believes.
And what the mind believes, it eventually does.[21]

Long before the birth of Christ, Buddha made this same point: "We become what we think about."[22]

To an extent, the religion teacher can deliberately design a process culminating in a personal act of faith. The practice of the early Church and current pastoral practice in some mission countries provide clues as to how this can be accomplished.[23]

The Bangkok Congress on Mission Catechetics (1962) describes the stages of an adult journeying from unbelief to conversion to baptism. The first stage, pre-evangelization, is an anthropocentric approach which addresses itself to the human condition of the adolescent.[24] It supposes that the catechist empathizes with and works from "all that is true, all that deserves respect, all that is honest, pure, admirable, decent, virtuous, or worthy of praise" (Phil. 4:8) in the lives of the adolescents. Appreciation for what is good in the life of the adolescent opens up possibilities for deep, personal dialogue and also strengthens the position of the catechist to remove whatever blocks the reception of the Christian message.

In addition to his knowledge of society at large, the catechist should ascertain personal knowledge, the specifics of the backgrounds of the adolescents who sit before him in the same room. To illustrate: family background, emotional health, school characteristics and the like.[25] With regard to family background, studies have shown that (hearing) children from families with missing fathers tend to show a low motivation for achievement, an inability to defer immediate rewards for later benefits, low self-esteem, and susceptibility to peer group influence.[26] Factors like these also apply to the deaf. For instance: Has the teenager "accidentally" observed aggressive behavior at home? Or does he still suffer from the opposite contagion of paternal child rearing by well-meaning but ill-advised hearing parents? How much violence does he watch on television or film? Does his deafness propel him toward television programs which carry their message with overt actions? Are these actions usually violent? How does his deafness affect parent-child communication?

Pre-evangelization also enters the residential school for the deaf, and consequently the catechist should scrutinize the school situation with the realization that the school may occupy the entire life of the adolescent except for weekends and holidays. As home environment recedes, with whom does the deaf teenager become closely involved on a day-to-day basis? Who are the models shaping his behavior and character development? Is the deaf adolescent segregated by age as well as by handicap? Can the hearing staff communicate easily in sign-language, and if not, does this reinforce segregation by age? Is intellectual achievement secondary, giving way to athletic success for boys and romantic success for girls? Is the attitude and performance level of the student determined not so much by the number of books in the library or the quality of classroom instruction, but rather by the attitudes and levels of the other deaf students in his class or dormitory section?[27]

Insights into questions such as these have a noticeable impact on the way in which the Christian message is to be communicated. As an example, consider the question of peer models, those in the forefront of the "leading crowd" whom the remainder of the school society imitates. A Christian peer model is a compelling witness and can strongly influence his followers to aspire to his own goals, and the teacher reinforces such influence by giving approval, affection and relevant doctrinal content.

Consider the question of athletic glory. The catechist may go to homecoming games and tournaments and teach teenagers that, like their coaches, Jesus expects them to perform to the limit of their abilities in the spirit of cooperation. Playing to win for God means exerting a full effort, for "while all the runners in the stadium take part in the race," St. Paul says, "the award goes to one man" (1 Cor. 9:24). Far from destroying athletics, the catechist can rotate a catechesis of Christian virtues around an athletic axis.

Some of these observations are, in a sense, pre-religious but necessary to prepare the ground for Christianity. If immaturities, for example, dominate a youngster, the teacher should address himself to these even while he is appealing to the area of faith, for it is improper to make demands at the level of faith when the human level remains underdeveloped. To fail to recognize this is to invite rejection of the Christian message, for the adolescent may fail to open to Jesus not because he deliberately ignores Jesus, but because his immature condition renders him powerless to let Jesus in.[28]

Within the realm of pre-evangelization, there remains a vital task: to ascertain the kind and degree of faith the adolescent already has. In the United States, for example, preoccupation with technical values at the expense of love and engrossment with the speed of everyday life at the expense of meditative quiet have produced what can be called an "immunized Christian," the meaning of which can be captured with a medical analogy. To illustrate: an injection against influenza brings just enough influenza bacteria into the bloodstream to immunize against the real influenza. Similarly, a small dosage of Christ makes one immune to the real Christ, the full Christ. The small dosage of Christ that is received actually prevents the struggle for a deeper understanding and religious experience of the real Christ. It is difficult to convince a person in this predicament that he has to be saved because he does not feel lost. His small dosage has lulled him into the deep sleep of thoughtless acquiescence with the contents of traditional creeds which have imperceptibly lost their real meaning. Needless to say, the catechist will do well to learn to what extent "immunization" has taken place.

Besides the "immunized Christian," the task of ascertaining the kind and degree of faith must also be seen against the background of the "anonymous Christian." Anita Röper explains the "anonymous Christian" as someone who is aware of his relationship with God, but has yet to join the visible Church which officially represents Christianity.[29] "Anonymous Christianity" directs itself toward men of good will who have met God in the depths of their own psyche but have never heard— or, for some reason, never understood—the contents of the Christian message. It is a Christianity which remains unformulated and implicit, a Christianity which is "unaware of itself."[30] If some of this applies to the deaf, the catechist will do well to utilize St. Paul's previously quoted dictum (Phil. 4:8) as a point of departure toward explicit Christianity. Alongside this should be placed Paul's speech to the Athenians: "Men of Athens, I note that in every respect you are scrupulously religious. As I walked around looking at your shrines, I even discovered an altar inscribed, 'To a God Unknown.' Now, what you are thus worshiping in ignorance I intend to make known to you" (Acts 17:22-23).

The work of pre-evangelization lays the seed for evangelization proper, the dynamic verbal (or signed) heralding[31] of the core of the Christian message: Christ is Lord; he loves us supremely; let us never separate ourselves from him. "Heralding" presumes that the catechist will spare nothing to share his cherished beliefs with his audience. The main features of evangelization have been summarized before: "Once the believer has acquired a sense of God and appears spiritually ready to accept God's message, a short resume of salvation history is to be presented in such a way that the compelling fact of Christ as the Lord appears with striking clarity."[32]

Christian truth customarily communicates itself through a Christian person[33] and evangelistic truth cuts back to the bone as it narrows to core Christianity proclaimed to convert someone. What core Christianity is for the deaf will be deferred to the concluding chapter. For now, it suffices to note the importance of a correct arrangement of content, which should be as follows:

A. A recalling of what God *did* for us in Christ. This entails the memory of his wonderful deeds contained in Scripture and listed in the creed.
B. What God *does* for us in Christ. This involves God's contemporary work through the sacraments and grace.
C. The response of man by prayer and a virtuous life.[34]

To complete the effectiveness of evangelization, essential truths should embody a form commensurate with the human condition of the deaf adolescent and his society as well as society at large. Catechesis proper, which hinges upon the conversion experience obtained by the evangelization process, can then begin. For the deaf, catechesis seeks to more deeply develop the basic Christian message: The fatherhood of God, the brotherhood of man, the sacrificial death of Christ, the resurrection, the Eucharist, establishment of the Church, some idea of divine grace, personal and group prayer, and finally the commandments and Christian morality.[35]

24
Identifying the Divine Persons

We have up to now analyzed the unbelief, doubt, and belief of deaf adolescents and suggested some remedies to bring the unbeliever and nominal believer to belief. Pertinent to conversion and belief is the process by which the deaf youth identify God. Clearly, a God with ungodly characteristics is hardly worth converting to, or a Christ with only human traits is easily relegated to historical archives like a Caesar or a Napoleon. Despite the current search for new perspectives, God remains as the "still point" around which all else is organized. Difficult to undertake, investigations into the deaf person's concepts of God are nonetheless essential to catechetics.

This section gets underway with the query, "Who is God?" (Question 3), a question which, although linguistically simple, bristles with difficulties for the deaf. Only 12.8% of the secular school deaf students said that God is Father, Son, and Holy Spirit, whereas 41.7% of the Catholic school pupils answered similarly. This notable difference is perhaps due to a more frequent exposure to religious teaching in the Catholic school. One must hasten to add that the control group performed worse than the Catholic school deaf and not much better than the secular school deaf: 25% of them responded with the three divine persons. No attempt was made to ascertain whether the three persons were perceived as three separate Gods or three persons in one God. The words of the adolescents are simple and straightforward. Daniel 20WAIS108A says that God is "Father, Son, Holy Spirit, Blessed Trinity." "God the Father, God the Son, God the Holy Spirit" is the comment of Linda 17WAIS113A. Likewise did the rest of the 19.6% of the deaf and 25% of the control group answer.

Staying with the same question, the replies of 39.2% of the deaf showed knowledge of only one or two persons of the Trinity. Some 39.7% of the secular school students and 37.5% of the Catholic school pupils responded this way, resulting in the average of 39.2% of all the deaf students. Of these one or two persons, the most frequent response is that Jesus alone is God, an observation which may indicate that, for numerous deaf teenagers, Jesus may be the clearest manifestation of God. Nevertheless, the deaf, as we shall see later, put so many limitations upon Jesus as to all but divest him of his divinity. Sample quotes from the deaf teenagers will elucidate the subject. Dorothy 20CNE98A says: "Jesus Christ. There is only one God"—perhaps implying that an admission of the divinity of the Father and Holy Spirit would be tantamount to a belief in three Gods. The handling of the question by Judy 18WISC97 shows uncertainty: Question—Who is God? Answer—"I don't know." Question—Does God have a name? Answer—"No."

Question—Is Jesus God? Answer—"Yes." Question—Any more persons? Answer—"No." Pearl 17_V likewise falters: Question—Who is God? Answer—"Heaven is God." Question—Does God have a name? Answer—"Jesus." Question—Any more persons? Answer—"Yes, Joseph and Mary." Larry 16_V hesitates as he says, "I don't know who God is. Maybe Jesus is God. Maybe. I think so." Although LeRoy 19_A evidenced no notion of God the Father and the Holy Spirit, he explains that Jesus is not wholly God. "Jesus can be part of God," he insists. Others stated briefly that Jesus alone is God.

The same "Who is God" question evoked another category of answers which again concern part of the Trinity. But now we see the deaf subordinating Jesus to the Father, reminiscent of the trinitarian disputes of the early Church. Before describing this relationship, it might be helpful to dwell on the Father for a moment. In-depth questions about God the Father were not asked consistently in this investigation. Therefore, questions concerning the Father were not subjected to statistical analysis. Yet it is safe to say that at least some deaf adolescents assign a sex to the Father. To them, the Father is either like a man or *is* a man, and he is elderly, white-haired, dressed in a religious habit, and in a place somewhere up in the sky.

The deaf are taught that God is a person and they naturally conclude that he is like a human person, not "person" in the philosophical sense. Hence, since one cannot dissociate sex from person, they conclude that the Father is masculine. To a minority of the deaf students, the Father is not only masculine, but he also has a family: Mary is his wife and Jesus is his child according to the natural congenital process. Furthermore, Joseph is sometimes identified as God the Father.

Here we come across the first of many links between the thinking of the deaf and that of the Hebrews and ancient religions. By assigning a sex, the deaf show a similarity to the ancient Egyptians and Greeks who thought of so many of their gods as masculine, feminine or bisexual. This, however, differs somewhat from the Israelite idea of the deity, which often lacks sexuality. Yahweh transcends sex; he has no family and no companion goddess.

The words of the deaf young people further elaborate the Father's masculinity and his relationship to Jesus. Robert 18MAT Adv.4.9V puts it this way: "God does not have a name. God's wife is Mary. Jesus is under God because Jesus is the son." An interview with Stephen 17MAT Adv.4.4A followed this sequence: "God is nobody." Question—Can you explain what you mean by the word "nobody"? Answer—"Nobody is a person that we don't know." Question—What about Jesus? Is Jesus God? Answer—"No, Jesus is the son of God." Question—Do you know anything about Joseph? Answer—"Yes, Joseph is the step-father. God is the real father." Question—Is God a man, a woman, or what? Answer—"God is a man." Kathleen 19WAIS119 was sincere in her initial profession of faith, but described God as nothing: "God is nothing." Question—Who is Jesus? Answer—"Jesus is the son of God, not God." Question—Who is the father of Jesus? Answer—"God is the father."

Additional quotes illumine the same topic. Charles 21RBE113— expresses himself thus: "God is the Supreme Being who made all the earth. God the Father—his wife is Mary—son, Jesus. Mary's second husband is Joseph, who took the place of God." Question—Is God the Father a man? Answer—"Yes. He is higher." Question—Jesus is the son of God; is he equal to God? Answer—"No. Jesus is under God. God wanted Jesus to come to earth to pull the people—to tell all the people about Father so the people would believe in him (the Father)." William 17_A sees the Father as the creator of Jesus: "The Father made Jesus. Jesus is the son of God." "God is a human spirit," says Paul 18CAT10.5A and "Jesus is God's son—under God, not even with God." Alyce 18CAT13.4A, a bright girl, gives this description: Question—Who is God? Answer—"God is the king of all humans and treats them equal and fair. And God is a teacher too. God teaches us to be good and help other people who need help." Question—Does God have a name? Answer —"I don't know." Question—Is Jesus God? Answer—"I have heard that before." Question—Are any other persons God? Answer—"The Holy Spirit." Christopher 18RBE104_emphasizes the divine family. Responding to the question "Why do we call God 'father'?" he remarked, "Because he has a family; mother Mary, and son Jesus."

Subordinating Jesus to the Father seemed reasonable to some deaf. After all, if the Father is a congenital father, it is logical that he was "born before Jesus" as a few of the deaf said, is older than Jesus and is entitled to the dignity, respect and authority of human fatherhood. The view of this group of deaf somewhat parallels the memorable response of a hearing man undergoing instruction in the Catholic faith. On being asked if the Son is God, the man pondered and said, "Well, no. But when the Father dies, the Son becomes God." This remark reflects a truth: to the deaf interviewees in this group, sonship subordinates. It seems that the task of the teacher is to point out, without unmaking his humanity, that Jesus is a divine person.

Latest New Testament scholarship can enrich "Son of God" for the deaf as it emphasizes that when the original authors used the term, they meant it literally, as do the deaf. Moreover, Jesus, as Son of God, experienced with God a nearness and solidarity unknown to other men (Mt. 11:27; Lk. 10:22). Pannenberg explains the term further. The title "Son of God," he says, was used in Israel at the enthronement ceremonies of a new king. Yahweh adopts him as a son. And the king witnesses to this by saying, "The Lord said to me, 'You are my son; this day I have begotten you'" (Ps. 2:7). Subordination is implied here, but in later

Gentile Christianity the title "Son of God" referred to Jesus' participation in the divine essence.[37] Perhaps the simple statement that Jesus is truly God and truly man would suffice for the deaf as long as it is taught so that the former preserves the latter.

Another group of deaf subordinate Jesus and regard him as a man only. Jesus' goodness turns him toward others and compels him to alleviate their needs and heal their illnesses; yet throughout he remains a man only. A total of 26.7% of all the deaf fell into this category: more specifically, 27.6% of the secular school students and 24% of the Catholic school students answered this way. An average of 16.8% of the deaf doubt whether Jesus is God: 21.1% from the secular schools and 4% from the Catholic schools. (A notable difference occurs in the control group, where 47.4% said that Jesus is not God and none doubted.) This deaf group fails to explain the uniqueness of Jesus, although they perceive his manhood clearly, a manhood which, to them, is real, not hollow or phony. Judith 18CMMS99V, for instance, acknowledged a historical personage named Jesus and continued, "Jesus was a nice man. Jesus helped people, was never selfish." Question—Yes, but is Jesus God? Answer—"No, Jesus is not God." Mary Kay 16WISC97A commented that God is like a man whose name she didn't know. Asked if Jesus is God, she observed, "Jesus' Father is God, not Jesus." Perhaps the same sentiments linger in the mind of Mark 17CNE130_: "No. Jesus is not God. Jesus is the same as people."

To explore further the view of the deaf on the person of Christ, all were shown a drawing of the Nativity. Asked to identify the infant, 97.1% responded that he is Jesus. The following question is, "If the baby is Jesus, is he God?" In response, 56.4% of the deaf said that the infant is God: 51.3% from the secular schools and 72% of the Catholic schools. A full 26.7% of the total group thought that the infant is not God: 27.6% from the secular schools and 24% of the Catholic schools. The sum of 16.8% of the total deaf group were uncertain: 21.1% from the secular schools and 4% from the Catholic schools. On this question there is no significant difference between the deaf and the control group, which responded thus: 100% identified the infant as Jesus; 52.6% said that the infant is God; 47.4% responded in the negative, and none didn't know.

The responses of the 26.7% of the deaf who held that the infant is not God deserve discussion. It is inconceivable to this group to join divinity to infancy. The prevailing sentiment here is that Jesus somehow became God in adulthood. A few even said that Jesus became God only after his death. None of them, however, offered an explanation of how this might have happened, e.g., did the Father bestow lordship on Jesus at his baptism in the Jordan, did Jesus become gradually conscious of his divinity, etc.? These deaf touch upon the question of the hypostatic union and self-consciousness of the pre-Easter Jesus, a question that can involve the most learned theologians in heated discussion.[38]

If, however, the deaf insist upon a clarification of the distinction between Jesus' divinity and the Father's divinity, the following summary may enlighten the mind of the teacher, who must, of course, simplify the language for the deaf.

It has been shown that Jesus' person cannot be separated from God's essence. . . . However, Jesus distinguished the Father from himself. Even though Jesus may not have spoken of himself as Son, the Palestinian community may have designated Jesus with this title in correspondence to the mode in which he himself had spoken of his Father. If Jesus' history and his person now belong to the essence, to the divinity of God, then the distinction that Jesus maintained between himself and the Father also belongs to the divinity of God. The relation of Jesus as Son to the Father may be summarized with primitive Christianity as "obedience." It is therefore a relation proper to the essence of God himself. God is not only "Father," but as the God who is revealed through Jesus' resurrection he is in his eternal essence also "Son." Thereby the expressions "Father" and "Son" are to be strictly applied to the relation to God of the historical man Jesus of Nazareth. Here the word "Father" means the God of Jesus, who was the God of the Old Testament, to whom Jesus directed his prayers and from whose hand he accepted his fate. The word "Son" here does not designate, as it does in other places in the New Testament, Jesus' place of honor in contrast to humanity and the cosmos, but primarily his relation to the Father, a relation of obedience and mission, but also of trust. The latter term may well be taken as a more appropriate expression for that which Jesus' addressing God as Father implied in his own understanding.[39]

Answers to the question "Who is God" can be grouped into still another classification: those deaf who admit human beings into the divine realm, a phenomenon common to 21.6% of the deaf—25.6% of the secular school deaf and 8.3% of the Catholic school deaf. The sum of 5% of the control group shared this thought. This observation uncovers another link between the deaf and ancient religions, many of which had a plurality of semi-human gods. Endowed with divinity are Adam and Eve, Moses, Peter, John, Joseph, Mary, angels and others. Usually these are included with Jesus or the Father. Joyce 18WAIS117A, for instance, says: "Jesus—maybe Moses—that's all." According to Michael 16CMMS118A, Jesus is God; but he added, "Mary, too, is God." The confusion of Francine 16MAT Adv.4.9A is evident: "Jesus is God—I'm all mixed up—is Peter God?" "Jesus, Mary and Joseph" is the simple response of Raymond 17WAIS112A. Likewise is the reasoning of Robert 20WAIS102A: "Father, Jesus, Mary and Joseph." "Jesus and the angels—that is all" answers Anthony 17WISC86V. Other samples are: "Lord Jesus and Hail Mary," "Jesus, Mary and Peter," "Jesus, Mary and the father's name—I think it is Joseph or Peter," "Mary is God. Jesus is the son."

Attributing divinity to Joseph is understandable, since some deaf confuse him with God the Father. Jesus' father is God, and the father's name is Joseph; therefore, Joseph must be God.

The same reasoning leads them to think that Mary is God. If the son is God, the mother can hardly be inferior. This tendency to deify Mary showed in the pre-testing and led to the formulation of a separate question dealing with the issue. After identifying the drawing of the Blessed Virgin, the deaf were simply asked if Mary is God. A total of 15.8% answered affirmatively: 19.7% from the secular schools and 4% from the Catholic schools. Note the significant difference between the Catholic and secular response. Some 11.9% of the deaf didn't know about the matter—14.5% from the secular schools and 4% from the Catholic schools. Again, there is a significant difference. The sum of 72.3% of the deaf said that Mary is not God: 65.8% of the secular school students and 92% of the Catholic school students.

The difference between the deaf group and the control group is also significant, as 100% of the control group responded that Mary is not God. The relatively inadequate understanding of the secular schoool deaf students as compared with the better comprehension of the Catholic group indicates that (1) the deaf can clearly grasp the proper meaning of Mary, and (2) any brief or inadequate treatment of her risks being misunderstood by the deaf.

The last category of teenagers grappling with the question "Who is God?" are the confused and the hesitant. Larry 16_V simply does not know: "I don't know who God is." Mary Beth 19_A also says she doesn't know and adds: "Maybe a ghost." Benjamin 18_A stared straight ahead and after a moment of thought remarked that God does not have a name; as an afterthought, he added: "Jesus' soul is God." When asked "Who is the Holy Spirit?" his reply was, "The Holy Spirit is Jesus." Asked if Jesus is God, Timothy 17_A could honestly say, "That is a hard question." After exhibiting no comprehension of God the Father and the Holy Spirit, Steven 17_A was asked about Jesus. His response: "I have been confused about Jesus." Ann 19CMMS128V, on the other hand, was aware both of a semi-divine Jesus and the effects of the Holy Spirit's action within. Asked who the Holy Spirit is, she offered, "It means that you receive a new, good heart." According to Judith 18CMMS99V, "The Holy Spirit is all people." Moreover, for Judith, God is "nobody."

The ineffectiveness of rote learning in childhood is reflected in the comments of some. Paul 17WISC108A, for instance, remarks, "I learned when I was a little boy, but now I can't remember."

Although the control group reflected more on the same question of God's identity, they shared the uncertainty, as this response indicates: "God could be a he, a she, a goat or anything. The best way to think of God is as an almighty presence." In this group of greatest confusion are 9.8% of the total number of deaf: 10.3% from the secular schools and 8.3% from the Catholic schools. A total of 15% of the control group is in this category.

Another classification is deserving of mention: those who conceive of God as either a non-person or as only persons other than the three persons of the Holy Trinity. Into this group fall 9.8% of the deaf: 11.5% from the secular schools and 4.2% from the Catholic schools.

The control group, which has 25% in this group, is notably different from the deaf. The hesitations of the control group stem partially from its reliance upon reasoning, which takes preference over revelation. The very existence of a personal, infinite being comes in for critical examination. These adolescents have weighed the witness value of influential people in their lives, their knowledge of Scripture, and the state of the present-day Church and found all of this wanting. They turned, instead, to subjective religious experience and to the powers of their own discursive reasoning. Only in this way, they felt, could the question of God's reality and nature be met.

Several examples follow. "I don't think of God as a Trinity," said one bright young man, "I have a different concept. God is a creator and sometimes there is something which touches people, forms their attitudes, and I can't go much beyond that. It is more like some kind of a force that moves between people or in people or something. It doesn't really matter who God is. It is better not to be concerned about that because man's capabilities are too limited." Steven, 17, phrases his vagueness this way: "I know there is something up there, a spirit or something like that. I go to one person, but I don't know much about this person or if it is a person. It could be a rock or something." Others within this category frankly said that they didn't know. Still others had vague notions: "I guess it is somebody superior to us," "I don't know—just a being," "It is very hard to say what God is."

Although the end result of the control group is similar to the deaf, the process leading to the result is different. The hearing group had greater exposure to Scripture and the teachings of the Church and a greater intellectual understanding of these than the deaf. The hearing group, however, would allow little to be imposed upon them by an external, structured source, such as church or school. The deaf, on the other hand, although they exhibited a lesser degree of understanding than their hearing counterparts, were willing to accept a greater degree of external imposition.

25
Literalism and Its Relationship
to the Paschal Mystery

If the phenomenon of literalism among the deaf puzzles experienced teachers of the deaf, it oftentimes drives the uninitiated to despair. It is for both the experienced and the beginning teacher of the deaf—to specify for them the nature of literalism—that the following discussion is offered. First, there will be an explanation of literalism, and then its appearance in the paschal mystery—the crucifixion, resurrection and Eucharist. Finally, clues are offered to alleviate the problem.

The phenomenon of literalism is illustrated in a casual meeting between a superintendent of a residential school for the deaf and a small group of teenage deaf students. The superintendent had just changed the time of the religious education program at the school from Sunday evenings to Wednesday evenings. Puzzled by the shift, the students stopped their superintendent in the corridor and asked how it is possible to conduct Sunday school on Wednesdays.

Another illustration of literalism happened at a recent workshop for religion teachers of the deaf where one of the instructors was teaching courtship and marriage to a class of deaf teenagers. Since the deaf are born actors, the instructor decided to introduce his topic with creative dramatics. Bringing in a male and female puppet and becoming the puppeteer, the instructor manipulated the puppets toward each other. As they drew close, the puppets mutually kissed and embraced. Suspending the show, turning to the class, and remarking that the puppets loved each other, the instructor asked if they could be married. "No" was the quick reply of 19-year-old Michael. "Why not?" inquired the instructor. To the astonishment of the audience, Michael explained what was uppermost in his mind—namely, that it was impossible for the puppets to marry "because they are not living."

Such adherence to the primary meaning of a word, accompanied by a failure to recognize its expanded, multiple or transferred meaning, is called literalism. This accounts for the deaf person's slowness in understanding some kinds of humor, idioms, and figurative language. It is also present in the deaf adolescent's understanding of religious stories. Literalism prevents him from going outside the story, from transferring it, stretching it, connecting it, or applying it to his own life. A deaf adolescent, for instance, will quickly comprehend the visible and tangible features of a parable of Christ, but he will have difficulty relating it to something else, making the point of comparison, and learning the lesson on a higher level.

As a random example, one may choose the parable of the treasure hidden in a field (Mt. 13:44). The problem of literalism has nothing to do with the details of the story: the man stumbling upon buried treasure, realizing that it was not his unless he bought the property, and rushing to sell everything he had to buy that field. But the deaf will falter badly if the teacher assumes that one cursory explanation suffices for the point of comparison—that Jesus is offering the valuable kingdom to us and that we should pay any price, endure any agony to get it. Literalism urges the teacher to slow down here and carefully guide the deaf through the higher lesson and the association of it with his own life.

It is not our intention to here treat literalism exhaustively, but before relating literalism to the paschal mystery, a final observation is necessary. Literalism is related to another stumbling block for the deaf: the formation of abstract concepts of immaterial realities. A detailed and popularized discussion along with a philosophical essay of the process of abstraction in general and its application to the deaf is given in the Appendix.[40]

Unfortunately for the deaf, the language of religion abounds with words, stories and events stretched beyond their normal usage. They are grossly misunderstood by the deaf, as we have seen, because of their proneness to take them in their literal sense. We now see this appear in the adolescents' comments on one of the central events of Christianity, the sacrificial death of Christ on the cross. For many of the deaf, religious language has communicated only a crude, physical understanding of the crucifixion. If language—whether signed, written or spoken—communicates a sharing of experience, the only crucifixion experience that has reached some deaf encompasses nails, cruel soldiers, spears, loss of blood, asphyxiation, death, and nothing more. Absent is the entire spiritual meaning of the experience: Jesus' death as a substitution for Israel and humanity, Jesus' death as a ransom and satisfaction for sin, and Jesus' own predictions of his passion.

This physical view is due to several factors. First, there is the literalism described above. Second, there is the deaf conception of the person of Christ. As we have seen, according to some deaf, Jesus is a normal man or an exceptionally good man, but just a man. It is logical for this group of deaf to scale down the death of Christ to a mere human event. Moreover, if one does not attribute divinity to Jesus, one can hardly view the crucifixion with an attitude of faith, an attitude which should be present before extended meanings of the crucifixion can be illuminated.

To complete our discussion, we now turn to the deaf young people themselves. For the reasons just outlined, short-sighted, literalistic responses were given by 55.8% of the deaf. This percentage, however, applies unevenly to the Catholic deaf schools and secular deaf schools. The Catholic school deaf registered 24% and the secular school deaf 65.8%, a notable difference. Contrast this with a mere 5% of the control group. The proportion of deaf who were uncertain of the reason for the crucifixion is 15.4%; of this 13.9% came from the secular schools and 20% from the Catholic schools. None of the control group expressed doubt and 95% of them attached a non-literal meaning to Jesus' death.

Examining the views of the 55.8% of literalistic deaf is insightful. The individuals were responding to the question "Why did Jesus die?"— and they had all been shown a drawing of the crucifixion, identified it correctly, and agreed that this was a true historical event. Moreover, they had all been asked follow-up questions to ascertain if further reflection would suggest an extended meaning to the crucifixion. Even after the follow-up question, the 55.8% failed to give an extended meaning.

Here is some of what they said. Stephanie 19WAIS98AV remarked: "The king and the soldiers were jealous of Jesus. They put him on the cross. They were jealous because Jesus loved all people." "Because the bad men put the nails in him, put the crown of thorns on him, made him die," is the interpretation of Karen 16WISC80A. To Judy 18WISC110A Jesus' own goodness was partially responsible for his death: "The people loved Jesus. The king got jealous and killed him." A jealous king appears again in the comment of James 18WISC96_: "Jesus wanted to become king. The other king got jealous and told the soldiers to kill Jesus." Patrick 18CMMS74V says: "Jesus died because the king did not free him. The people tried to help Jesus, but the king was too powerful. Jesus died and the sky became dark and the earth shook." Jesus' peace fills the remark of Richard 19MAT Adv.3.0V: "Jesus was nice, good character, walked around, didn't bother anybody. Some men got mad, took Jesus away, killed him." Richard did not know why the men became angry.

More typical of the 55.8% is a restricted, graphic description of the bloody scene at Calvary. "Three men put nails in Jesus"; "Some crazy people killed him, maybe lightning from the storm, I don't know"; "His hands and feet were bleeding, hurt him a lot"; "The soldier put a spear in him"; "He did not have enough food, long time hanging on the cross"; "Soldiers cut Jesus, blood came out"; "Jesus was bleeding from the thorns"—all of these sample responses reflect a literalistic interpretation that stays at the Calvary scene.

Yet closer examination of the 55.8% reveals the ability of some to move beyond the physical Calvary. Although their comprehension of the reasons for the crucifixion remains literal, it is less literal than that of the first group. Here we meet the themes of regal jealousy, a desire to maintain power, the goodness of Jesus and a refusal to believe in God as motives for the killing. According to these deaf, the jealousy of the king is aroused as Jesus' goodness elevates him as a possible rival, and therefore Jesus had to be eliminated. Also deserving of mention is Jesus' pressuring the people to believe in God. Some refused, rebelled and had him killed. This group assigned motives but could not elevate their reasoning beyond this or connect the crucifixion with humanity, then or now.

Finally, we turn to the group which moved farthest away from literalism. The responses of this group offer refreshing evidence that some deaf have broken out of the literal-concrete prison. They expressed some awareness of the crucifixion as the atoning work of Christ. While this group acknowledged that Jesus' death "opens heaven" and "forgives sins," they did not see that they must make Christ's cross their own. Nor were they clear—aside from their statements above—on how to apply the atonement to man's contemporary situation. Daniel 17WISC111A comments: "He washed our sins so we could find our way to heaven." Michael 17WISC120A conditions forgiveness on belief: "Jesus died for the forgiveness of our sins—if we believe in him." A few of the deaf expressed the notion of Jesus' strict obedience to his Father, the motive for which, however, remains unknown. Thus according to Charles 18WISC121_, Jesus died "For God's sake. God the Father told Jesus that he must die. Jesus obeyed God the Father." Kenneth 19MAT Adv.4.2V expresses the forgiveness theme but does not apply it to himself: "People say that Jesus died to forgive the sins of others." Question —Did Jesus die to forgive *your* sins? Answer—"I don't know." Like Kenneth, Margaret 20MAT Adv.4.4A saw a connection between the crucifixion and forgiveness, but could not contemporize it: Question— Did Jesus die to forgive *your* sins? Answer—"No. Jesus died before I was born." Blaming Adam and Eve's sin for the crucifixion is David 17CAT8.0A: "Jesus died to forgive sins and open heaven for us. Adam and Eve closed heaven. God punished and closed heaven. Jesus opened heaven again." The idea of heaven first closed, then opened, is expressed by Daniel 20WAIS108A: "Jesus died to save us from our sins. Before Jesus died, heaven was closed. After Jesus died, heaven opened for us."

A final follow-up question was asked about the crucifixion: Whose fault is this? Anyone else's? Obviously, there is no intent here to fix subjective guilt or culpability, but only to see if the deaf youngsters put an expanded meaning on the crucifixion. Most of the students placed the fault on some individual or group present on Calvary or in the vicinity. Sample responses were: "The man who speared Jesus," "Judas," "the king," "the soldiers who nailed Jesus" and "the temple leaders." Some answers from those deaf who put an extended meaning on the crucifixion were: "all of us," "Adam and Eve," "all people" and "God."

The statistical analysis of the crucifixion question shows a notable difference between the secular school deaf and the Catholic school deaf. Also noteworthy is the difference between the deaf and the control group. Some 55.8% of the deaf gave a literal reason for the crucifixion (only 5% of the control group responded this way). Of this number,

65.8% were from the secular schools and 24% from the Catholic schools. Answering this question non-literally are 28.8% of the deaf—20.3% of the secular school deaf and 56% of the Catholic school deaf. Again the difference is noteworthy.

The pupils in the control group, on the whole, gave answers noticeably superior to the deaf. The sum of 95% of them gave non-literal reasons for the crucifixion. Their answers were neither as trivial as the deaf nor as restricted to the physical aspects of the crucifixion. Forgiveness and love are in the response of Sarah, 16: "Jesus died to take away our sins and to show us that he loves us that much—because I don't think the people of his time realized how much he loved them. They didn't really believe in his love." Joseph, 17, is impressed with the reconciliatory power of the crucifixion: "Jesus died to bring us back to God. Christ was our offering which allowed us to be saved." Frances, 17, says that expiation is a dominant motive: "He died to pay for our sins. Every wrong we do is forgiven because he died."

Two investigators at the University of Notre Dame surveyed 2,937 Catholic young people in the Archdiocese of St. Louis. This total figure includes both Catholic and public school enrollments, where most of the respondents were either in the eighth or the twelfth grade. Over one-half of them said that the chief value of the suffering and death of Christ is that he thereby showed his unlimited love for us. Others explained that he thereby reconciled us with the Father or opened to us a real sharing in the life of the Trinity.[41]

While many of the deaf, especially those who answered literally, attributed the blame for Jesus' death to a specific individual or group, the control group blames no one or everyone. Typical of their comments are these: "It was nobody's fault. Jesus did that for mankind. If he didn't want to be crucified, he didn't have to be crucified." "Indirectly ours." "Everyone's fault." "Actually, it could be anybody's fault, because we sinned."

Before making reflections on the crucifixion responses, a final set of statistics must be given. Some 15.4% of the deaf did not know what to make of the crucifixion: 13.9% of these were from the secular schools and 20% from the Catholic schools. These responses hedged in doubt or simply did not know any motives for the crucifixion.

We remarked earlier that the spiritual meaning of the crucifixion eluded numerous deaf, an observation which is applicable to primitive New Testament traditions. Recall, for instance, that, like the deaf, Luke sees no spiritual meaning, that Matthew does have his death "for many," and Paul has his soteriology; but only later, in Hebrews, is there a full-scale theology of Jesus' death.

The deaf youths' occasional use of the term "kill" rather than "death" deserves notice, since here again the deaf align themselves with primitive Christian tradition. The crucifixion was thought of as "the killing of Jesus" before it came known as "the death of Jesus." To illustrate: Peter, in Acts 2:23, tells his audience: "You even made use of pagans to crucify and kill him."

Perhaps the most dominant reason for literalism is the language deficiency which is a direct by-product of deafness itself.[42] Weakness in language comprehension is doubly debilitating for the deaf in the area of religious language. The writings of religion and theology are strewn with words and expressions that would lead to utter misunderstanding if they were taken in their literal sense. Analogies, symbols, imagery, and figures of speech are common in religious language. They are man's attempts to capture and express sublime truths not verifiable by the senses.

One of these truths is the idea of Christ's vicarious death. To try to put this point across, St. Paul uses four comparisons. First, in 1 Corinthians 5:7 he compares Christ to the Passover lamb. Second, in Colossians 2:14 he uses an image from the criminal law of his day, explaining that our sins are written on the tablet above the head of the crucified. Third, Paul takes a comparison from the institution of slavery; thus, in 1 Corinthians 6:20 and 7:23 we see the death of Christ redeeming us from slavery. Fourth, in Romans 5:18ff. and Galatians 4:4ff. the obedience of Christ offsets the disobedience of Adam.[43] Paul chooses these images to illustrate that Christ died "for us," the sinless one taking the place of sinners. Unfortunately, however, it is figurative language like this that makes little sense to the deaf. If left on their own, they would perhaps wrestle with it for a while, gain a piecemeal understanding and then give up. It may be simpler and clearer in the long run for the teacher to say simply "Christ died for us" and then underline and show them the "for us" in the various passages of the epistles.

Besides the language deficiency, other reasons, mostly pedagogical and theological, steal the significance of Jesus' death from the deaf. First, it is impossible to understand the crucifixion apart from the public life of Christ. Since the deaf in general have little taste for the printed word, they can hardly be expected to learn much of Jesus' life from Bible reading.[44] Neither have they learned much of Jesus' life from the visual-aids, total communication, or other techniques used in the once-a-week religion sessions. To the extent that there is a lack of knowledge of Jesus' life, there will be a difficulty in seeing the deeper side of the crucifixion, since his cross is connected with and summarizes his whole life and work.[45] Second, any satisfactory understanding of the crucifixion supposes the existence of the kingdom of darkness and demonic powers, for by the cross of Christ did God "disarm the principalities and powers" (Col. 2:15). The crucifixion took away the power of the evil spirits over man. Some of the deaf cannot see the cross as a victory because, according to them, there is no such thing as evil powers. Many of the deaf scoff at the devil, dismissing him as a harmless fantasy character existing only in the minds and canvasses of the artists who created him. When questioned about the existence of hell, only 37.9% of the deaf thought that it was real. This point will be examined later. A third reason flows from the second. If the deaf reject belief in a kingdom of darkness capable of distorting their lives, there is no need for struggle, victory and allegiance to a kingdom of light.

We now turn to the resurrection. As mentioned earlier, no attempt is made to ascertain whether the deaf young people grasp the significance of the resurrection. They are simply asked if they believe in the resurrection, if Jesus rose body and soul or only in spirit, and if Jesus is still alive. Question 18, on the contemporary Jesus, is asked as a check. Some of the deaf believe that only Jesus' spirit rose. This led the investigator to divide the responses into the categories of full resurrection and part resurrection, the latter designating a mere spiritual rising.

It was found that 72.8% of the deaf believe that Jesus' body rose from the dead. Of this number 67.1% represents the secular schools and 91.7% the Catholic schools. The sum of 18.4% of the deaf responded that only Jesus' spirit rose: 24% of the secular school young people and none of the Catholic school pupils. This notable difference indicates that belief in Jesus' complete resurrection is more prevalent among the Catholic school deaf. None of the deaf maintain that Jesus did not rise from the dead. Expressing doubts on this matter are 8.7% of the deaf: 8.9% from the secular schools and 8.3% from the Catholic schools. The views of the control group are somewhat similar to the deaf. A full 73.7% of the hearing teenagers believe that Jesus, body and soul, rose from the dead. Some 15.8% of them believe that only Jesus' spirit rose, and 5.3% did not believe in Jesus' resurrection. A small 5.3% harbored doubts.

The thinking of the deaf on this matter is conditioned by several factors. First is their conception of Jesus' divinity. If Jesus is "under God" or "the son of God, but not God" or a man only, it is logical that he will remain in the earth—yet St. Paul's passive expression of God raising him up (Acts 2:32; 1 Cor. 15:13) is compatible with this understanding of Jesus. Confusion about Jesus' identity, therefore, leads to confusion about his resurrection. Second, although the doubting Thomas incident and other appearances of the post-Easter Christ have impressed the deaf, we have to say that the public did not witness the resurrection as it did the crucifixion. This lack of evidence disturbs some of the positivistic deaf. Third, if the deaf divest the faith dimension from other miracles, they may do likewise to the resurrection. Fourth, and perhaps most significant, is the deaf adolescents' understanding of the idea of a spirit. This has a bearing on the after-life, the resurrection life of man, and the spirituality of God.

What is a spirit according to the deaf? Although a direct probe into this question was beyond the scope of the survey, scattered responses enable guarded observations to be made. Reactions to the questions on heaven, hell, the resurrection and the nature of God contain spin-off information on the spirit and hence clear the way for some discussion to be made. We can say that at least some deaf regard a spirit as a corporeal entity, recalling the ancestral worship of spirit-souls in China. One young man, for instance, said that at the time of Jesus' death, a spirit departed from Jesus' heart, went straight up and disappeared into the sky. Whether most deaf conceive of spirit as fine, perhaps gaseous matter that darts about the universe, appearing and disappearing, influencing men and withdrawing from men, is not apparent. Other deaf see the departure of something physical from man's body at the time of death. Still others commented that God comes down to snatch this out of the body at death. To declare to the deaf that "God is a spirit" is to invite a connection between "God" and "fine physical matter." Most people presumably would describe a spirit as a personality without a material body, but such a thought is far from that contained in some responses of the deaf. It must be added that for these deaf the spirit is enclosed in a human form. God is one of these and he thus becomes like a ghost.[46] For the percentage of the deaf mentioned earlier, it is only this spirit that survived the death of Jesus. More will be said later about the spirit. Our purpose here was only to see it as related to the resurrection.

"Only the eschaton will ultimately disclose what really happened in Jesus' resurrection from the dead. Until then we must speak favorably in thoroughly legitimate, but still only metaphorical and symbolic form about Jesus' resurrection and the significance inherent in it."[47] Largely lacking metaphor and symbol, how do the deaf describe the resurrection? Marilyn 18WAIS111A thinks that a transformation took place: "Jesus' body became a spirit and rose up to heaven." Sharing this view is Joan 19MAT Adv.4.7A who says: "Jesus' body became his soul." For others Jesus sat up, walked out, overpowered the soldiers and left. Thus says Thomas 19WISC106A: "Jesus opened the door, defeated the soldiers and rose to heaven with his body." Karen 16WISC81A comments: "Jesus became alive in God. Just his heart and soul went up to heaven." Joseph 17WISC118A, echoing the thoughts of several others, remarks: "Jesus is a ghost." Bypassing the reality of the soul but acknowledging the resurrection of the body, Linda 18RBE109_ says: "The people touched Jesus' body, not his soul." "He rose body and soul because he came back to earth to show his wounds to his mother and some saints" is how Charles 21RBE113_explains the resurrection.

The 8.7% of the deaf who doubted were uncertain for varying reasons. Patricia 18WAIS96A was never told of the resurrection: "I never heard anything like that before." A future resurrection is on the mind of

William 17_A: "Jesus' body went back to earth. It will rise again later." Reluctant to admit a resurrection, Joseph 17WISC118A concluded that perhaps "Jesus is a ghost," an expression fairly common among those deaf who acknowledged only a partial (spiritual) resurrection. Some of the deaf in this category, and others besides, still search for observable evidence. Andrea 18WAIS117A, for instance, wishes to physically see Jesus: "People say that Jesus rose. But he doesn't have his body now. I can't see anything. Maybe Jesus is a ghost now." Another respondent, a deaf young man, thought similarly until he saw a religious movie which satisfied him that Jesus rose physically. Experiencing disappointment over his failure to physically see God, Robert 18CMMS104V wonders about the resurrection: "Maybe it's only a story."

Although they were more familiar with Scripture and showed more finesse in their reasoning, the control group percentages parallel those of the deaf. The sum of 95% of the control group believes the resurrection happened (5% deny the resurrection). A full resurrection is the belief of 73.7% of the control group, whereas 15.8% espouse a partial (spiritual) resurrection and the remainder are uncertain of the nature of the resurrection. To Frances, 17, the resurrection confirms Jesus' identity: "Jesus rose with his body and soul to show people that he really was God and not just another man." Reflecting St. Paul's passive expression in 1 Corinthians, Edward, 16, says: "Yes, I believe. Jesus was raised from the dead by God's power." Others simply said that Jesus, body and soul, rose from the dead. Those entertaining uncertainties expressed these variously. The resurrection delayed Sarah, 16, who finally shook her head: "I don't know how to answer that. When you come right down to it, Christ is just a spirit." According to Christina, 16, only Jesus' soul rose: "Some people saw him—but I guess it is just his soul." "There was the shape of him," says Adrien, 18, "but it wasn't his physical body—it was his soul." In their search for evidence, several others parallel the deaf. Here are some sample responses: "Jesus rose—body and soul—but I don't think Jesus is alive now. I don't see any evidence of him." "By the facts of historians that I read, I would say, yes. I don't know if he rose with body and soul. I don't think that Jesus is alive now." "I don't personally believe that Jesus rose; but I won't say that the resurrection is beyond belief." "According to the records and all that stuff, he rose; but I'm not sure."

Remembering is an important part of worship, prayer, and liturgical celebration (Gen. 8:1; 19:29, Ex. 32:13; 1 Sam. 1:11; Lk. 22:19; Jn. 14:26). Memories bind Christians through recalling common sources of faith; besides, memories make the future. The resurrection of Christ, which should be *the* memorable event, is meaningless to many deaf because it offers nothing for their future and tells them nothing about themselves for their present.

Reversing this thought and elaborating the Heideggerian insight of history that man organizes his past around the direction of his future, Navone says: "Thus the Christian, seeking his divinization with and in the risen Christ at the second coming and the beatific vision of God, finds a past that is sacred, marvelously transcending the purely human with its wonderful works of the Lord."[48] Do those deaf who believe in the resurrection understand it as more than a mere historical story? Do the resurrection believers bring the risen Christ to the present? Do they associate him with themselves? As explained earlier, Question 18 was designed as a check on the resurrection. The question seeks insights as to whether the adolescents believe that Christ is still alive and with us after the resurrection. That a large number of deaf, as well as the control group, relegate Christ to the obscure past is evident from the responses.

Those deaf who place Christ alongside John F. Kennedy, Abraham Lincoln, and George Washington number 41.1%—43.8% from the secular schools and 31.8% from the Catholic schools. To these deaf either he rose only spiritually and vanished to a separate world or rose not at all. A few thought that Jesus rose and then died again. At any rate this group ranks Jesus as an historical figure only—historical in life-span, historical in ability, historical in stature. Jesus is somehow alive but irrelevant to Linda 17RBE113__who says: "Jesus is alive, but he disappeared. He is gone. He doesn't visit me." Timothy 19WAIS124A says: "Jesus' soul is in heaven. His body is with Row A" (the deceased historical figures). Looking for material evidence is Raymond 17WAIS112A who says: "Maybe Jesus is with Row B (the living figures). But I don't know. There is no proof. We do not see Jesus." "Jesus is alive now," comments Karen 16WISC81A, "but just his heart and soul go up to heaven." According to William 18WISC121A: "Jesus rose to heaven. He is not here." To Ralph 18WISC107__ not even Jesus' spirit exists: "Jesus died once—finished. He can't die again. A spirit is nothing." Edna 16_A acknowledges the resurrection but adds: "Jesus rose, yes. But he became very old and died again. Now Jesus is dead."

Perhaps a well-meaning liturgist put Rita 20WAIS98 and a few others in a category by themselves. This small group holds that Christ physically dies on Good Friday and rises on Easter Sunday each year. A perplexed Rita finally indicated that Christ belongs with both Row A and B because "Jesus dies and rises again each year." She means, as she later explained, that he dies and rises in the same way as he did originally.

It is somewhat satisfying that 46.3% of the deaf align Christ with Row B, a total figure which is broken down to 45.2% of the secular schools and 50% of the Catholic schools. In doing so, this group of deaf assign life and a contemporary presence to Jesus—a presence, however, which may be characterized by aloofness and physical remoteness, having little in common with the everyday lives of the deaf. This concludes our discussion for now, although the theme of God's presence will be studied again later.

It must also be observed that 12.6% of the deaf, which includes 11% of the secular school deaf and 18% of the Catholic schoolers, remarked that Christ is with both Row A and B. They placed Jesus with Row A to account for his crucifixion and with Row B to account for his resurrection and present life.

Because of their notable difference from the deaf, the control group results are worthy of examination. Placing Christ with Row A is the view of 29.4% of the hearing teenagers, whereas 70.6% of them put Christ with Row B. None assigned Christ to both rows. Some sample Row A answers are as follows: "His body is dead. So you'd have to put him with Row A." "Christ is only an historical man." "God is a dormant force. It doesn't do anything. In that sense it is with Row A." Typical of Row B responses are these: "Jesus is contemporary." "God is alive." "He is alive in his Church and sacraments." One adolescent cared little about objective reality as she made Christ's life or death dependent upon the subjective view of the individual: "If a person thinks of God as dead, he is dead to that person. So it depends on the person's opinion. I think God is—for that person—what the person thinks he is."

In making a critique of the deaf view on Christ's contemporary presence, one must consider several contributing factors. First is the deaf position regarding the divinity of Christ. For if Christ is a man only, one can hardly expect him to be the master of life. Second is their understanding of the realm of the spiritual. To some, a spirit "is nothing," "a ghost," or an unearthly transparent entity and consequently only remotely connected with contemporary life. Third is the positivistic view held by some deaf; for them, if Christ is physically absent, he is entirely absent. That Jesus can be mysteriously, though really, present eludes such a mind. Fourth is a survey on the deaf understanding of God's transcendence and immanence. And last is God's spirituality. The fourth and fifth points are yet to be analyzed. It is obvious that all these factors interweave and place their mark on the adolescents' comprehension of the presence of Christ. Therefore, to insulate Question 18 from them would be a mistake.

26
The Eucharist

While recognizing that Jesus' manhood and his activity as an historical personage are part of his great importance to us, we still have to view him against the thinking of the deaf youth. Previous evidence indicates the difficulty with which the deaf transfer or connect one thought to another: literalism forbids the easy use of such transfers and connections. Hence, even though we hardly desire to totally spiritualize Christ, Hellenistic style, we ask how the deaf of the twentieth century can hold on to a Christ who, to them, labors under the limitations of an historical figure whose work was fixed in Palestinian times.

How can the deaf transfer Christ to the present? It is more accurate to say that the deaf must participate in the transfer, since Christ himself has already made it possible by giving us intermediary signs, the sacraments. For the sacraments push Jesus' work, life, and death beyond the frontiers of time and place. The sacramental dynamic process occurs at the level of mystery—and therefore beyond sense perception—through the use of symbols. Unfortunately, this process has not brought Christ to the present for numerous deaf.

Partly because it is so far-reaching and profound, and partly because it is received so often, the Eucharist was chosen as a topic for interviewing the deaf. Incorporation into Jesus' mystical body, participation in his death and resurrection, and sharing in his holy communal meal as sisters and brothers are all included in the Eucharist. These dimensions, however, were not explicitly asked in the testing. The emphasis, rather, was on the making-present of the real Christ in bread and wine, material which distinguishes the Eucharist from the other sacraments.

Baptismal water and confirmation chrism, for instance, remain water and chrism after the sacraments have been given. But in the Eucharist, what was bread and wine before the consecration becomes Jesus' body and blood afterward. It is precisely to this that our question addresses itself. Do the deaf see the Eucharist as the body and blood of Christ? Or do they comprehend it in a different way? A check on the real-presence aspect of the Eucharist is made in Question 21m, which asks why people genuflect in church.

It should be an object of concern to all those involved in religious formation that numerous deaf put a single interpretation upon the Eucharist—the literalistic one. It is true that a teacher can elicit correct rote responses from young deaf children, but their answers that "Communion is Jesus' body," while satisfying the teacher, often masks a verbalism which later vanishes into perfunctory belief or unbelief—a process common to deaf and hearing alike.

The disappointing statistics support the above remark. Only 37.2% of the deaf believe that the Eucharist, or Holy Communion, is the body and blood of Christ. The Catholic school deaf contribute significantly to this percentage, since 62.5% of them understand the Eucharist in this way. Only 28.6% of the deaf in the secular schools affirm this same belief. A total of 44.7% of the deaf do not believe in the Eucharist (at least as it was presented in the interviews): 20.8% from the Catholic schools and 52.8% from the secular schools. Answering that they did not know or doubted about the Eucharist are 18.1% of the deaf—16.7% from the Catholic schools and 18.6% from the secular schools. The control group fared worse, as 35% of them expressed belief, 55% expressed unbelief, and 10% didn't know.

As they did elsewhere, very many deaf expressed their Eucharist views freely and their words were recorded verbatim by the investigator. Careful study of these enables one to group their thoughts into several categories.

One characteristic that appeared is a fragmented understanding of the Eucharist. The deaf here allow for the wine changing into blood, but hold that the bread remains unchanged. The answer of Kimberly 16CAT6.9A is typical: "The bread stays the same, but the wine becomes blood." "Holy Communion is not Jesus, but the wine becomes the blood of God" is the comment of Stephen 17MAT Adv.4.4A. John 20WAIS114A says: "The wine becomes blood. Nothing happens to the bread. The people eat it." That a piece of bread can become someone is perhaps too mind-clouding for this group. Yet wine changing to blood remains a liquid and retains its color, a phenomenon which, because of its more evident symbolism, is more plausible to them than the former assertion.

The dominant view of the next group is the strong connection made between Communion and forgiveness of sin. "Communion," says William 20RBE85_, "is holy bread, for the forgiveness of sins." Carol 18WAIS91AV is vaguely aware of something sacred as she says: "Communion is for sin." "People who receive Communion," Charles 21RBE113_explains, "have their sins forgiven and they follow the spirit of Jesus." After watching the investigator sign (with Ameslan) the consecration, Charles added: "The priest does not have authority for miracles. Only Jesus can do that. There is only one Jesus." Several other deaf similarly separated the priest from Jesus.

Accenting the physical idea of Jesus' bodily (or soul) presence *in* the bread is the position of another group. After watching the signing (Ameslan) of the consecration. Sandra 18_V remarked that the bread remains such, but "Jesus' body is inside." Steven 18CAT7.3A says likewise: "Jesus is inside of the bread." Richard 19_A alters this somewhat as he says: "Jesus' soul and heart are in the bread." Pointing to the drawing of the host, Linda 18RBE109_ replies: "Jesus' body is in that."

Another group of deaf unwittingly express a thought in accord with 1 Corinthians 11:30 where Paul mentions illness and death resulting from unworthy participation in the Eucharist. These deaf claim that the bread and wine become different or holy and make people strong. To Larry 16_V the bread becomes slightly different and "priest and people eat the bread and body becomes strong." "Communion is bread that makes people strong," remarks Julie 17MAT Adv.4.4V. The following sequence took place with George 17WISC116A. He began: "I read book. Book says, 'This is my body.'" Question: What does that mean? Answer: "That the bread is for the body. The bread is for my body to help it become stronger." Question: What about the wine? Answer: "Wine becomes blood. Blood makes clean, makes strong. Blood makes good body—I think." The view of Michael 18WAIS112V is similar: "You eat the bread and the bread helps your soul. The wine helps the priest's soul."

Another category of deaf search for sensory evidence of Jesus' eucharistic presence. "I never saw that (i.e., bread changing) happen," protests Judy 18WISC97_. Several said that since they cannot see or hear the words of the consecration, they are uncertain of what happens. Margaret 20MAT Adv.4.4A remarks: "I don't know. I can't see it. I sit far back in the church." For similar reasons, Peter 17MAT Adv.4.9V doesn't think anything happens at the consecration: "I don't think so. I never look. I'm too far away in the church." Evidence from the sense of taste eluded Ellen 18WISC125A: "I say that Communion is the body of Christ, but I don't believe it. Before, my girlfriend—she is a little devil —stole a host. And then we went to Communion. The host she stole and Communion both tasted exactly the same. What was the difference? That is why I don't believe." Question: Can the power of God change the bread so that it becomes the body of Jesus? Answer: "Impossible. I don't believe it." Disappointed in their expectations of hard evidence, this group found the Eucharist difficult or impossible to accept.

Still another category of responses shows that some deaf have no idea of the Eucharist, as surprise was commonplace in their comments. At the interview they were learning about the Eucharist for the first time. After viewing the drawings and witnessing a signed (Ameslan) explanation of the consecration, a startled Dora 16WISC104A asked: "Do you mean the bread becomes a person—Jesus?" Answer: "Yes." Dora: "Impossible!" "I never heard about that before," protested Phyllis 19WAIS94V. Other samples are similar: "Nobody ever told me about that before," "I didn't know about that," etc.

Other remarks are noteworthy but too few to be categorized. They have to do with equating faith with feelings ("How many people feel excited? How many people feel anything different? It must be just bread"), divorcing the priest from Christ ("Maybe God can change the bread but the priest can't"), and speaking of the Eucharist as an academic subject ("I think I learned that when I was young, but now I forget"). This last group is more numerous than the previous two.

A criticism could be made that the study treats only one aspect of the Eucharist—the real presence. Theologically, it is less preferable to look at the real presence by itself than to consider it in the context of the entire mystery, including covenant, thanksgiving, sacrifice and repast. Yet these would lose their dynamism without the real presence. It is because of this and to preserve simplicity of communication that the "real presence" aspect of the Eucharist was chosen for investigation.

So important is the deaf adolescents' sense, or lack thereof, of the eucharistic presence of God that a follow-up question was designed as a check. Question 21m asks the deaf why people genuflect in church. Ameslan and mime were sometimes used to eliminate misunderstandings on this question. The categories of answers—namely, eucharistic presence (in the tabernacle), the cross, God's general presence, don't know, and other—are based on feedback from the pre-testing.

Exhibiting some understanding of the permanence of the Eucharist and of the eucharistic presence in the church (in the tabernacle) are 3.4% of the deaf. (The control group registered 11.1%.) Explaining that people genuflect only to honor the cross are 24.7% of the deaf (and none of the control group). The same percentage of deaf said that genuflections are made to respect a general presence of God—a presence which can pervade the church, but which sometimes does not even "focus" on the church, much less the tabernacle. A total of 27.8% of the control group gave a "general presence" answer. Having no idea of the motivations for genuflections are 28.1% of the deaf (22.2% of the control group likewise has no idea why people genuflect) whereas 19.1% of the deaf and 38.9% of the control group gave trivial or irrelevant reasons for genuflections. From all of this, one conclusion is clear; if a minority of deaf see the Eucharist as the real presence, even fewer see it as a permanent sacrament. Question 21m therefore reinforces the findings of Question 10.

Closely paralleling the deaf is the performance of the control group. Joseph, 17, is among the believers, and an adequate summary of his believing group is his remark: "The host becomes Jesus and you have a chance to have Jesus inside you. That is what the idea is." Others see the Eucharist differently. Among these is Edward, 16, who says: "Christ is not there. It is not really Christ. It just symbolizes him." "Communion is remembering," says Steven, 17. "You remember about the Last Supper. That's all. I don't think he is really there." Adrien, 18, is hesitant as she says: "I think it is like the bread at the Last Supper. But at Communion, it is a part of God. Right? Well, tell me if I'm right, or I'll be all mixed up." Peter, 15, says: "It represents the body and blood of

Christ. But it remains bread and wine." A few gave authoritarian answers. Such is Frances, 17, who says: "It is Catholic teaching that this is the body and blood of Christ and I have not questioned that teaching." Yet she was unconvincing as she admitted that the Eucharist left her unaffected. On the question of the Eucharist, the statistics between the deaf and hearing were similar.

Yet there was one important deviation which the statistics left undetected. The hearing young people had wider knowledge of pertinent Scripture passages, the Last Supper, and the words of consecration. Still, only 35% of them believe that the Eucharist is really the body and blood of Christ. The deaf, on the other hand, burdened with a marked deficiency in these areas and strait-jacketed by literalism, demonstrated a similar end-result.

No discussion of deaf eucharistic thinking can be made without including other topics which impinge upon it. First of all, one may ask why, from the deaf point of view, it was appropriate for Christ to even want to institute such a sacrament. The reason for raising this issue, excluded from the statistical analysis, is a question on the meaning of the Mass that was sometimes asked of brighter deaf adolescents. Their reflections indicate that most of them understand the Mass almost exclusively in terms of its physical characteristics, i.e., sitting, standing, singing, sermons and the reception of Holy Communion. These deaf, if they see the Eucharist as Christ's body and blood at all, fail to see it as offered to God and offered for them. The *why* question for them is logical.

An event related to the Eucharist was already examined—the crucifixion. The Eucharist, St. Paul explains (1 Cor. 11:26), is a memorial and proclamation of Christ's death. Hence, the deaf (as well as the hearing) understanding of the Eucharist is contingent upon their understanding of the crucifixion. Tying in, too, is Christ's divinity, or lack thereof, and his relationship with his Father.

Pursuing the subject further, we may remark upon two categories of deaf—one which viewed the Eucharist as academic and the other which thought of the Eucharist positivistically. For both groups, the Eucharist was something learned in a classroom, only to be forgotten with the onset of adolescence.

Perhaps a revision of religious language would serve these deaf. Feedback from the deaf indicates that in some instances the language used to communicate the Eucharist was objective, historical narration which over-appealed to memory. Rather than objective language, what is called for is a balance between it and a language tied to experience and existence. When talking about the Eucharist (or Trinity), human language labors under "great poverty of speech."[49] For help we turn to symbols.

Are symbols, for some deaf, synonomous with confusion rather than clarification? In a broad sense, all language is symbolic, since words themselves are symbols. While this is true, it is also correct to say that, in a more restricted sense, "symbol" is an intermediary between the language and its ultimate referent. The symbol, understood in an indirect sense, bounces off the direct, literal object and embeds itself in the more remote subject matter to which the speaker is referring.[50] For instance, in John's Gospel Christ refers to himself as a door, a vine, a light, etc. Furthermore, symbols can be distinguished as conventional and intrinsic.[51] The conventional symbol is arbitrarily designated, e.g., Uncle Sam representing the United States. The intrinsic symbol, on the other hand, has a built-in kinship with what it stands for, e.g., the cross representing Christianity, the dove representing peace. This second kind has less to do with abstract language than the first and therefore can ease the task of illumination for the deaf.

Modern advertisers are learning that the intrinsic symbol can communicate not indirectly but even more directly than other modes of communication. Intrinsic symbols, they say, can stand alone insofar as their own power enables them to telegraph a wordless eloquence. The Prudential Life Insurance Company, for instance, finds it superfluous to explain its stability verbally: the Rock of Gibraltar does that without support from words. Indeed, man has yet to build the words that can dislodge the rock. For the hearing as well as the deaf, the rock is sign-language.

Numbered among the intrinsic are also many ancient religious symbols, such as fire, water, plants, stones, light and darkness. Added to this list are bread and wine, representing nourishment and consequently all life. With some imagination the teacher can coalesce the bread and wine with life and then with life personified. The Old Testament employs this symbolism as it joins a name to a person: the name stood for the person's dominant characteristic, even becoming an essential part of him—in a way, identical with him.[52] A development of the intrinsic symbol approach would perhaps reach the positivistic deaf group and those who were untouched by a language which communicated little of the Eucharist to them.

This method can converge with another to bring the Eucharist to the deaf adolescents, a method which presupposes that the teacher (1) genuinely believes in the Eucharist and (2) is competent in sign language and mime. By play-acting the teacher can re-present to the deaf the skirmish between Christ, his wavering disciples and the skeptical onlookers (Jn. 6:35-70). Patiently explaining that *he* is the bread of life (Jn. 6:49ff.) and that, unlike those who ate manna in the desert and died, those who eat this bread will live forever, Jesus had made himself unmistakably clear: he is the "living bread that comes down from heaven" (Jn. 6:51).

That Jesus had shocked his audience is only too obvious from the ensuing argument. Shattered, the people turned to one another and asked, "How can this man give us his flesh to eat?" (Jn. 6:52).

Sensing the shock and seizing the initiative, Jesus repeated, "Let me solemnly assure you, if you do not eat the flesh of the Son of Man and drink his blood, you have no life in you" (Jn. 6:53ff.).

Still, they could scarcely believe what they were hearing as they protested: "This sort of talk is hard to endure! How can anyone take it seriously?" (Jn. 6:60). Then they began to leave.

But Jesus, refusing to yield, stood adamant. Rather than dilute his teaching, he let them walk away. As a teacher, Jesus was obliged to adhere to truth and therefore call them back if they had misinterpreted him. He did not. As they walked away, they knew perfectly well what he meant and they rejected it. "From that time on, many of his disciples broke away and would not remain in his company any longer" (Jn. 6:66). Saddened, Jesus turned to the Twelve and asked: "Do you want to leave me, too?" "Simon Peter answered him, 'Lord, to whom shall we go?' " (Jn. 6:69ff.).

At this juncture, the teacher may call for a decision from the deaf. Does this shake their faith? Do they wish to join the departing disciples or stay with the Twelve and Jesus? Perhaps this episode can be enclosed in a para-liturgical ceremony with the decision as the climax. Qualifying this entire incident for use with the deaf are its color, literal language, and straightforwardness.

Another eucharistic insight comes from ancient Greece. Perhaps because of their popularity or perhaps because they held beliefs closely similar to Christianity, ancient Greek mystery religions frustrated the spread of Christian belief. They consequently came under sharp attack from the early Christian Fathers who were aggravated by rites which rivaled those of Christianity. One of these was a Dionysian rite which could have competed with the Eucharist. The god Dionysius was closely associated with vegetation—especially vine and ivy. Greek followers of this cult believed that partaking of the fruit of the vine brought about union with Dionysius. The rite emphasized wine drinking, not for the pleasure of intoxication, but for sacramental significance: in drinking wine, the Greek was taking into his body the god Dionysius himself. And this transformed the Greek worshiper into a "Bacchus," a divinized being. Both Plato and Euripides attest to this in their writings.[53]

The nominal believers among the deaf will sometimes raise the question: "Communion? What for?" Since teaching the deaf by comparison and contrast is often effective, perhaps St. Augustine's famous remark is a fitting answer. Augustine compares communion and ordinary bread. Since it is naturally assimilated, ordinary bread becomes part of the recipient's body. But holy bread has the opposite effect. People who eat holy bread become like it (Christ).[54]

We have laid out for ourselves the various facets of deaf eucharistic thinking. Equipped with this, we can move on to ask how all of this affects a deaf person's reception of the Eucharist. Staying with the norms of Pius X and allowing the continued reception of First Holy Communion by younger children, it becomes clear that the Eucharist must be recycled into and treated more at length in adolescent catechesis. A confused, minimum awareness of the holy bread suffices for a younger child, but not for an adolescent. Often bereft of understanding, verbalisms issuing from a child can be discarded in adolescence. Unless he or she is disposed properly, an adolescent's reception of the Eucharist can be sterile. Although God takes the initiative, his objective action is joined to the recipient's subjective dispositions toward and participation in the Eucharist. This is a prerequisite for the grace of the eucharistic Christ to nourish the person. More meaningful dispositions are dependent upon a more effective catechesis.

In conclusion, one can say that a sense of reverence and appreciation of the Eucharist alone can sustain a deaf person's faith and survival in a hearing church where the religious language is so often unintelligible to him. A catechesis which saves them from their worst blunders and helps them recognize that the Eucharist can be understood only in the light of mystery and by the inclusion of intrinsic sacramental symbol and scriptural drama will lead them to deeper reverence and appreciation.

27
The After-Life

Unflinchingly, life moves toward its end—and toward its perfection. For some, the day of death is the day of greatest triumph; for some, the day of greatest failure; for some, both. From time immemorial poets and thinkers have struggled mightily to articulate what they believe happens next. Surely the question of life after death captivates any religion.

For cosmic, community, and individual destiny, the Christian looks to the Scriptures for guidance. But even the Bible throws a veil over the subject, and St. John declares: "We are God's children now; what we shall later be has not yet come to light" (1 Jn. 3:2). Thus does the field of after-life study abound with theological implications and speculations.

Revelation does render some basic tenets clear. For both the community and the individual there are the judgment, eternal life, heaven, hell, purgatory, resurrection and, with its cosmic dimensions, the paramount idea of the kingdom of God. On the surface, these may appear simple enough. But they can become quite difficult for several reasons: (1) without any development, childhood after-life ideas are often carried into adolescence and adulthood, where they are grossly distorted or rejected; (2) the language is entangled in much mythological imagery; (3) some of the concepts, especially heaven, so easily become associated with egocentric longings—heaven becomes "reward" and hell "punishment."[55]

In an ambiguous world, to see any of these "last things" requires an eye of faith. And even with an eye of faith, "we see indistinctly, as in a mirror" (1 Cor. 13:12). How dimly do the deaf see in this mirror? The eschatology covered in the interviews represents neither completeness nor depth. It is restricted to the individual level and encompasses only continued personal existence, heaven, hell and, in a few instances, purgatory. Yet the comments of the deaf youth provide clues which, taken with others, give an important glimpse into their religious thinking. Let us now meander through their minds to see what is there.

Gazing at the tombstone drawing, 96.2% of the deaf affirmed a belief in life after death: 96% from the Catholic schools and 96.2% from the secular schools. None of the deaf responded negatively. Some 3.8% expressed doubt, 4% from the Catholic schools and 3.8% from the secular schools. On this question, the control group registered as follows: 80% of them believe, 15% do not believe, and 5% are not sure.

If the deaf affirmed a belief, they were then asked what happened to the man after death.[56] Most of their replies demonstrate that they are wedded to the classic distinction between "body" and "soul"—a distinction that contemporary biblical theology is trying to move away from. If the deaf express the continued existence of a detached spirit-soul, they fail to reunite it to the body at the last judgment. As noted earlier, numerous deaf comprehend the spirit, or soul, as corporeal. Furthermore, they see the soul as encased in the body, but, unlike the ancient Egyptians who made every effort to preserve the body and thereby keep the soul from escaping, the deaf are willing to allow the spirit to depart. They are willing to make this allowance because, according to some of them, God himself comes down at the moment of death and frees the soul. For the deaf teenagers death consists in a radically changed relationship between their body and their soul-spirit, which many regard as a material reality existing per se after death.

Their own comments testify to the above summary as well as to their fondness for concrete expression, a tendency which we have seen many times before. Diane 19CAT7.0A remarks: "Jesus comes down to take his soul to heaven or to hell. But I'm not sure about the soul. I can't see anything." "His soul comes out of his body," says Timothy 17CAT6.7A, "and can go up or down." Charles 21RBE113_ explains that the fate of the soul is contingent upon the person: "If the man had a strong faith, God will pick him up, but if he had only a so-so faith, his soul stays in the body. It does not separate." To Rita 20WAIS98_, a person's skin as well as his soul survives: "His skin and soul goes up to heaven. His skeleton stays." According to Donald 16CMMS133V, Jesus waits for the man to die, and then "Jesus will touch him and order him to wake up. Then Jesus takes his soul to heaven. His body stays here."

Observations made earlier about the deaf comprehension of "spirit" also bear upon this question. Michelle 17MP80V, perhaps believing the soul to be an ethereal substance, answers: "The soul of the man goes up to Jesus. We cannot see it, but God can see it." The idea of the soul "traveling" or "spiraling upward" appeared in scattered responses. To Margaret 20MAT Adv.4.4A, lack of soul movement is tantamount to punishment: "His soul goes to heaven. If he was bad, God sees that and leaves his soul with the body. God does not take the bad man's soul to heaven."

Besides ability to travel, several deaf endowed the soul with other characteristics. Such a one is Patrick 17WISC107_who says: "His soul goes to heaven to talk to Jesus." According to Arthur 18_V, his soul comes into existence at death: "I don't have a soul now. When I die, God gives me a soul."

Analysis of responses enables still other categories to be assembled:

(1) Several deaf students introduced reincarnation. The spirit goes up and then comes down again to live as an animal.
(2) A few deaf explained that their spirit is not within them, but behind them, constantly following them.

(3) Several deaf persons, without being asked, volunteered a description of the soul's composition. To them the soul is: (a) a personalized ghost, (b) their heart, (c) something substantial which only God can see, (d) nothing.

Contrary to the ancients who felt themselves surrounded by unseen personalized forces,[57] the deaf relegate the soul-spirit to heaven. Either God himself comes at the moment of death and takes it to heaven, or the soul frees itself and travels there.

This specific and colorful description recalls the concreteness of the ancient conception of death. The cupbearer Siduri, for instance, pities Gilgamesh in the Epic:

Gilgamesh, whither are you wandering?
Life, which you look for, you will never find.
For when the gods created men,
they let death be his share,
and life withheld in their own hands.[58]

Notice the concreteness of the concept of life in the statement that the gods withheld life in their hands. If the temptation arises to see this as a mere figure of speech, recall that Gilgamesh and, in another myth, Adapta are given a chance to gain eternal life simply by eating life as a substance.[59] But a serpent unfortunately steals the "plant of life" from Gilgamesh. A cunning god, Enki, dissuades Adapta from eating the bread and water of life when he enters heaven. In both instances the eating of food makes the difference between death and immortality.[60] To the extent that this is concrete, it parallels the deaf mode of expression.

The above is discussed to propose that, since the deaf and the ancients express themselves similarly, the language of the ancients may be more communicative and existential to the deaf than the objective, speculative language we are so accustomed to using. The concrete expressions of ancient religion are precise, particular and strong. They derive their vigor from (1) experiences of nature—sunrise, sunset, soil fertility, fire, weather and seasonal changes; (2) life experiences—birth, growth, marriage, illness, death. Ancient man integrated these experiences, turned some of them into intrinsic symbols, and presented them in a language outstanding for vividness and color. The recapturing and reassigning of this language to Christianity will place it on the wave length of the deaf, since they themselves are so fond of using it.

Control group statistics differ noticeably from those of the deaf on the question of life after death. A full 80% believe in life beyond the grave, 15% deny this, and 5% don't know. The believers express themselves simply, relying for the most part on their own reasoning rather than faith, revelation, or authoritarian teaching. The sole exception is Peter, 15: "Religion says that he can go to any one of three places: heaven, hell or purgatory."

Several others among the 80% subjectivize to the point of nullifying an objective after-life that could exist independently of their thoughts. Such is Christina, 16, who says: "If he does not believe in a life after death, he won't have any life after death. If he does believe, I don't know what would happen. It depends on what he did when he was alive. But I'm not sure." Steven, 17, reflects a weaker version of Christina's thinking: "I'm not sure about this question. I tend to think that maybe if he believes in more life, he will have more; if he doesn't, he won't. But I'm not sure."

Sheila, 16, remarks: "His mind lives on, freed from the burdens of earth, and he is in heaven or hell according to his worth."

Other samples include: "If he had faith, he will have eternal life." "There is life after death." "His soul goes to heaven." "He goes to heaven, a place for the spirit."

Among those who deny further life is Cheryl, 16: "No. There is no more life. Heaven is an idea for the living, to console people and lessen their fear of death." Gerard, 18, says: "No. I don't believe. Philosophically, the person is no longer subject to time and is outside of time; so how can he continue to exist? I haven't developed my thought on this yet."

If the soul or spirit leaves the body, it is logical to ask its destination. The deaf supply the answer—heaven. Question 11b asks if heaven is real, followed by Question 11d's inquiry: "Where is heaven?"

A total of 77.9% of the deaf explain that heaven is real: 68% from the Catholic schools and 81% from the secular schools. Expressing doubt on the matter are 18.3% of the deaf—of these, 28% are from the Catholic schools and 15.2% from the secular schools. Control group believers in the reality of heaven number 75%, close to the figure for the deaf. But a noticeable difference appears in that 15% of the hearing group deny that heaven is real and 10% doubt.

As stated previously, in the field of eschatology "heaven" is a most unmanageable idea. How can one ascertain if the deaf (and hearing) conceive it as reward, or as the fruition of a budding earthly life of faith, hope and charity, or as beatific vision and eternal bliss? Following the principle of linguistic simplicity, the investigator merely asked: "Where is heaven?" A criticism could be made that (1) responses to such a question would reveal nothing of "what" heaven is, and (2) this is a leading question insofar as it presumes a location somewhere. The criticism has merit. Still, the final responses lay out much information—especially the differences between the deaf and hearing young people upon whom the same procedure was used.

The three categories, "place," "state" and "don't know," were culled from the answers themselves. Admittedly, these three were sometimes awkward to handle, for the responses varied nearly as much within each category as they did among the categories. In spite of these shortcomings, however, some deductions can be made.

Giving answers that come under the category of "place" are 84% of the deaf, representing equally the Catholic and secular schools. Contrast this with a mere 16.7% of the control group. A small 5.7% of the deaf (4% from the Catholic schools and 6.2% from the secular schools) believe that heaven is a state of being. Thinking similarly are 44.4% of the control group, a significant difference. The sum of 10.4% of the deaf answers fell in the "don't know" category: 12% in the Catholic schools and 9.9% in the secular schools. Again, this contrasts sharply with the control group, which placed 38.9% of the responses in the "don't know" category.

The second category, of "state," refers to heaven as a *state* of fulfillment as distinguished from a *place* of fulfillment. The few answers which left a specific physical *place* unemphasized were put in this category. For example, Judith 18CMMS99V and a few others said: "Heaven is anyplace. It can be around here." Mary 17CAT12.9A, too, rises above *place*: "Heaven is spiritual,[61] but I don't know if it is real. Maybe it could be anyplace."

"God himself, after this life, be our dwelling-place," sighed St. Augustine long ago.[62] Any exposition of other-worldly "places" can hardly improve on this. Yet the deaf responses are more than idle superfluities. They give us a glimpse of something of the nature of their heaven. The heaven of the deaf ranges from the closeness of the earth's surface to the remoteness of other galaxies—with clouds, atmosphere, and stars in between. Several were disappointed that they could physically see nothing of heaven. Such is Timothy 17WISC100A who says: "Heaven is out of the earth, maybe. I can't see." Question: Can a rocket take you to heaven? Answer: "I can't see. People live there. Ghosts live there." Julie 17MAT Adv.4.4V likewise sees nothing: "Maybe in the sky, but I can't see where souls go." "Sometimes I think heaven is real, but I never saw it," comments Peter 17MAT Adv.4.9V. "It is above the earth and all around the earth." Paulette 18_A settles the issue: "Far out in the sky. At night you see it, but during the day you can't." The response of Joan 19WAIS116A is dreamlike: "Heaven is where that man lives now . . . millions of miles above the stars." Some introduce a note of heavenly happiness, as did James 19WAIS123A: "Up. I don't know how far. Heaven is a place where you talk to Jesus and enjoy yourself and experience pleasure." Echoing St. Augustine, Linda 18RBE109 gives this answer: "My teacher told me that heaven is anywhere the people are happy with God. And God can go anywhere. So heaven can be anyplace." Other samples are: "Straight up." "Heaven is in the clouds." "In the sky, above the clouds."

Such views parallel beliefs that are fairly widespread throughout Oceania, Polynesia and Micronesia. The people of the Torres Straits, for example, hold that somewhere to the west is a mythical island, Kibu, where the wind blows the souls of the dead.[63]

Halfway around the world, fourteen-year-old Gerald, deaf from birth, had never heard of the beliefs of the Pacific islanders, yet his own after-life thought, in its concreteness, was akin to theirs. This became evident when literalism erupted from him as he stood in a suburban Philadelphia cemetery. His religion had been taught to him somewhat systematically for several years and he had retained in his mind the notion that heaven was up and hell was down. Now he was standing at graveside pondering the casket of his deceased uncle as it was about to be lowered in the ground. After a moment of silence, tears appeared and then uncontrollable weeping. At home after the ceremony, his mother, seeking to console him, asked why he had broken down so utterly. "My uncle," replied Gerald, "was a good man—a very nice man. Why were they going to lower him in the ground?" Puzzled, his mother pursued the issue and drew this explanation: hell was physically in the earth and therefore the graveside lowering was the equivalent of his uncle's descending into hell. This incident, though true, is extreme in its intensity and in this regard untypical of the reactions of most deaf; yet it demonstrates what literalism can do. Perhaps it is this same type of thought which oftentimes leads to a rejection of hell in later adolescence.

The specter of hell crumbles beneath the skepticism of many deaf who dismiss it lightly and disparage the devil. Affirming the reality of hell are 37.9% of the deaf: 56% from the Catholic schools and 32.1% from the secular schools. Contrast this with the control group, 75% of whom believe in hell. The term "hell," however, is understood differently by the control group, as will be treated shortly. The sum of 37.9% of the deaf deny the existence of hell and 25% express doubts.

Ironically, lack of physical evidence, which was mentioned but proved an insignificant factor affecting belief in heaven, is now invoked to uphold a denial of hell. Compare, for instance, Larry 16_V: "I think heaven is real, but I never saw it," with Joyce 18WAIS117A: "Hell is not true. I never see anything in the earth."

In addition to those who gave simple "yes," "no" and "I don't know," a great many deaf had more to say. Charles ?1RBE113_believes in heaven, but he asked the investigator for evidence of hell: "Hell is like an oven. But where is it? No proof." Caught in the same inconsistency is Debbie 16WISC133A who accepts heaven: "I never saw hell. If I die and I see hell, then I know it is real."

Others who believe in hell express themselves like Joseph

17WISC118A: "Hell is in the middle of the earth, because there is a bright hot fire there." Mary Lou 18WISC89_says: "Hell is in the earth.ᵧ Bad people go there." Still others gave more advanced answers. Consider the apocalyptic remark of Daniel 17WISC111A: "Hell is real. All who accepted the mark of the beast will go to hell." "If God judges you and you pass," explains David 17CAT8.0A, "you go to heaven. That means your soul is free. You can go anywhere. But if you go to hell, you ᵪ have to stay there and suffer." "Hell is suffering," says Diane 19CAT7.0A. The remarks of Linda 18RBE109_ are a fitting conclusion: "The bad people punish themselves. They are in pain. They suffer. They are separated from the good people. Limbo is for people with small sins. God cleanses them, forgives them. Then they move to heaven."

Those deaf who hold that hell is a physical place in the earth compare with the Hebrews who call such a place "sheol." Mentioned 65 times in the Old Testament, "sheol," the abode of the dead, is characterized by a shadowy, subterranean, sub-existence from which it is impossible to praise God or return to the living. Core, Dathan and Abiram tumbled into it alive when the earth split open and closed over them (Num. 16:30-33). Job, the Psalmist and some deaf (referring to hell) describe it as the deepest place of creation (Jb. 11:8, Ps. 86:13).

Turning to the control group, we find that 75% of them—a significantly greater percentage than the deaf—accept the reality of hell. But they differ from the deaf in that most of them moved away from the concept of hell as a physical place. Bruce, 17, admittedly hesitant about the issue, is content to say that "hell is another plane of existence." "Heaven and hell are states of existence—union with God or separation from God," says Frances, 17. Peter, 16, emphasizes the mental aspect: "Heaven and hell are both like mental states." Patrick, 17, similarly says: "Hell, like heaven, is not a real (physical) place. It is something like having a dream, but the dream is real." "Hell," explains Joseph, 16, "is the life of a separated soul that has turned away from God." Joan, 18, describes hell as a place for the spirit and adds: "But we can't comprehend the things of the spirit until we are dead." The control group and deaf group alike caught glimpses of selfishness and selflessness, and an understanding that selfishness leads to alienation and selflessness to union. The ultimate outcome of alienation is that rupture of relationship with God which we call "hell."

A study of the responses enables an observation to be made. As mentioned earlier, there is the difficulty, for both the deaf and the hearing, of communicating heaven and hell in a language overlaid with mythological imagery. Although Jesus himself used images, the hell of the twentieth century is partly derived from the imagination of medieval painters and writers. Even Dante, for instance, employs devils to work day and night to make hell as hot as possible and to mete out punishment corresponding to each kind of sin.[64] It is this kind of hell that the deaf first accept, then reject. Such a dismissal is to be expected, since this hell is an inaccurate mixture of artistic imagination, accidentals and essentials.

What the deaf need is the essential hell (and heaven) presented in straightforward, existential language and consonant with the substance of revealed truth. The beginnings of heaven and hell can be felt here and now; they can therefore be communicated in a language rooted in personal experience. As a pedagogical technique, one can, for instance, ask the deaf to ponder about those individuals against whom they nurse a grudge, or those whom they refuse to forgive or refuse to speak to, or those toward whom they feel jealous. Then it can be demonstrated how this conceit and jealousy lead to a false relationship or severed relationship. To carry this over the human/divine bridge requires further demonstration.

Suppose that an ideal person seeking deep friendship became the constant companion of the deaf. He is a dignified person of splendid appearance whose heart is crowded with all that is noble, rich and beautiful, whose love for the deaf is unsurpassed, and whose gaiety is infectious and draws the entire deaf population around him. Yet he wants to give himself utterly to one deaf individual. Such a person is God. He catches the deaf person and holds him and asks for a response of love.[65] Will the deaf person love him?

The same inertness, conceit or jealousy that severed the human relationships above can sever this one too. To lose such a person must be considered a catastrophe. And the ultimate outcome is eternal separation, hell. But the final product of a responsive love is eternal life, eternal embrace, heaven. Thus the teacher will not only be pointing out the last things, heaven and hell, but likewise will be existentially teaching how sin works itself out into loneliness and despair and how sin's opposite, love, works itself out into union and happiness.[66]

A final note concerns the devil. No question was asked about the devil, but many deaf voluntarily raised the issue. Those rejecting hell also rejected the devil. *Who* was rejected is less important than *how* he was rejected. Sometimes laughing sincerely, the adolescents often derided the devil, reducing him to a trifling character from a world of make-believe. It is the subjective opinion of the investigator, supported in part by pre-test drawings, that what they are rejecting is not so much the devil himself as a childhood caricature. Crudeness of concept, it seems, inclined the deaf to dismiss the devil; refinement of concept inclined the control group to retain him. This seems likewise true of the broader concept of hell.

28
Divine Activity in Heaven

We now turn to the next question, God's locale. The responses of all groups were nearly identical; 94.2% of the deaf place God in heaven, 92% from the Catholic schools and 94.9% from the secular schools. A full 94.1% of the hearing adolescents share this view. This question reveals little in itself, but assumes added weight when taken in conjunction with Question 11f concerning God's activity in heaven. Later, Question 11f will be tied to Question 19 and together they will account for considerable insight on the deaf identification of the divine.

Previous glimpses of thoughts of the divine have already been discovered. For instance, the deaf have a personal, even sexual, God. What is commonly applied to human nature, e.g., personality, feelings, and the like, the deaf apply to God. Now if God is a person, then to the deaf youngsters he can only be in one place at one time. His proper home is heaven, which, as previously noted, can extend from the earth's atmosphere to outer space. There he sits on a throne of majesty, sometimes surrounded by serving angels. But does he merely sit? What other activity occupies his time? Can he leave his throne and go wherever necessity calls him? What kind of necessity would justify his leaving? The explanations to these and related questions must come from the deaf themselves.

With the Catholic school and secular school responses nearly identical, 65.9% of the deaf answers involve divine observation and 31.1% involve an intervention of God. Some 3% of the deaf did not know. Contrast this with the control group, where only 33.3% of the answers involve observation and 55.6% contain intervention.

Implicitly housed within the comments of the deaf are their views on several aspects of God: his transcendence, his immanence, his providence, and something of his knowledge. But before elaborating these, we pause to pass on some preliminary remarks which will have a bearing on these main points.

God, as the deaf have already presented him, will come forward again as a person with human attributes, male sex, and a ghost-like human or quasi-human form. Although they present him as almost human, few deaf volunteered the term "Father" for this person and none used the term "Holy Spirit." The earlier uncertainty about Jesus' identity recurs and his relationship to the Father and Holy Spirit compounds the confusion. The deaf sometimes speak of Jesus alone, sometimes of Jesus being sent by someone else, and sometimes not of Jesus but only a nameless being in the sky. It is already sufficiently clear, and will become even more so in forthcoming sections, that to many deaf God is above and man below. This, coupled with the "person" restrictions the deaf put upon their celestial being, largely provides the basis for their understanding of divine activity and divine communication. Activity will be elucidated now, communication later.

The nature of divine activity according to the deaf commands attention, for it gives clues to the overall deaf view of divine providence. Much of God's activity is taken up in observing people, an activity which is done sometimes with the assistance of angels, sometimes by dispatching Jesus here, and sometimes when God himself either comes down to make inspection tours or watches from a fixed abode above. If he remains above, however, the surveying must be accomplished with physical eyes (and ears)—magnified, to be sure, but still physical. They enable him to see (and hear) at distances that are out of the question for human beings. Other deaf called up more elemental substitutes. One explanation, for instance, was that God finds it necessary to strengthen his fallible memory by "making movies" of people's lives. Still other deaf, however, offered more subtle explanations as they somehow perceived that God can extend his personality—perhaps through an effluence—to people as he "warned their minds" and "changed their dreams," thus recalling the Gospel incident involving Matthew's military official (Mt. 8:5-13) whose slave Jesus cured from a distance.

However accomplished, God's constant surveillance leads him to his single most oft-mentioned operation: either he, Jesus, Jesus' friends or the angels become present at the moment of death and whisk the soul to heaven. His less important activities on earth include: (1) the growing of plants and inspection of farms to satisfy himself that crop growth proceeds on schedule, (2) the manipulation of the weather, (3) assistance at giving birth, (4) localized interferences to "stop trouble," (5) aid for the sick and (6) blessing the people and listening to prayers. When aloof from earthlings, he rests, he works, he enjoys himself by eating and drinking, he listens to music, he gives commands to angels, and he meets and introduces the souls of the most recently deceased to others to facilitate their getting acquainted.

In the manner of its execution and in the object of its attention, the deaf view of God's providential activity somewhat parallels the actions of the Mesopotamian god, Enki. One myth has Enki making a tour throughout his territory, which includes most of the world then known.

> Enki stops in each country, blesses it, and by his blessing endows it with prosperity and affirms its special functions. Next he organizes all bodies of water and what has to do with water. From the sea Enki turns to the winds which bring the rains and then to agricultural pursuits. He looks after the plow, opens up the furrows, and lets grain grow on the field.[67]

From the fields he moves on to towns and villages making sure that everything is running smoothly and appointing divine overseers to perpetuate what he had begun. In places the Old Testament follows Enki and the deaf. Yahweh, for instance, locally manifests himself to the Jews wherever his name is remembered: "In whatever place I choose for the remembrance of my name I will come to you and bless you" (Ex. 20:24). Another passage almost repeats the words of the deaf: "The Lord, your God, you shall worship; then I will bless your food and drink, and I will remove all sickness from your midst; no woman in your land will be barren or miscarry" (Ex. 23:25-27).

Absent in these deaf responses is a providential guidance that is ongoing, positive and personal; present in the responses is a providence that is sporadic, negative, impersonal, and nature-inclined. To the deaf, God's providential care extends more continuously and positively to nature than to human beings. For instance, almost without exception it touches personal life only when the individual is in difficulty, where there is disharmony or sickness, and at the time of death. Altogether lacking is any expression of divine guidance of human history and of the entire community as a corporate body belonging to him, i.e., history interpreted as a covenant relationship with God. This is due in part to the limited scriptural knowledge of the deaf.

Perhaps the life of any believer sooner or later confronts him with the profound question: "Is God malicious or benign toward me?" The deaf person's attainment is that, despite his restricted understanding of the divine providence, he goes through life confident that a benign eye is upon him and is prepared, in the end, to save him. An analysis of the entire body of deaf responses discloses three main classifications: (a) those indicating that God primarily observes and sometimes intervenes, (b) those holding that God primarily intervenes and sometimes observes, and (c) those maintaining a more central position, placing less emphasis on either extreme and saying that God's activity involves much of both observation and intervention. Attention is now turned to each.

(a) *God primarily observes and sometimes intervenes.* The largest fraction of the 65.9% of the responses involving divine observation fall in this category. Because the words of the deaf illuminate this issue clearly, they are now presented:

у "He watches the people and sometimes he helps. If there is trouble in a family, Jesus sees it—and maybe he'll help. If other families have no trouble, Jesus doesn't bother." (Julie 17MAT Adv.4.4.V)
"God watches everybody. A long time ago I thought God had millions of eyes to see all the people. But now I know that God has only two keen eyes to watch with. He keeps records of what people do so he can judge whether to send them to heaven or hell.

God also comforts people, helps people, listens when they pray. Finally, God controls the weather." (Lucy 19WAIS116A)

✗ "God stays in heaven. When people die, God introduces them to other people, helps them make friends. After they die, God helps the deaf become hearing and the blind people see. Now Jesus gives food to people." (William 20RBE85_)

"God works there (in heaven). When people pray, he stops and listens. He forgives the people, and when they die, he takes their souls to heaven." (Robert 18MAT Adv.4.9V)

✗ "He watches the people. If the people sin, God stops watching them and later they go to hell. But God keeps watching the people who believe in him. Jesus' friends also help to watch. So later, when the good people die, Jesus knows right away and he takes them." (John 20WAIS114A)

"God studies the people. He sees how the people live—if they are improving. God wants people to be friendly, good neighbors. He wants mothers and fathers to take care of their children." (Charles 21RBE113_)

✗ "God sits down and talks to the people who died yesterday. He asked them what happened, what was wrong, what kind of sickness they died from." (Patrick 17WISC107_)

✗ "God walks around and talks with his friends in heaven. He does not eat or sleep. There is no trouble there. He wants it peaceful. Sometimes in the morning and evening, God watches the people on earth to see how they feel—if they are sick or healthy." (Stephanie 19WAIS98AV)

✗ "He controls the world from heaven. And he sees the people. He watches because he loves us and wants to find out who prays, who loves him and who goes to church." (Janet 17CAT10.6A)

(b) *God primarily intervenes and sometimes observes.* This second classification differs from the first in two ways: (1) rather than having God fixed in heaven or en route to earth, these deaf youth often place him on or around the earth, flitting about in ways consonant with a spirit; (2) but if he must remain in heaven, his prime activity there includes more than observing. The number of respondents here largely fall within the 31.1% who stress intervention. A sampling follows:

✗ "God works with Christians here. For instance, God works with me now through prayer, through listening. And God judges too. Sometimes he sends angels here to help people." (Daniel 17WISC111A)

"I don't think God is in heaven. He must be out somewhere. I think he watches people, grows plants and helps give birth to babies." (Judy 18_A)

"God comes down. He follows the people to see if they are good or bad." (Donald 16CMMS133V)

∨ "God walks around here (on earth) to help people who get hurt and he sees if people are getting along all right together." (Karen 16WISC117A)

∠ "God moves the air. God lifts the water to make the rain. He gives lightning and thunder and he can move the sun around to make a beautiful day." (Donald 19WAIS122_)

(c) *God both observes and intervenes.* These responses only slightly favor either observation or intervention. Some, therefore, allow themselves to be aligned with the 65.9% stressing observation, others with the 31.1% stressing intervention:

✗ "God sees the people and helps them from heaven. He helps us by removing our sins and he helps us decide what is the right thing to do. Sometimes he comes down and walks around here. He tries to help people to be good like himself." (Debra 16WISC133A)

✗ "God sees the people, takes care of them and answers their prayers. God forgives their sins when they go to confession. God takes the souls from the dead bodies." (Alan 17MAT Adv.5.5A)

✗ "Jesus sees things all over the world. He wants to stop trouble. He wants to keep track of people, find out who starts wars, and fights." (David 17WISC124A)

Lastly, typifying the 3.0% of the uncertain deaf are the remarks of Mark 17CNE130_: "Jesus used to help the blind and the crippled. But what does he do now? Where is he now? I don't know."

Turning to the control group, one finds that, both statistically and qualitatively, they differ from the deaf on the question of divine activity in heaven. The sum of 33.3%—as compared with 65.9% for the deaf—of their responses involve observation and 55.6% (31.1% for the deaf) involve intervention, while 11.1% of the control group were uncertain.

Like the deaf, the control group responses shed light on the areas of divine transcendence, immanence, and providence; unlike the deaf is their understanding of these—although the differences are sometimes less than one would expect. The control group has a sophistication which enables them to lift or lessen some of the severe limitations the deaf assigned to the divine. Occurring less often in these responses, for instance, are some of the anthropomorphisms and more mundane matters mentioned by the deaf, e.g., God's "listening to music," "eating and drinking," and his bookkeeping. Less frequent also is the same degree of circumscription of the deity in place, i.e., to many deaf, travel or visual surveillance from a distance is a prerequisite for divine knowledge of earthly events. The control group, on the other hand, more readily places God everywhere "at the same time."

The control group comments also reveal a greater understanding of divine immanence. The hearing young people were, to a greater degree than the deaf, aware of God's uniqueness and his special closeness to his creatures. The kind of providence coming from this is more stable, personal, and dynamic and acts before, not after, misfortune strikes. Here are some examples. Ritamarie, 16, says: "God is everywhere at this moment. He is guiding us to do the right things in life because he loves us. I'm not sure if he eats and drinks and does things like that." The thoughts of Frances, 17, are similar: "God loves us and guides us. And the most important thing is that he loves us. God is right here, next to me." "What does God do in heaven?" says Adrien, 18. "He helps people, he watches everybody. He is everywhere at all times. People die every minute and he judges them. That's enough to keep him busy." "God lives there and goes about his business," explains Peter, 15. "He oversees everything and every person because we are all his children. He watches what we do." Joseph, 17, is one of few who ties providence to pre-vision and the problem of evil: "God observes. But if a car is about to hit a kid, God will not stop the car. This question really puzzles me." "God is all over," says Jeanne, 17. "He 'knocks at the door' and spends time trying to get into the hearts of people. I don't know if he has any other activity or not."

In concluding, it can be said that the evidence presented here gives clear insights into the deaf view of divine transcendence, immanence and providence. These, along with divine knowledge which is also contained here, will be elucidated in a forthcoming section. Still, at the risk of some overlapping, it will be helpful to pause now for related observations.

Probing the evidence discloses that the deaf, differing somewhat from the control group, accentuate God's transcendence and overlook his immanence. This means that the deaf perceive God as (1) substantially distinct from the world and (2) having no need of the world. To the theologian, but not to the deaf, transcendence also includes God's incomprehensibility, awe-inspiring mystery, and exalted holiness.[68] What the deaf are implying here, and correctly so, is that they fail to see the world as an expression of God's nature. The material world, in other words, is in no way a part of God, although it is a created likeness of his perfection. Deaf teenagers concretize transcendence by expressing it in spatial imagery and by placing distance and height between God and the world, almost repeating the words of Jesus to the Jews: "You belong to what is below; I belong to what is above" (Jn. 8:23). Regarding the second point, the deaf understand God as self-sufficient. He turns his attention toward the people, but nothing the people give him can add to his life or happiness. He helps people for their sake, not his.

In the history of religions, placing God in the sky, as do the deaf, has been risky. While many great gods of ancient civilizations have been deities residing in the sky, these figures oftentimes tended to fade out of the picture, and for the *coup de grace* they were often removed from the rituals and replaced by less remote gods. The successors of the sky gods were connected with life and represented fertility.[69] If deaf adolescent thinking parallels this, one ponders whether, to the deaf, Jesus' resurrection-ascension was a disappearance into oblivion and irrelevancy. To re-establish for the deaf a relationship between transcendence and providence, one must re-emphasize divine immanence, connect God with life, and make him existential.

To come face to face with an approachable God affected by human affairs, the deaf adolescent needs the Hebrew revelation—at least for a beginning. As already noted, God, in some traditions, was on familiar terms with Adam, Noah, Abraham and Moses. To the judges, prophets and kings, he was equally close. Furthermore, it was unnecessary for the psalmists to make themselves heard in outer space or to invoke angels or other intermediaries. The Lord himself was close and compassionate. Consider the concretisms in Psalm 139:

> O Lord, you have probed me and you know me;
> you know when I sit and when I stand;
> you understand my thoughts from afar.
> My journeys and my rest you scrutinize,
> with all my ways you are familiar.
> Even before a word is on my tongue,
> behold, O Lord, you know the whole of it.
> Behind me and before, you hem me in
> and rest your hand upon me.
> Such knowledge is too wonderful for me;
> too lofty for me to attain.

Appropriate for the deaf, both for its literary qualities and for its clear claim of personal providence, is the Old Testament story of Joseph (Gen. 37—50). Stripped of some of its secondary ramifications and made existential, it can show the deaf how God thwarts the intentions of human agents and makes Joseph's story end well.

Numerous other Old Testament passages point out a Hebrew mind so keenly aware of the workings of divine providence that it bypasses the realm of secondary causes in natural phenomena and makes God directly responsible for them (cf., for example, Ps. 103:10-32). Moreover, God's utter dependability prompts the Hebrews to praise him repeatedly, and his locked-in relationship to his people compelled these words from the pen of Isaiah: "Can a mother forget her infant, be without tenderness for the child of her womb? Even should she forget, I will never forget you" (Is. 49:15).

Moving into the New Testament, Jesus himself affirms God's providence. "Look at the birds of the sky. They do not sow or reap, they gather nothing into barns; yet your heavenly Father feeds them. Are not you more important than they?" (Mt. 6:26). Elsewhere Jesus says: "As for you, every hair of your head has been counted" (Mt. 10:30). Furthermore: "He is not far from each one of us, for in him we live and move and have our being" (Acts 17:28).

Liturgically, a practical way to strengthen deaf awareness of God's immanence is to take maximum advantage of their belief that God is in church—a point we shall return to later.

29
The Deaf, the Hebrews and Other Ancients

The flow of thought is here interrupted to divert attention to a major finding underlying this entire study. In their assignment of a sex to God, their proneness to deify humans, their construction of an anthropomorphic God, some of their after-life thinking, their ideas of a spirit, and above all in their concrete and colorful expressions, the deaf stand on common ground with some views of the Hebrews and other ancients. The Israelites, however, differed conspicuously from their contemporaries in that they kept Yahweh sexless and refused to exalt anyone else to divinity. But aside from these, many insights into the Semitic religious mind are likewise insights into the mind of the deaf and both have similar language patterns. Some Hebrew traditions, especially as found in the Pentateuch and the Psalms (in the New Testament the Gospel of Mark may be included here), because of their language characteristics, are on the wavelength of the deaf.

Besides parts of the Old Testament, the language of some rabbinic literature achieves great beauty with an uncomplicated, concrete style and is therefore pedagogical to anyone pondering a more meaningful catechetical language for the deaf.

Consider, as an example, parts of *Mekilta de Rabbi Ishmael*. Compiled in the third or fourth century (circa 250 to 300 A.D.) and attributed to Rabbi Ishmael, the *Mekilta* is the classic Hebrew commentary on the book of Exodus.[70] Rabbinic Judaism held a dual revelation from Sinai, i.e., the books of Moses[71] and the oral tradition later written in the Mishna, a tradition which was believed to have been literally spoken by God to Moses. Illustrated below are *Mekilta* passages that are akin to (a) the simple, concrete language used by the deaf, (b) the literalism of the deaf and their construction of an anthropomorphic God and (c) deaf thinking on heaven. Let the *Mekilta* illustrate each.

(a) *The Simple, Concrete Language Used by the Deaf*

Used so often by the deaf, concrete words, like precise and particular ones, are strong words. Although some theologians dismiss them as childish, concrete words can contain the seeds of more advanced insights. The following passage derives its beauty from its simplicity, which, in turn, is rooted in the basic elements.

Some time ago Rabbi Eliezer was sick and the four elders, Rabbi Tarphon, Rabbi Joshua, Rabbi Eleazar ben Azariah and Rabbi Akiba went in to visit him. Rabbi Tarphon then began saying: Master, you are more precious to Israel than the globe of the sun, for the globe of the sun gives light only for this world, while you have given us light both for this world and for the world to come. Rabbi Joshua began saying: Master, you are more precious to Israel than the days of rain, for rain gives life only for this world while you have given us life for this world and for the world to come. Then Rabbi Eleazar ben Azariah began saying: Master, you are more precious to Israel than father and mother. For father and mother bring a man into the life of this world, while you brought us to the life of the world to come.[72]

(b) *The Literalism of the Deaf and Their Construction of an Anthropomorphic God*

Scripture hereby teaches that God spoke the ten commandments with one utterance—something impossible for creatures of flesh and blood—for it says: "And God spoke all these words, saying, If so, why then is it said: I am the Lord thy God, thou shalt have no other gods before me?" It simply teaches that the Holy One, blessed be he, after having said all the ten commandments at one utterance, repeated them, saying each commandment separately.[73]

A footnote to this passage explains that after hearing the voice of God speak the first two commandments, the people became frightened and asked Moses to intervene. God ceased speaking and Moses repeated the other eight commandments, referring to God in the third person.[74]

(c) *Deaf Thinking on Heaven* (N.B. The heaven quoted is not inhabited by humans)

One passage says: "I have talked with you from heaven," and another passage says: "And the Lord came down upon Mount Sinai." How can both these passages be maintained? The matter is decided by the third passage: "Out of heaven he made thee to hear his voice, that he might instruct thee; and upon earth he made thee to see his great fire (Dt. 4:36)."—These are the words of Rabbi Ishmael. Rabbi Akiba says: Scripture teaches that the Holy One, blessed be he, lowered the upper heavens of heaven down to the top of the mountain and thus actually still spoke to them from the heavens.[75]

The purpose of this pause is not only to point to a connection between the deaf and the Israelites and other ancients, but, more important, to see this connection as a factor in making catechetics more existential for the deaf. The starting point is the deaf person as he is. And since he already thinks religiously like a Jew, we can talk—manually or orally—to him as we would talk to a Jew.

The whole question here is one of religious language. The language used in the catechesis of the hearing needs to be re-examined and reformulated before it is presented to the deaf. It is pointless, for example, to tell the deaf that Christ is a "sacrament" when hearing teenagers and perhaps even the teacher are unsure of the meaning of the term. Equally meaningless to the deaf are such common expressions as "Christ is the Word," "God's saving mystery," "celebrate life" and numerous others. But to point to the early Israelites and other ancients is to point to a coherent, intelligible way to use religious language with the deaf.

Yet it must be said that this is a starting point and not the complete endeavor. Even though the Hebrews can give the deaf a pertinent theological language, if it is to be a living language, its words, signs and expressions must be experienced in a community of faith. Allowing for this, Hebrew thought patterns and expressions are an interpretative key that unlocks a sensible theological language for the deaf. To this extent it is today more relevant for the deaf than the detached, sophisticated, and esoteric language we have grown accustomed to.

30
God's Nature and Attributes

(a) *Pantheistic Tendencies and the Deaf*

In view of the many similarities already seen between the deaf and the Hebrews and other ancients, one wonders whether the deaf share the relationship that the ancients (but not the Hebrews) saw between God, nature and upper levels of being. Question 12 is a package of drawings progressing in a hierarchy from nature (the tree), to man-made objects and people (the city), to human beings (the children), to a supernatural being (the angel), to the Blessed Virgin, and, finally, to God. The accompanying question "Is the tree, etc., God?" seeks to determine whether and to what extent the deaf equate divinity with any level of being. A complete equation would indicate that pantheism affects the deaf.

Pantheism is a belief signifying that every existing thing, from nature to beyond the human, is, in some way, divine. Such a belief destroys the distinction between creator and creature, the finite and the infinite, good and evil, truth and falsehood, and one human person and another. Though pantheistic views differ (e.g., Spinozan, Hegelian, etc.), they unanimously agree in their denial of the distinction between God and the world. Taken strictly, pantheism means that God is everything and everything is God.

Question 12a, the first of the package, concerns the identification of God with a tree. In ancient times, trees had been associated with the sacred or a sacred power in nature. Gilgamesh, for example, comes upon a miraculous tree in a garden and it was identified with the "herb of life." In the garden of Eden stood the tree of knowledge of good and evil and the tree of life (Gen. 2:9). The sacred tree of Mesopotamia and Elam was religious because of what it expressed. It had power to grow, to lose and regain leaves, to reproduce, and to resist the wind. The tree re-enacts the life cycle of the universe. It became what we earlier called the intrinsic symbol. To the ancient mind, moreover, the tree did not lose its observable natural qualities when it became symbolic. The date palm, for instance, was sacred and symbolic to the Mesopotamians, the oak to the Scandinavians, and certain specific trees to the Hindus.[76] In view of the many similarities already observed between the deaf and the ancients, is the attachment of the sacred (or God) to the tree one more bond?

The percentages indicate otherwise. A full 92.9% of the deaf (and 89.5% of the control group) answered that the tree is not God. On this issue the deaf part company with the ancients, insofar as the ancients saw the tree as a sacred power in nature, and align themselves with the

Hebrews. The idea that the individual is part of society, that society is rooted in nature, and that nature is a manifestation of the divine was accepted by the peoples of the ancient world with the single exception of the Hebrews.[77] Yahweh, said the Israelites, is nowhere to be found as a part of nature. Both the Hebrews and the deaf hold that God is absolutely transcendent; yet the deaf compound this with their unawareness of God's immanence, his involvement in this world.

The next drawing in the series is the city. Hardly anyone either associated God with the city or identified him with it. This, again, is in keeping with the tendency of the deaf to accentuate transcendence. Most of the deaf answered with a simple "yes" or "no." A few spontaneously explained. Such is Steven 17_A, who says, "God is not the city because people made the city." "The city is not God," observes Paul 17WISC108A, "because the city is new and God is old."

As we move on to the third drawing, the children, the percentages remain similar to those on the city. Only 3.9% of the deaf think that children are God, and there are no significant differences between the deaf and the control group on this matter.

But as the progression reaches the fourth drawing, the angel, a difference occurs. The sum of 21.6% of the deaf, all from the secular schools, claim that the angel is God. Contrast this with the 5.3% of the control group. This reinforces our previous observation of the deaf youth deifying others. On the other hand, keeping the angel below God are 74.5% of the deaf. These made some spontaneous remarks. Charles 17_V, for instance, observes: "The angel is a servant. He will take care of God." "But the angel follows the children and helps them," is the explanation of Margaret 20MAT Adv.4.4A. According to John 20WAIS114A, "The angel is under God. He helps God look at the people." Anna Marie 18WAIS117A believes that she will become an angel after death. "Before, the angel was a man. He died and became an angel in heaven. Same with me. When I die Jesus will bless me and I will become hearing."

Other deaf understood a hierarchy of beings with God as the apex and the angel near it. Their angel is the traditional one in human form fashioned by art and handed down in Scripture and theology. According to these deaf, the chief activity of the higher being is the guardian angel role, i.e., "following the children" and serving and aiding God in his continual surveillance of the world. One can take advantage of this and relate to the deaf the numerous uplifting angel episodes in Scripture (e.g., Gen. 28:12; 1 Kgs. 22:19ff. and elsewhere) and use the doctrine of angels to open their eyes to God's love for them and to the vastness of creation, "for there must be many higher orders of beings whose service is joined with ours under God."[78]

The next drawing, the Virgin Mary, evoked a 23% deaf response that she is God. Of this total 4% were from the Catholic schools and 28.7% from the secular schools. These percentages recall the earlier confusion about the Blessed Virgin. Besides, the notable difference between the Catholic and secular schools indicates what more frequent religion teaching can do.

The culmination of the progression is the last drawing, Jesus. Besides its proper function in the question, it is also a cross-examination of earlier probes into Jesus' identity, and the responses reinforce the previous confusion elicited on this subject. A total of 58.2% of the deaf said that Jesus is God: 52.6% from the secular schools and 76% from the Catholic schools. The 63.1% of the control group parallels the deaf. As before, one source of confusion is that the deaf apply to divine sonship the subordination of a son in the father-son human relationship. Consequently, to call Jesus "the Son of God" is to make him less than God —at least for numerous deaf youth. "Jesus is not God: he is the Son of God," is a common comment among the 28.2% of the deaf who, although they adhere to New Testament usage, deny Jesus his divinity.

To sum up, what this package shows is an absence of pantheistic trends or associations on the nature and human level. The deaf are unlike those ancients who saw a sacred power in nature (trees and vegetation) and society. The deaf leave God unconnected with the city and likewise with the children. But the divine begins to be associated with the angels, the Blessed Virgin and Jesus. Surfacing here again are two previously noted difficulties—the tendency to deify creatures (i.e., the angel and the Blessed Virgin) and confusion over Jesus' identity, especially as manifested by his title, Son of God.

(b) *God: Real or Fantasy?*

As said earlier, the purpose of the Question 13 package is to ascertain whether the deaf adolescent associates religion with unreality. The progression of drawings proceeds from pure fantasy (the Disney characters), to fantasy mixed with the human (Superman), to fantasy, human and holiness (the Flying Nun), to holiness and humanity (the bishop), to reality (Jesus as consecrated host). Since God is spiritual and unperceived by the senses, does his spirituality work against him in the minds of the deaf? Are the Disney characters and other fantasy characters and experiences in the same category as God?

In the pre-testing a few deaf remarked that God, but not Jesus, resembles the fantasy characters. Furthermore, the response that God is a ghost gives credibility to the possibility that he is a product of the imagination and nothing more. Some religion teachers of the deaf, in the casualness of social conversation, voiced a suspicion that perhaps the whole dimension of the invisible, the supernatural, eludes the deaf because the auditory intake is lacking. According to these teachers, perhaps the deaf discern real relationships only among objects (or persons) perceptible to the senses and within their frame of reference, and therefore whatever the deaf consider divine they also consider unreal. Question 13 addresses itself to these suspicions.

The responses of the deaf obliterate the above fears. None of the deaf placed God in the category of fantasy characters.[79] To all of the deaf, God is real; the fantasy characters are not. This holds, moreover, for the entire progression, excluding the consecrated host.

These responses resemble earlier confusion evidenced in our question about the Eucharist (Question 10). The sum of 27.7% of the deaf said that the consecrated host is really Jesus: 60% from the Catholic schools and 17.1% from the secular schools. Answering that the host is not really Jesus are 43.6% of the deaf. Of this total, 16% are from the Catholic schools and 52.6% are from the secular schools. A total of 28.7% of the deaf did not know: 24% from the Catholic schools and 30.3% from the secular schools.

Curiously, the control group differs noticeably from the deaf—except on the host. Some 15.8% of them placed God in the realm of the fantasy characters, Superman and the Flying Nun, while 36.8% said that the host is really Jesus.

(c) God's Love for the Deaf

The deepest need of the deaf and hearing person alike is to overcome his separateness. A question that has confronted men of all ages and cultures, separateness has been conquered by a variety of loves, the most profound of which have been brotherly love and love of God.

Today's theology is stressing the unity—indeed the identity—of the love of God and the love of one's fellow man. However viewed, true love is the touchstone of Christianity. Brotherly love, for instance, marks a person as a genuine disciple of Christ (Jn. 13:35). No one that we know of before Jesus had ever demanded a love of neighbor so unqualified, so universal, so thorough. As a yardstick for Christians to use in measuring their love for one another or how much they should love one another, Jesus points to himself and his love for men (Jn. 13:34; 15:12; 1 Jn. 3:16). Consequently, love of neighbor is joined with love of God.

While acknowledging the unity of love, this study limits itself in Question 14a to the love God has for the deaf. St. John's beautiful phrase, "God is Love," captures God as well as human language can: his nature is love and we and our world are the result. As even a hurried reading of the New Testament will verify, Jesus has spoken often and eloquently of God's love for men. This kind of love coming from the realm of God confers a distinct character on Christianity.[80] Whether and to what extent the deaf appreciate God's personal love for them will have far-reaching effects upon their understanding of Christianity.

Question 14a proposes to discover the degree of the deaf youths' awareness of God's personal love for the individual. It gives the respondents specific comparisons. They are asked to list five persons who have been most wonderful and loving to them, starting with the best and ranking them in order down to number five. The love of God for the respondent is then compared with the love each listed person has for the respondent, until the teenager indicates that God's love is less than or equal to numbers one through five or surpasses number one.

God's self-giving love penetrates the deaf as it does anyone else. And yet the recipient's unawareness, misconceptions, and immaturity are walls that impede penetration. Only 38.2% of the deaf responded that God loves them more deeply than the highest listed human being. Of this number, 37.7% were from the secular schools and 40% from Catholic schools. The 45% response of the control group is a slight improvement over the deaf. An identical 38.2% of the deaf (32% from the Catholic schools and 40.2% from the secular schools) reduce the love of God to human proportions and equate his love with the love of someone from #1 to #5 on the scale. A total of 25% of the control group does likewise. A small 2.9% of the deaf (and 10% of the control group) place the love of God below #5. Having doubts on the entire question of God's personal love are 20.6% of the deaf: 24% from the Catholic schools and 19.5% from the secular schools.

The deaf in the first category place God's love above the human and exhibit an understanding of the depth of his love. They were conscious that the heavenly Father cares for all the needs of his children, that God's love shows itself in his boundless mercy, and that God loves them as individuals with an intensity unmatched by humans. The only disturbing note is that some of the deaf in this category acknowledged God's universal love, but not his particular love. This comes up again as we turn to the other main category of deaf—those who reduced God's love to human proportions.

As explained above, this group placed the love of God alongside numbers 1 through 5. A study of their responses, including some in the doubting category, reveals several common denominators which partially account for their restricted view of God's love.

1. *God loves everybody in general and nobody in particular.* The deaf in this category express the principle of a divine love which is almost exclusively universal and collective and therefore almost fails to filter down to the individual level. God relates himself to the community only and to the deaf individual hardly, in much the same way a President of the United States loves America in general and few citizens per-

sonally. The quotes and categories which follow allow some insights as to why God's love weakens or collapses at the individual level. Let us now turn to the deaf themselves:

Ann 18WISC89_listed (1) mom and dad, (2) my sister Theresa, (3) Kathy, (4) Mike Brinker, (5) Carl Kuchner. She placed God between (4) and (5) and added, "I know that God loves everybody. But I don't know if God loves me or if he loves me very much."
Joseph 18_V made his listing hesitantly, placed God next to #5, and remarked, "God loves all people together, not one—all."
Geraldine 17CMMS108A listed (1) mom and dad, (2) Ann Waitt, (3) Aunt Betty, (4) grandparents, then said: "I think God belongs somewhere in the list." After further reflection, she added, "God loves all people. Maybe he loves me, too; I don't know."
Paulette 19RBE116_ranked the people who love her, reprimanded the investigator for attempting to make comparisons, and said, "God loves everybody, not one person—everybody."
William 18WISC121A at first did not know where to put God on his list. Finally deciding to put God between #1 and #5, he commented, "But I don't feel any love. God loves all people."

We have seen elsewhere several similarities between the deaf and some Hebrew traditions. The difficulty of the deaf in comprehending God's personal love for them as individuals, while readily admitting God's collective love for the community, is another link between the deaf and the Hebrews. For nowhere in the extant literature of Palestinian Judaism of the first millennium is God addressed as "my Father" by the individual Israelite.[81] The very idea of Israel was communitarian, and the community as a whole faced God together in a corporate relationship. This is not to say that the individual was totally unrelated to God, but to underscore the lack of awareness of divine fatherly love given to the individual. It is thought that Old Testament priestly and prophetic religion had little to say to the individual Israelite. Only later in the Wisdom literature does the Jew see God at work in his everyday life.[82] The deaf, however, keep God's love on the collective or universal level, not because they are community-conscious as the Israelites were, but because of the restrictions they place upon the deity and their own lack of felt love. Both these reasons surface in categories 2, 3 and 4 below.

2. *Owing to the billions of people inhabiting the earth, to expect God to love each one individually is to expect a herculean task, impossible even for God.* This need not be surprising, especially when viewed in the light of the limitations we have already seen the deaf place upon

God, e.g., God as a celestial being, circumscribed in place and enjoying an aerial view of the earth. In addition to distance, the divinity is also handicapped by limited knowledge and power, areas to be explored shortly. Here are some sample comments:

Nancy 18_A ranked (1) parents, (2) Aunt Peg and Uncle Kenny, (3) grandparents, (4) Bob, and (5) Bertha. "God is first," said Nancy, but her response broke down under the follow-up question: "How do you know that God loves you more than your mother and father love you?" She answered: "Jesus' book says so. But I'm confused. There are so many people. I don't know how God can love me."

David 17WAIS109_ listed (1) mother, (2) father, (3) brother, (4) grandmother, and (5) grandfather, and had this to say: "I never see that God loves me. My family loves me more than God. Besides, God has many, many other people to love. How can he love me?"

Michael 16MAT Adv.3.5V ranked the people and said: "Jesus loves me less than my parents love me. Jesus helps. But my mother and father help me more. Jesus has to help many people. How can he do it? My mother and father help me."

3. *Parental love surpasses the love of God because not God but parents work and do specific favors for their deaf.* Instead of understanding love as an attitude or orientation of character, these deaf look upon love as activity done for them. Here are samples:

Steven 17_A wrote (1) mother and father, (2) Grandpa Barney, (3) Aunt Pat, (4) Uncle and Aunt Barney, and (5) Carolyn. "Maybe God is better than #1," said Steven, "but my father goes to work every morning, takes care of me, makes money to help me. God does not work for me."

Stephen 17MAT Adv.4.4A wrote (1) Mary, (2) Cecil, (3) Norman, (4) brother Mike, and placed God between (2) and (3). "My mother," explained Stephen, "washes my clothes, gives me good things. But God does not wash my clothes or give me things."

Helen 20WAIS94_ likewise listed the persons who love her and remarked that her parents love her more than God because "my father goes out to work for me, my mother cooks for me. God doesn't do that for me."

4. *The love of God is conditioned upon the deaf person's sensory experience of him.* According to these deaf, seeing God and meeting him (physically) are necessary prerequisites to making judgments about his

love for them. These deaf also imply that knowledge of God is impossible without meeting or seeing, and to love a person without knowing him is equally impossible. The literalism expressed here recalls what was seen earlier. The remarks of the deaf follow.

> Dorothy 20CNE98A wrote (1) parents, (2) brother and sister, (3) aunt, (4) boyfriend, and offered: "God loves everybody the same. I would give God the last number because I don't know much about him. If I had no mother, I would never see my mother. I wouldn't know who she is. It's the same with God."
>
> David 17CAT8.0A made a listing, conceded that God loves him about equal with number five, but added: "I never see God. I never meet God. I don't know God. But I heard that he loves all people."
>
> Phyllis 16MAT Adv.3.8V ranked the people and said: "God is last, number 5. My aunt and uncle love me more than God. I was never with God."

Staying with the question of God's love, insights into deaf thinking deepen when it is compared to that of the control group. We find a slightly higher percentage (45%) of hearing teenagers expressing God's personal love as higher than human or supreme and a smaller percentage (25%) lowering his love to human proportions. But the four characteristics common to much of the deaf thought seldom appear in the control group responses. Basically this is because the hearing teenagers keep divinity free of the defects which the deaf assign to it. Consider these responses:

> Bruce, 18, says: "God loves everyone and he can forgive faults. He loves anyone who has faith in him. I know that God loves me. It is a more intense love than my parents' love. It would have to be. It is so intense that it overlooks a lot of things."
>
> Frances, 17, remarks: "God loves me. God can love more than any person can. He has a great capacity to love us and that is his job."
>
> Joan, 18, comments: "After I began to trust in Christ as my Savior, I began to realize that God loves me with a perfect love. I accept his will in my life. Whatever he wants is fine with me."
>
> Joseph, 17, says: "My mom is human, right? Okay. So she would not be able to love a person as much as God could."

Nevertheless, not all the members of the control group thought differently than the deaf. There were a few similarities. Edward, 16, for instance, fits into category 1 above as he says: "I would say that this

Being knows me and loves me." When asked: "Does God love you as an individual?" he answers: "No. It is part of an overall love. God loves everybody." Maureen, 17, fits into category 4 and remarks: "I feel God's love from my parents. But from my contact with God, I was not aware that I am loved."

To recognize better what is happening, we pause to look at related factors which help to shape the deaf adolescent's conception of God's personal love for him. The basic factor, supported by evidence already presented, is that the God of the deaf is finite and the love he communicates is therefore finite. Some features of this finiteness are elaborated below.

One feature is God's exclusively universal love, which some deaf students described before in category 1. These, as well as some deaf in other categories, not only emphasize his universal love; they also stress that he loves everyone exactly alike, the only exceptions being a few bad people whom he ignores. Light is shed on this point by studying it in connection with Question 26f, "Does God love the deaf or hearing people more?" One would expect at least some deaf to blame God for their handicap and consequently agree that God loves the hearing people more. Yet a surprising 90.9% of the deaf responded that God loves the deaf and hearing people equally. Almost no deaf comment reproached God for burdening them with the handicap of deafness. This may be due to the deaf person's concentration upon God's transcendence without immanence, forcing God to love from afar with an undiscriminating love that gets no farther than mankind in general.

God's personal love is also restricted when an almost exclusive transcendence is tied to another feature—namely, God's limited knowledge of his individual creatures. To illuminate divine knowledge, we introduce Questions 15f, g and h: "Does God know you?" "Does God know your name?" "Does God know your address?" As the questions advance from f to h the percentages drop steadily: 74.3% of the deaf believe that God knows them as individuals, 65.7% feel that God knows their names, and only 55.2% hold that he knows their addresses. The control group differs widely with the deaf on this question: 84.2% of the hearing teenagers responded that God knows their names and addresses.

Accompanying quotes are withheld until later when they will be given with the remainder of Question 15. For now, it suffices to summarize their content: God is ignorant of some names and addresses because to gather complete information he would have to inspect an immense number of streets, homes and people. Scant personal knowledge leads to scant personal love, for love presumes knowledge. Moreover, God's knowledge depends chiefly not upon his intellect but upon his sight: God knows much because he sees much, and what he fails to see he fails to know—a point to be substantiated shortly.

Another finite feature affecting the deaf person's understanding of God's personal love is the aspect of love as an activity. Loving means giving. It means ability to help in need or to change the status quo. But ability presumes power and the deaf adolescent's God is power impoverished. This will emerge in Question 16, which shows how some deaf (approximately 25%) reduce divine power to human proportions.

Finally, loves means nearness. Even on the human plane, distance connotes separation, which means being cut off without capacity to use human powers; therefore separation means helplessness.[83] Since the deaf adolescents' obscure understanding of immanence puts distance between them and their God, it is logical that the result is a somewhat helpless God. Distance plus helplessness combine to make God a stranger, someone with whom it is difficult to achieve union.

In concluding, it is obvious that the question of divine love for the deaf is as crucial as it is massive. Much more could be said: for instance, how maturity of character helps the deaf person to receive both human and divine love, how the nature of love can be clarified, how to achieve prerequisites (e.g., humility) to love, and how love works in contemporary society. But these issues are all larger than our purposes here.

In the last analysis, the deaf can be reassured that Jesus is the best proof of God's love for men (Jn. 3:16; 10:11; 1 Jn. 4:9ff.). Jesus' nearness and knowledge, his compassion and power, have prefaced his unique love and his supreme concern for the individual which have compelled people across the world to dedicate their lives to him even to this day. Simone Weil was speaking of brotherly love, but her words also apply to Jesus' desire to relate to the deaf adolescent:

> The same words (e.g., a man says to his wife, "I love you") can be commonplace or extraordinary according to the manner in which they are spoken. And this manner depends on the depth of the region in a man's being from which they proceed without the will being able to do anything. And by a marvelous agreement they reach the same region in him who hears them. Thus the hearer can discern, if he has any power of discernment, what is the value of the words.[84]

It is his intense love which makes Jesus require all men to decide whether they shall be for him or against him (Mt. 12:30).

(d) Negative Aspects of God's Character

Four questions (14b, c, d and e) are analyzed together in this section. The aim is to investigate what are regarded as negative or unfavorable aspects of God's moral character: anger, punishment and fear. In the pre-testing, attempts were made to delve directly into divine justice, but these efforts were dropped for reasons already explained. Instead, three simple questions were asked: Is God angry like this man (the respondent is shown the accompanying drawing)? Always? Sometimes? Never? (Question 14b); Does God punish people? Often? Sometimes? Never? (Questions 14c and d); Are you afraid of God? (Question 14e). The adolescents' spontaneous explanations of these questions contain enough reasoning to allow observations to be made. But before these commentaries are made and statistics given, we pause now to present a general preface and then a brief preface for each of the three qualities.

Although these qualities are negative, their importance can hardly be underestimated. For this examination seeks to determine whether and to what extent the deaf have constructed the caricature of a capricious deity, eternally prepared to punish, unpredictably angered and striking fear in his followers. Such a loveless deity justifies rejection of religion and severance of the fragile bond that is fear. Just as on a human plane our lives are shaped by those who love us or refuse to love us, so too on the divine plane our lives are shaped by God whom we conceive as loving us or refusing to love us. If the deaf accentuate the above caricature, it is hardly surprising that they cannot accept the demands of such a God and therefore will abandon him in adolescence.

The anger that we are concerned with here is not the holy anger that Jesus directed at the buyers and sellers in the temple (Mt. 21:12ff.) and at the hypocrisy of certain Pharisees (Mk. 3:5). Nor are we primarily concerned with Old Testament divine anger which brings God's retributive justice to men and which flares because of Israel's lethargic response to his covenant love (Ex. 32:1-10; Dt. 11:16-17; Hos. 13). Nor are we concerned with God's final wrath which is being stored up for the Day of the Lord. Rather, the anger meant here is merely an anthropomorphic emotion in God's character as written in Psalm 77. The question seeks the place of anger in God's emotional make-up in the same way that we inquire of anger in a human being. Along with this, we are concerned with the attitude of God—whether, to the deaf, it is habitually kind and fair or hateful and arbitrary.

Punishment is another negative idea with which God is so readily associated. This question is again a simple open-ended inquiry and deliberately leaves untouched such themes as punishment and responsibility, punishment and compensation, effects of punishment, and punishment and hope. Consonant with notions common throughout the ancient Near East, the Israelites attributed to Yahweh all the misfortunes that struck them.[85] Do the deaf share this view? And can the deaf see any medicinal value to punishment and respond with Job as he says:

"Happy the man whom God reproves!

The Almighty's chastening do not reject.
For he wounds, but he binds up;
he smites, but his hands give healing" (Jb. 5:17ff.).

Or, on the other hand, do the deaf envision God as meting out punishment for punishment's sake?

The final negative idea is fear of the Lord, a term which likewise stands in need of clarification. In this study, we are unconcerned with the Old Testament idea of "fear of the Lord," which often must include reverence and a desire and love for God, coupled with hatred for sin.[86] The fear that we are concerned with is the human emotion of fear and the deaf adolescents' experience of it in their relationship with God. This entire matter is far from trifling, for the debilitating effect of fear upon love is obvious and need not be elaborated here.

Keeping in mind the prefacing remarks just concluded, we now turn to the three qualities, beginning with divine anger. Statistical analysis shows a strong similarity between Catholic school deaf, secular school deaf and the control group. A total of 1% of the deaf and none of the control group say that God is always angry, while 43.7% of the deaf and 45% of the control group say that he is sometimes angry. And almost the identical percentage, 45.6% of the deaf and 45% of the control group, say that he is never angry. Saying that they don't know are 9.7% of the deaf and 10% of the hearing teenagers.

As done previously, we can gather up insights and group thoughts from analyzing the comments of the young people. The following patterns emerge clearly.

1. *God is never angry.* John 19WAIS116AV, for instance, says: "God is always serious, not angry." "God is never angry," explains Karen 16WISC117A, "but God feels bad when I do something wrong." "God is never angry because he is very patient," is the comment of Shirley 17MAT Adv.4.2A. Other sample remarks are: "God is never angry because he always understands people," "He is peaceful," "God is quiet, smiling and happier than people," "He always forgives everything."

2. *God's intention is to remain calm, but sin and repeated refusals to accept his help provoke his anger.* Carl 20WAIS119_ says: "God is sometimes angry because people do not obey his rules." "God gets angry at sins," says Debra 16WISC133A. "He does not like sins." According to Richard 19_A, evil places God in a dilemma and the result is anger: "God is sometimes angry. People fight, kill each other. God sees them. And God says 'Stop! Stop!' But the people don't care. They fight

again and God gets mad." William 17WISC89V has similar thoughts: "God advises, advises. People still do wrong and God gets mad."

3. *God's anger is relegated totally to the historical past.* For Dean 20WAIS121_, the historical event is the crucifixion: "When Jesus died, God became angry and started a lightning storm and earthquake." "God was mad in the past," says Phyllis 16MAT Adv.3.8V. "God used to get mad," says John 17WAIS96A, "many, many years ago, not now."

4. *This group is uncertain since they have never seen God and therefore have no sensory evidence of divine anger.* Thus Daniel 17WISC111A explains: "I don't know God's feelings. I never see his face. I don't know if he is angry or not. God was angry with Moses for striking the rock." Ann 19CMMS128V simply says: "I don't know. I never see God." Robert 19_A echoes the same thought: "I don't know. I never see his face."

Moving over to the area of punishment, we first give the statistics, then examine the responses. The sum of 4.7% of the deaf said that God punishes often: none from the Catholic schools and 6.2% from the secular schools. No one from the control group answered that God punishes often. Responding that God sometimes punishes are 61.7% of the deaf: 59.3% from the Catholic schools and 62.5% from the secular schools. A total of 58.8% of the control group answered likewise. The deaf who say that God never punishes number 18.7%: 14.8% of the Catholic school students and 20% of the secular school students. Some 29.4% of the control group responded similarly. The average of 14.9% of the deaf (25.9% from the Catholic schools, 11.3% from the secular schools) and 11.8% of the control group gave other answers.

As in previous questions, very many deaf here aired their views at some length, and an analysis of these enable the following observations to be made. To most of the deaf, God is free of caprice. He is larger than a petty deity who punishes arbitrarily, since a sufficient reason accompanies his chastisements. According to many deaf, expiation of a sin or crime seems to be uppermost in God's mind as he metes out punishments which may often be physical (e.g., sickness or accident) and sometimes emotional (e.g., sadness). God can allot these misfortunes swiftly or delay a number of years or even until death. Furthermore, some deaf resemble those apostles who struggled within themselves as they passed a blind man and finally asked Jesus, "Rabbi, was it his sin or that of his parents that caused him to be born blind?" (Jn. 9:1ff.). Personal misfortune, these deaf persons say, comes directly from personal sin. A few of the deaf have seen divine chastisements as medicinal, but more of them limit their explanation to God's need for vengeance: someone does wrong and therefore deserves censure. Sharing this view is the Psalmist who opens Psalm 94 with the words: "God of vengeance, Lord, God of vengeance, show yourself." These and other trends common to their thoughts are classified below and accompanied with quotations from the deaf.

1. *To repay a wrongdoing, God sometimes inflicts a physical or emotional punishment now or later, but before death.* "God sometimes punishes," says Ronald 19_V. "He makes the people feel pain." Mary Lou 18WISC89_remarks: "People are so bad. Maybe the bad people go driving and God punishes them. He lets them get in an automobile accident." "Jesus can send bad weather, put people in accidents or make people die," is the view of Raymond 17WAIS112A. According to Debra 16WISC133A, "God punishes bad people. He can make them feel sad." Alice 19WAIS118A said that God punishes by withholding answers to prayer: "The people pray, want something. God will refuse to give it to them."

2. *God either desires or is compelled to withhold all punishment until after death.* Stephen 17MAT Adv.4.4A says: "On earth it is hard for God to punish people. After death, God punishes people for a reason. God will make them work." "He waits until the bad people die," says Ann 19CMMS128V, "and then he puts them in hell." "If a man steals, lies, makes big sins, God will wait for him to die and then send him to hell," is the observation of Dean 20WAIS121_.

3. *God's punishments are not contemporary, but historical only.* "Before Christ," explains Sandra 18WISC110A, "God punished people more often. But now not much. I didn't read about any punishment in the New Testament." Anna Marie 18WAIS117A comments: "Jesus punished before, when he was alive. I saw Jesus punish some men in a movie. But now—I never see that happen now." "God punished only once," says Margaret 20MAT Adv.4.4A. "He punished Adam and Eve a long time ago. That is all."

4. *Sensory evidence supporting divine punishment is lacking.* "How can God punish?" asks Paula 17WAIS108_. "God never punishes. God can't hit you. You never feel anything from God." Kathleen 18WAIS119_expresses similar views: "Never. I never see him punish people. How can he punish people? How?" John 17_V says: "Never. God can't punish. Do you know anybody that God punished?"

In other scattered responses, some deaf, perhaps enough to constitute a trend, described the Old Testament idea of "an eye for an eye."

Paralleling the above-quoted blind man incident, Peter 17MAT Adv.4.9V, who has several sharers of this thought, remarks: "If a mother and father do wrong, the baby is born deaf, blind or crippled. God can give people a shorter life."

Lastly, we observe the deaf adolescents' fear of God along with an examination of their comments. As already seen in the statistics, 66% of the deaf have no fear of God. The reasons which the deaf advance for their absence of fear center predominantly around one main theme: lack of physical evidence of God's presence. To these deaf, God is present only if he is met and experienced by the senses, especially sight and touch, and, for some others, an interior "feeling" of his presence. Some of this is in harmony with our previous findings on the deaf understanding of divine transcendence joined to a minimum of immanence. Given this premise, the rest is logical, for to be remote is to be innocuous and there is no need to fear the innocuous. Here are some examples:

Shirley 17MAT Adv.4.2A says: "No. I'm not afraid. Maybe if I see God—if God comes down here I will be afraid." Joanne 17WISC93_ remarks: "No. But I would be afraid if I met him." "No," says Karen 16WISC117A. "If God sees me and talks to me, I would be afraid." "I don't feel anything. God never bothers me," says Robert 18_V.

Included in miscellaneous answers are those of the deaf who said that God will automatically forgive everyone, so why be afraid. Ignoring the necessity of sorrow and repentance, Ronald 17_A remarked: "God is good. He will forgive me." Also included in the miscellaneous answers are those who said that they were too young to fear God; they will grow old and wait for death before they become afraid.

Other deaf (26.8%), however, do exhibit a fear of God. The only fear they describe, however, is akin to the theological notion of servile fear—a fear which is concerned with serving God minimally to avoid punishment. There is hardly any mention of filial fear, which inspires the person to see himself as God's son and shun everything that would threaten the God-son relationship. Nor is there any thought of reverential fear on account of God's sovereignty. The fearful deaf youth feel afraid mainly because God's vigilance over them is unceasing and seems to intensify when they are guilty of wrongdoing. Below is a typical sampling.

Tom 19WISC106A admits his fear because "God is always watching me. If I want to tell a lie, God knows it right away. I feel it inside." Echoing similar thoughts, Kathleen 19WAIS119_ says: "When I do something wrong, I feel afraid of God." Ruth 17_A remarks: "When I do bad things, God says, 'I will see you,' and then I am afraid. But I must be brave."

It is now time to lay out for ourselves the anger-punishment-fear insights of the control group and compare them with the deaf. Although the comparative statistics are very similar, an analysis of the control group remarks opens up differences. For instance, 43.7% of the deaf and 45% of the hearing teenagers said that God is sometimes angry, while those who say he is never angry number 45% of the control group and 45.6% of the deaf.

The statistical similarity is striking, but the reasoning of the control group diverges from the deaf. The hearing young people sense that human language applied to God must be stretched or used analogically or indirectly, whereas the deaf are less aware of this and thereby make God different from his creatures not in kind but in degree (i.e., God is a magnified man). The responses of the hearing teenagers recognize anger in God but are able to purify it, at least to some extent, and raise it above the anthropomorphic level which the deaf assign to it. Consequently, the hearing young people see through divine anger to God's spirituality, uniqueness and steadfast love.

Here are some examples of divine anger as expressed by the control group. Sheila, 16, explains that God may be angry, "but not as men are angry. Jesus may act humanly, but not God the Father, who has no human attributes. The Father may give sudden correction, but not from anger." "God is not human," says Christina, 16, "but we have to explain him in human terms. He gets 'angry,' but he knows how to control his 'anger.' " "If he is perfect," says David, 16, "I don't think he's going to get angry." According to Frances, 17, "God is sometimes angry. But God's anger is a sign of his love—like parents get mad at their children because they love them and want what is best for them."

While acknowledging these differences, it is also noted that some of the hearing group resemble the deaf in one aspect: restricting divine anger to history. Peter, 15, for instance, explains that "God was angry once, when they crucified Jesus." Similarly, Kathleen, 16, says: "Very seldom does God get angry, but he is always forgiving. I think the last time God was angry was during the time of Moses—the plagues."

On the question of divine punishment there were some similarities between the control group and the deaf, although the control group elevated the issue to a higher level and showed a more objective comprehension. For the hearing young people, God's punishments resulted not from his human-like anger and need for revenge but from his desire to reform the individual. Punishment is seen as part of God's overall design. The control group, therefore, stabilizes the issue of chastisement and frees it from the vicissitudes of God's personality—something that some of the deaf are less capable of doing.

Behind the punishment, the hearing young people detect a noble motive: God's concern for his people. Just as the Babylonian captivity (597 B.C.) remade the Israelites into "good figs" (Jer. 24) and converted them wholeheartedly to God, so does the contemporary hand of God strike for medicinal purposes only. Equipped with such generous motives, God proceeds to assess the guilt and grade the punishment accordingly. At times, he even designs the chastisement as an antidote for the specific crime or sin (e.g., nausea to counteract gluttony).

Those control group members who remarked that God never punishes reasoned that God acts in ways completely above the human. They implicitly allude to God's utterance through Isaiah: "For my thoughts are not your thoughts, nor are your ways my ways, says the Lord. As high as the heavens are above the earth, so high are my ways above your ways and my thoughts above your thoughts" (Is. 55:8-9).

Recurring most often in the control group responses is the concept of medicinal punishment: God's periodic chastisements are from a motive of remedy, not mere retribution. Sheila, 16, for instance, explains that "God doesn't even consider it a punishment. He thinks of it as a correction. People call it punishment because it interferes with their happiness." Joseph, 17, simply says: "God punishes, but only to help the person." Frances, 17, has similar views: "God sort of punishes—but not exactly. He doesn't punish to hurt, but so that people may learn from it."

Another view is that God fits the punishment to the crime and designs it as a cure for that crime. An example is Kathleen, 16, who says: "If I often act selfish in front of the television set, maybe God will black out the set—or something." According to Adrien, 18, "God punishes people as often as they need it—maybe by making them lose something of value. If a lady's jewels are making her vain, maybe God will see to it that she loses them—to wake her up."

Typical of those who hold that God never punishes is Patrick, 16: "Never. He never does that. God does not act like human beings."

Peter, 15, shares the deaf view of delayed punishment. He says: "God punishes people, but not before they die. And these people deserve the punishment. God is fair."

We now move over to the control group view of fear, where we find little mention of continuous fear. However, there is much mention of a temporary fear which wrongdoing or sin activates and which then fades until subsequent wrongdoing or sin reactivates it. That this kind of fear is really conscience is evident. Perhaps both the deaf and hearing young people are aware of the ancient Hindu saying that conscience is "the invisible God who dwells within us."[87]

Here are samples from the control group. Sarah, 16, expresses her thoughts: "Sometimes I feel afraid of him. I feel uncomfortable when I do something wrong." "I'm a little bit afraid of God," says Kevin, 17. "I feel it when I do something wrong." Patti, 16, shares this and explains: "Not all the time. I do something wrong, then I feel bad. That is

God reminding me that I did something wrong." "When I serve him and do his will, I'm not afraid of him, because he is on my side," is the explantation of Joan, 18.

Other control group views are less prevalent and include the concepts of (1) a childhood fear of God that was outgrown in adolescence, (2) a lack of fear because God is too wonderful to be afraid of, and (3) a fear of God because he is unknown and mysterious.

In conclusion, we return to our original aim, which sought to determine if the anger-punishment-fear syndrome inhibited or prohibited the deaf adolescent from approaching God. We can now say that it did not. Although he is basically benign, a human-like anger occasionally issues from the God of the deaf. Evil works provoked his anger, which was also sometimes an outlet for his punishments. Yet many deaf failed to move beyond this and therefore saw retributive justice as God's sole motive in punishing.

Their earlier emphasis on divine transcendence and the remoteness of God undoubtedly led some deaf youth to the conclusion that the earth is out of God's reach and therefore he must withhold punishment until after death. Despite great distances, some deaf at least understand themselves as capable of influencing God, even if this means stimulating his wrath. The alternative would be a stoic, static God aloof from the affairs of men.

Finally, some of these responses again show us the deaf conception of God as a person with a semi-human form. Those deaf who were uncertain of divine anger because "I never see his face" presume that a face is there to be angry.

(e) God's Knowledge

Einsteins, Da Vincis, Aristotles and peasants alike recognize something they have in common—partial knowledge. Even a genius, after years of education, confesses that his limited knowledge handicaps him. Standing in sharp contrast to this is the awesome knowledge of God, reflected in the thoughts of young school children as they mechanically say: "God knows everything." The Catholic Church and Scripture introduce us to an infinite God possessing both intellect and will.[88] His knowledge is exhaustive. "Nothing is concealed from him; all lies bare and exposed to the eyes of him to whom we must render an account" (Heb. 4:13). "The nether world and the abyss lie open before the Lord; how much more the hearts of men" (Prov. 15:11). God has perfect and infallible knowledge of himself and everything and everyone that existed, exists, will exist or can exist. In short, God is omniscient. This also implies that God is freed from knowing something only from a single perspective, such as is characteristic of human knowledge, "for God both transcends every perspective and occupies every perspective at once."[89]

This investigation is unconcerned with some areas of omniscience—whether God foreknows with certainty the future freely chosen actions of men and whether he knows temporal events timelessly, i.e., whether historical events that happened in the remote past are as present to his mind as what is happening now. We are, on the other hand, concerned with the deaf view on the process, content and extent of God's knowledge. To learn anything, does God have to study, experiment, classify and compare? Does God have to bother with a learning process or is his knowledge more direct and intuitive? How much does God know and how does he know? Does he have personal knowledge of each human being? Does he know what is happening inside each human mind? These are the areas in which the deaf will make known their views.

As explained earlier, to examine omniscience a package of five drawings with accompanying questions and three additional questions without pictures were devised. Each successive drawing demands more knowledge of God. The last three questions (i.e., Does God know you?, etc.) seek to determine the adolescents' thoughts on God's personal knowledge of themselves as distinguished from God's general knowledge covered by the previous questions (i.e., $2 + 2 = 4$, etc.).

Because this six-part question is bulky and the statistics numerous, the table arrangement below gives a clear statistical overview of the entire question.

GENERAL KNOWLEDGE

	Q. 15a $2 + 2 = 4$		Q. 15b GOD VS. TEACHER		Q. 15c GOD VS. PRES. NIXON		Q. 15d GOD VS. BOY		Q. 15e GOD KNOWS THE MOST	
	Deaf	Control	Deaf	Control	Deaf	Control	Deaf	Control	Deaf	Control
Yes	87.5	94.7	79.4	94.7	82.5	89.5	67.6	94.7	76.2	94.7
No	4.8	0	17.6	0	13.6	5.3	21.6	0	13.9	0
Don't Know	7.7	5.3	2.9	5.3	3.9	5.3	10.8	5.3	9.9	5.3

PERSONAL KNOWLEDGE

	Q. 15f YOU		Q. 15g NAME		Q. 15h ADDRESS	
	Deaf	Control	Deaf	Control	Deaf	Control
Yes	74.3	89.5	65.7	84.2	55.2	84.2
No	14.3	5.3	17.1	10.5	24.8	10.5
Don't Know	11.4	5.3	17.1	5.3	20.0	3.3

As seen in the table, 87.5% of the deaf hold that God knows that $2 + 2 = 4$. A question about the new mathematics (i.e., Does God know the new math?) was added here, but had to be occasionally dropped since some deaf were unfamiliar with the new math. Hence, the new mathematics question eludes statistical analysis. The deaf who did respond, however, fell into two categories: (a) God knows the new mathematics thoroughly and "sees the mistakes before we do," and (b) new mathematics is unknown to Jesus, since he died before it was invented. Category (a) is more numerous than category (b).

Question 15b demands more knowledge of God and the percentage drops to 79.4% of the deaf who think that God knows more than the chemistry teacher. Some deaf go outside the question and explain that God's general knowledge is greater but the teacher knows more chemistry than God.

Question 15c presumes that, to the deaf adolescent, President Nixon's knowledge would surpass the teacher's.[90] Yet the percentage rises as 82.5% of the deaf readily assign a greater knowledge to God than to the President.

Question 15d inquires whether the deaf give God credit for knowing a boy (likewise all human beings) to the roots of his being. Understandably, the percentage drops to 67.6% of the deaf who say that God knows that the boy is dreaming about baseball.

Question 15e approaches omniscience as it asks the deaf whether God knows the most—and 76.2% agree that he does.

As in other questions, the explanatory remarks of the deaf reveal their reasoning to support their convictions on God's knowledge, and certain trends emerge.

1. *The single most predominant pattern is that, to many deaf, omniscient means all-seeing and, less often, all-hearing.* God's knowledge is rooted in and contingent upon his physical visual ability. He knows because he physically sees and sometimes with a vision that can even penetrate into a boy's mind. But what he fails to see he fails to know. The Greek word *oida*, "I know," more strictly means "I have seen," a meaning which coincides with the thinking of this group of deaf adolescents.

Here again the deaf forge a connection with ancient forgotten religions. For example, the peoples of the Andaman Archipelago in Asia worshiped Puluga, their anthropomorphic sky god. Puluga's knowledge was vast, but encumbered by one embarrassing restriction: he knew men's thoughts only during daylight hours. At night he could see nothing and therefore know nothing and had to tolerate his ignorance until morning.[91]

Furthermore, in the Old Testament, Amos, Sirach and the Psalmist give Yahweh a pair of eyes without commenting whether or to what extent his knowledge is dependent upon them.

We now turn to the deaf themselves for their affirmations of divine visual knowledge.

According to Francine 16MAT Adv.4.9A, God knows more than President Nixon because "God was born before President Nixon and knows how everything was. God knows more about the world now because he will see what happens before President Nixon." Robert 18MAT Adv.4.9V asserts the reason for God's knowing his address: "God sees me leave the house. He sees me write my address." Jesus may not know Gary 19WAIS105V personally because "maybe there are too many people for Jesus, I don't know. Jesus can't look at them all." Steve 18CAT7.3A affirms that God knows all mathematics books because "he watches. He sees when the man is writing the book." To Mary Beth 19_A, God's surveillance is the source of his knowledge: "God knows the most. He learns a lot about how to make buildings (construction) from watching the people." "God can see outside my house," says William 20RBE85_, "but he can't see in the house."

2. *Another trend which appeared is divine knowledge based on creation.* Although they lacked theological terminology, these deaf reasoned simply that if God makes something from nothing, he must know it completely. Julie 17MAT Adv.4.4V, for instance, says that Jesus knows her personally because "Jesus makes babies." Mario 19MAT Adv.4.2V likewise says: "God knows the boy's dreams. He made the boy's mind—everything; he knows." "I did not see God," replies Joseph 18_A, "so it is hard to compare him with the teacher. But God made people and animals. He must know more."

3. *A third trend is that Jesus' historical situation both determined and restricted the extent of his knowledge.* These deaf say or imply that Jesus had need of going to school, subjecting himself to the piecemeal learning process, and building up his knowledge as do human beings. For instance, Michael 16MAT Adv.3.5V says that "Jesus does not know math." Moreover, Jesus knows less than the teacher and President Nixon because "Jesus did not study anything. The teacher went to school and studied more. President Nixon has meetings, discussions, talks. Jesus doesn't talk. He watches. That is all." Richard 19MAT Adv.3.0V replies that the new mathematics is unknown to Jesus: "He died before the new math started." "The teacher went to college," says Kimberly 16CAT6.9A. "God did not go to college."

4. *Finally, there are those who throughout the package exhibited a consistent awareness that God knows the most.* "God knows that the boy is dreaming about baseball," says Margaret 20MAT Adv.4.4A. "God made him and nature. God knows his dreams." Basing divine knowledge on creation, Margaret further explained that God knows everything in the series, including future events. Alan 17MAT Adv.5.5A

asserts that God knows more than the teacher because "God is perfect." ✗
"God knows everything better than we do," is the contribution of Joseph 17WISC118A to the question. Charles 21RBE113_ reasons that "God is very intelligent. He never gives the wrong answers. He can see through the boy's mind. And God knows all that will happen in the future." Larry 17_A sums up the question well: "God not only knows the most; he knows everything. He knows what the boy is dreaming because he made the boy's brain. How wonderful! It is impossible for a human ✗ being to make a brain."

As we move over into the area of God's personal knowledge of individuals (i.e., Does God know you? Your name? Your address?) there is a noticeable percentage drop. However reluctant the deaf were in allowing omniscience into general knowledge, they are even more unwilling to allow a divine knowledge of themselves personally. To some deaf, *what* God knows is deeper and more extensive than *whom* he knows. Undoubtedly the already examined notion of divine visual knowledge partially accounts for the numerous deaf admissions that God is somewhat ignorant of names and addresses.

Let us illustrate. Lorraine 17WISC121A remarks that God knows her, but not her name and address, because "there are too many people. ✗ It is too much trouble for God to remember all those names and addresses." Linda 18RBE109_ likewise says: "There are so many people in the world. Some move away, change homes. It's all mixed up. How can God know?" Jesus is ignorant of the name and address of Michael 16MAT Adv.3.5V, for "Jesus never asks: 'Where is Mike?' He is up ✗ there looking at the world." The name of Pearl 17_V escapes God because "many, many people have names. It is too hard for God." Arthur 18_V follows Pearl as he says: "Too many streets, too many houses." Phyllis 16MAT Adv.3.8V may remain unidentified, since "there are a lot of people. And many people have the same name—Phyllis, Phyllis." Other brief samples follow: "There are too many people. Jesus can't look at all of them" "My mother gave me my name. I doubt if God knows it." "God knew when I was born; but God does not know my name." "He knows my face, but not my name—too many ✗ people."

On the other hand, some deaf use the principle of visual knowledge to uphold God's personal knowledge of them. Peter 17MAT Adv.4.9V, for instance, emphasizes sight: "God learned my name from my friends. They call me (make my sign) Peter or they fingerspell P-E-T-E-R. God has seen that many times." Moreover, God knows Peter's address be- ✗ cause "he has seen that on my letters." God knows the name of Robert 18MAT Adv.4.9 inasmuch as "he made my mother think what name to give me" and "he sees me leave my house. He sees me write my address. He knows."

Pursuing the control group, it becomes apparent that they differ from the deaf in several ways. A study of the statistics, for instance, demonstrates that a higher percentage of hearing young people more readily attribute a more extensive and even perfect knowledge to God. The control group more frequently uses such expressions as "God is all-knowing," "God knows everything" and "God knows all." Moreover, the reasoning of the control group differs somewhat from the deaf. Although present, the concept of visual knowledge in the control group is trifling—a sharp contrast with the deaf.

The control group also testifies more strongly to a divine knowledge based on creation: God understands his own creation and presides over all of it. Edward, 16, remarks that "God would have to know an awful lot to create the world." "If he gave us our minds," says Joseph, 17, "he must know mathematics." "God gave Edison the talent to invent the light bulb—he knows the future," explains Patti, 16.

In addition, the hearing young people displayed a greater awareness of divine personal knowledge of individuals. "God knows all about me," says Maureen, 17. Frances, 17, comments that "God knows what I am dreaming before I have the dream." Kathleen, 16, ties personal knowledge to judgment: "God knows what I think and do because he has to judge me." These and other remarks yield a divine knowledge that is immediate and specific, whereas the deaf leaned more toward a knowledge that is successive and generic (i.e., God may know their faces, but not their names and addresses). One final remark concludes our comparison of the control group with the deaf. As mentioned earlier, the hearing group more strongly emphasizes divine knowledge based on creation, which means that God's knowledge comes from his causality: God's knowledge is causative. In other words, the hearing group implies that they as well as the rest of creation pre-existed as possibilities in the divine mind and that God's creative power brought them from possibilities into actual existence. Consequently, God knows them as individuals.

We now address ourselves to related factors, for the deaf necessarily carry their views of omniscience over into other characteristics of the divine and conversely. The first point for study is the influence of transcendence-immanence upon divine knowledge.

Even though transcendence-immanence belongs more properly to Question 19 and therefore is still to be examined, we have already seen sufficient glimpses to allow the observation that many deaf have lost the balance between the two. They go to extremes in stressing transcendence to the neglect of immanence, and this is bound to affect their interpretation of divine knowledge. By emphasizing God's remoteness, the deaf are likely to diminish his power over and knowledge of mundane affairs, as happened to some sky gods of ancient religions. And when remoteness combines with the restrictions of divine visual knowledge, the problem becomes doubly acute and the deaf youngsters must then contend with a far-away deity whom distance reduces to a state of near ignorance of them. Responses to Question 11g support this inasmuch as they reveal that, according to the deaf, God's knowledge of earthly events derives largely from physical sight. What saves the deaf from such an extreme, however, is their view that God is present in church. This is at least a beginning of immanence and, when coupled with the incarnation, can lay the groundwork for a clearer deaf perspective upon divine knowledge.

The idea of divine knowledge stemming from physical sight deserves more attention. Perhaps this thought, more than any other, underlies the statistical drop in the category of divine personal knowledge. The premise of visual knowledge, as many deaf pointed out, has its own logical consequences: God cannot possibly see everyone at once, he may notice only important people, and his gaze is not fixed upon an individual long enough to know the on-going details and developments of that person's life. Still, one can use to good advantage the deaf accent on the visual by (1) explaining that divine vision far surpasses human vision, (2) assuring them that God is never very far from any one of us, and (3) teaching that if God's eye is constantly on the sparrow (Mt. 10:29) it must certainly be on them too. The deaf can also be assured that if they love God, they come under his constant, loving gaze: "The eyes of the Lord are upon those who love him; he is their mighty shield and strong support" (Sir. 34:16).

Another related factor is the bearing of knowledge upon love and providence. We have already seen how God's restricted knowledge impedes his love of the individual, and we now expand the discussion to see how restricted knowledge affects corporate love, or providence. Since they realize God's role as an overseer, the deaf already understand the connection between providence and divine knowledge, restricted though it may be. With some effort, they can progress to the more advanced idea of divine planning or designing—an awareness that God not only sees but dynamically rules the world and that therefore events will ultimately work themselves out constructively. One can, for example, bring the deaf back to the Spirit hovering over the waters (Gen. 1:2) from which have come temperate climate, rain, food, plants and life. Let the deaf stand in awe before the earth, tilted at an angle of 23 degrees, just right to give us our seasons; let them stand in awe before the sun, 92,000,000 miles away, a distance just right to support our life; let them stand in awe before the moon, 240,000 miles away, just right for gentle ocean tides.[92] Such careful calculations, the adolescent would conclude, are impossible without divine planning, without divine providence.

As previously studied, many deaf characterize God's providence over individuals as sporadic, negative and impersonal. No doubt, excessive anthropomorphism is responsible for these distortions, and once they are embedded, the task of cleansing and purifying becomes all the more arduous. What the deaf lack in this area, they might well make up by an understanding of key Scripture passages which assure them of God's intimate knowledge of individuals and that everywhere the hand of God is present, perpetuating life on this planet. Outstanding among Scripture passages is Matthew 10:30: "As for you, every hair of your head has been counted."

Also outstanding and numbered among the most beautiful chapters in all Scripture, opening up the vast expanse of divine knowledge and its coalescence with providence and power, is the blistering exchange between the Lord and his critic, Job. Its dramatic climax in Job 38 sustains itself through Job 42. With some deletions and language adaptations, it can elevate the deaf to new heights, since its concreteness and color, along with its pedagogical principle of teaching by comparison and contrast, qualify it for use with the deaf.

Lastly, we turn brief attention to the insights of the deaf on divine knowledge and God's comprehension of the prayers of the deaf, although this subject will be discussed again. Question 23e probes God's knowledge of sign-language. A total of 35% of the deaf, which includes 16% from the Catholic schools and 42% from the secular schools, either deny or doubt that God knows sign-language. The various related factors already discussed have a bearing here and need not be repeated. Furthermore, when these statistics are placed alongside the 32% of the deaf (Question 15d) who doubt or deny God access to man's innermost thoughts, questions in regard to the prayer life of the deaf are immediately raised.

(f) Divine Power

Nothing exceeds divine power, which refers in general to God the almighty, the all-powerful, the omnipotent. More specifically, omnipotence refers to God's absolute sovereignty over everything he has created and to his ability to do all things "which are in accordance with his nature."[93] The quoted qualifier is significant, for it is impossible for God to do something which is logically contradictory or absurd. Nor can he reverse one of his laws, for this implies a change in divine planning, which in turn implies the acquisition of fresh knowledge. (This, of course, is untenable since it means that God's knowledge is discursive.) Examples to illustrate the above come easily. Making a square circle, changing a vice into a virtue, announcing that 2 + 2 no longer equals 4, eliminating a commandment, or violating a person's free will are nowhere to be found within omnipotence—not because God's power is limited but because the activities themselves are non-existent. The ideas within each activity cancel themselves out and thereby remove the activity from reality. The examples entailing a change of law or design fall outside omnipotence for the reasons outlined above.

To omit omnipotence is to reconcile oneself to an obscure understanding of the God of the deaf, for men of all ages unanimously assigned power to their deities. In particular, Scripture raises divine power to almighty realms, utterly beyond the reach of contemporary gods and pharaohs of Egypt as God becomes known as "El Sadday," "God (the) Almighty" (Gen. 17:1) and "Mighty One of Jacob" (Gen. 49:24). The importance of this attribute becomes more evident when analyzed in conjunction with other divine characteristics. Power, for instance, is the basis of confidence in God's ability to fulfill his promises (cf. Jer. 32:16ff.). Power makes his love and our salvation efficacious. Power, finally, puts meaning into prayer, providence and pardon.

Previous sections of this work have already yielded glimpses of the deaf view of divine power. What is particularly striking is the debilitating effect of power impoverishment upon divine love for the individual. Those deaf who remarked that "it is too hard" for God to love each individual were numerous enough to be grouped together under the proposition, *Owing to the billions of people inhabiting the earth, to expect God to love each one individually is to expect a herculean task, impossible even for God*, as we have seen earlier.

The deaf expose further views in their thinking on divine activity in heaven, his interventions on earth, and the consequences of his unceasing surveillance of the earth. In his observations, God sometimes needs the help of the angels and sometimes sends Jesus here on specific missions. According to some deaf, God uses his power to forgive sins, help people get along together, take souls at the time of death, grow plants and manipulate the weather.

As with Question 15, the clearest statistical presentation can be made by arranging the statistics as below.

| | Q. 16a | | Q. 16b | | Q. 16c | | Q. 16d | | Q. 16e | |
| | BOY | | WEIGHTLIFTER | | TRAIN | | ROCKET | | DIVINE POWER | |
	Deaf	Control	Deaf	Control	Deaf	Control	Deaf	Control	Deaf	Control
Yes	88.1	94.7	75.5	94.7	68.0	94.7	65.0	94.7	68.4	89.5
No	8.9	0	22.5	5.3	29.1	5.3	32.0	5.3	28.6	10.5
Don't Know	3.0	5.3	2.0	0	2.9	0	2.9	0	3.1	0

Before examining the statistics, a prefacing remark is in order. From its wording, the question seems to concern itself with arbitrary power and approaches to omnipotence that may just as easily originate from a force as from a person. There is merit to this criticism, yet it was felt that attempts to refine the question to fit more exactly our explanation above of omnipotence would leave the adolescents confused. What the question lacks in refinement, it makes up by the illumination found in the many clues in the respondents' explanations.

The question begins by asking the deaf to compare God's strength with that of the boy pulling the wagon. A total of 88% of the deaf said that God is stronger than the boy. Many of those who answered otherwise defended their position with the explanation that "a spirit can't pull." Question 16b demands more strength of God as it compares him to the weightlifter and the percentage drops to 76% of the deaf who believe that God is stronger. Question 16c brings in the power of a locomotive and shows a decline to 68% of the deaf who make God stronger. The percentage remains somewhat unchanged for Question 16d as 65% of the deaf place divine power ahead of the rocket. Finally, 68% of the deaf approach omnipotence in their response that God is the strongest.

The noticeable percentage decline enables one to say that, unlike the Hebrews who called God "the Almighty" and who were awed by the Sinai theophany and Yahweh's sovereignty over Egypt's rulers and magicians, a number of deaf adolescents are lightly impressed with divine power.

Again, many deaf youth had something to say about omnipotence and their comments now call for discussion. Running through the response were common denominators which can be grouped as follows:

1. *Those deaf who understand God as either extremely powerful or all-powerful.* Speaking of the train, Geraldine 17CMMS108A says: "God gave the people the idea to make the train. So maybe he is more powerful than the train." According to Peter 17MAT Adv.4.9V, God is stronger than the weightlifter because "God can pick up anything. He is not like people. He is stronger than people." "God must be the strongest," says Robert 18MAT Adv.4.9V, "He made the earth." Michael 17WISC120A echoes the same thought: "God is strongest because he created everything." Raymond 17WAIS112A expresses power this way: "Jesus is stronger than any man. He can destroy the train. And Jesus has to control the stars and keep the earth at the right distance from the sun."

2. *Those who assign to Jesus the strength of an ordinary man.* This group falls largely within the 23% who make the weightlifter stronger than Jesus. Thus does Marion 17_V reason: "Jesus is God and Jesus is a man. So he must be stronger than the boy, but not the weightlifter." "Jesus is stronger than the boy because he has better muscles than the boy," is the comment of Judy 18WISC110A. "The weightlifter is stronger than Jesus," explains Michael 16MAT Adv.3.5V. "The weight-

lifter practices and becomes strong. Jesus doesn't practice." Andrew 16MAT Inter.3.7V says: "The weightlifter has a bigger body, weighs more, has bigger muscles than Jesus. Jesus is thin." Wayne 18WAIS98A, acknowledging that Jesus is stronger than some people, then adds: "But some machines are stronger than Jesus."

3. *Those who explain that God's weakness comes from his inactivity or old age.* This group is found throughout the "no" and "doubtful" categories from Question 16a through Question 16e. William 18WISC121A, for instance, says that the boy, weightlifter, train and rocket are all stronger, since "God has nothing to do." John 19WAIS116AV attributes divine weakness to old age: "God is not stronger than the weightlifter because God is old." Rita 20WAIS98_ cites inactivity: "God is stronger than the boy, but not the weightlifter, because God gets no exercise." Anthony 17WISC86V reflects Rita's thoughts as he says: "The boy pulls. Jesus never pulls. Never. Jesus never exercises." "The weightlifter gets exercise," says John 17WAIS96A, "but God stays quiet, peaceful."

4. *Those deaf who associate strength with the possession of a physical body and therefore conclude that, since God has no body, he is either weak or powerless.* "The boy is stronger than God," explains Judith 18CMMS99V, "because he can pull and God can't. God is a spirit—nothing—can't pull." Carol 18WAIS91AV likewise remarks: "The weightlifter exercises. God is a soul—nothing." "The weightlifter and train are stronger than God because God is a ghost," is the observation of Paulette 18_A. "The weightlifter has muscles," explains Kimberly 16CAT6.9A, "but God has only the soul."

William's 20RBE85_ remark fits no category, but its simple beauty makes it a compelling last quote. After acknowledging that God is stronger than the boy and weightlifter, but not the train and rocket, William added: "The boy pulls the wagon and God pushes it from behind to help the boy. But the boy doesn't know that because God is a spirit. If the boy knew, he would turn around and say 'thank you.' "

We now turn to the remarks of the hearing young people. A look at the statistics shows that fewer control group responses come under the "no" and "doubtful" categories and that consequently they more closely approach omnipotence. Question 16e, for instance, reveals that 90% of the respondents ascribe supreme power to the deity. Less common in these comments are some of the anthropomorphisms mentioned by the deaf—especially the association of divine power with a physical body, physical activity and chronological age. Instead, the control group more readily differentiates spiritual strength from the physical, more readily distinguishes Jesus' human strength from his divine power, and more often uses banal but accurate phrases such as "all-powerful" and "almighty." Like the deaf, some of the hearing group base divine power upon the wonderful works of God in creation. Some samples will elucidate matters.

Patti, 16, for example, says: "God is stronger than everybody or everything. He has the power to make us." Maureen, 17, says that God is strongest, since "God has spiritual strength, which is different from physical strength. You can't prove spiritual strength to other people." "God is stronger than the train," says Jeanne, 17, "since God can stop the train if he wanted to."

It is now opportune to open a wider discussion of omnipotence, its usefulness, its implications and its relationship to other attributes. For the Israelites as well as the disciples of Jesus, divine power evoked more than academic interest; the dynamics of their God could revolutionize not only nature, but the nations and their own lives. Awed, the Jews began speaking of God's power in concrete religious images—his outstretched arm, his hand, his fingers, my rock, my fortress, my deliverer, my shield.

Moreover, as we said earlier, the prophet Jeremiah teaches that confidence in God is based upon divine power. Expanding this principle, a wider view opens out and throws light upon the further fact that a correct understanding of divine power is a prerequisite for inviting prayers of gratitude and petition and for appreciating the effectiveness of providence and the dependence of all things upon God. It is distinctly possible for some deaf teenagers to conclude that a good but weak God desires to assist but lacks the ability. If power is distorted or withheld, weakness rushes to the vacuum and the absorption of weakness into goodness produces an innocuous deity, unworthy of worship and ineffectual in his actions. He would command little respect, much less adoration, he would have little ruling power, much less absolute sovereignty, he would attract little allegiance, much less genuine discipleship, and his laws would be broken with impunity. Although not predominant, such thinking has occurred occasionally. Typical would be Robert's earlier quoted remark that he can do whatever he pleases since God is so good that he will overlook and forgive anything. This implies a unilateral relationship from God to man and would turn around St. Augustine's famous saying from "Love God and do what you wish" to "God loves you and therefore do as you wish."

That the courtship between weakness and goodness can bring dire consequences to goodness is evident from what happened to the good-weak gods of early religions. For example, an important Bantu tribe of the Kilimanjaro area of Africa venerated Ruwa, a god so kind that the tribe lost its fear of him.[94] Another good-weak god of a tribe from southwest Africa, Ndyambi, elicited this reaction from a follower: "Why should we sacrifice to him? We do not need to fear him, for he does not do us any harm, as do the spirits of our dead."[95] So the good but power-impoverished gods were seldom the recipients of prayers and sacrifices. One wonders to what extent those deaf in categories 2, 3 and 4 share some of these insights.

One contrast between the control group and some deaf may yield a helpful clue. Less aware of the mysterious element in divine strength, some of the deaf group wonder *whether* or *how* God is strong; more aware of the mysterious, the hearing group wonder *at* divine strength. An uplifting attitude of wonder and contemplation of omnipotence can change the deaf from wondering *how* and *whether* to wondering *at*. This, of course, applies to the entire realm of Christian mysteries.[96]

But in trying to open the deaf upward toward mystery, we recognize a challenge: if there is truth to the philosophical theory that the mind's journey from sense perception through symbolization and into abstraction is thrown into disarray in the mind of the deaf, it is quite possible that the deaf person's perception of the world unduly focuses upon sensible phenomena.[97] This would mean that the deaf need special assistance to penetrate to the trans-sensible. Here again, religious language is called to the rescue.

The literary form of the myth, which we shall discuss again later, has a communicative impact not found in abstract language and can therefore awaken in the deaf a sense of the divine mystery of omnipotence. Instead of telling the deaf that the Word of God is powerful, let us invite the ancients to tell them the same thought this way: "Now the Ennead of Atum came into being from his seed and by his fingers; but the Ennead (of Ptah) is the teeth and the lips in this mouth which uttered the name of everything and (thus) Shū and Tefnūt came forth from it."[98] Hence, the all-powerful mouth of Ennead (of Ptah) creates what it utters.

(g) *God's Eternity*

Eternity signifies "what endures without beginning or end, or what is inherently timeless, or what is utterly outside the created order of the universe and time."[99] A thought which held the rapt attention of St. Thomas Aquinas, the classic definition of Boethius is: "Eternity is the simultaneously whole and perfect possession of interminable life."[100] Psalm 90 applies eternity to God: "Before the mountains were begotten and the earth and the world were brought forth, from everlasting to everlasting you are God" (Ps. 90:2). Hence, anyone attempting to attribute eternity to God would have to ask (1) whether God began and will end, and (2) whether God is timeless, whether his life exists perfectly all at once or whether his life comes under the successions—the befores and afters—of time.

To ascertain the thinking of the deaf, a series of drawings depicting age spans from infancy to old age was devised (Question 17), as previously explained. After the testing had progressed, it became obvious that the package of drawings was superfluous, since many deaf interjected after the second or third drawing that God cannot die. Therefore, only one question "Can God die?" was subjected to statistical analysis. A total of 63% of the deaf said that God cannot die: this includes 84% from the Catholic schools and 56% from the secular schools. Those deaf responding that he can die total 14%: 8% from the Catholic schools and 17% from the secular schools. And 23% do not know: 8% from the Catholic schools and 28% from the secular schools. Unfortunately, the correlative question "Was God born?" was asked inconsistently and therefore omitted from the statistical analysis, since this would have distorted the percentages. The spontaneous remarks of the deaf, however, do yield information on divine beginnings as well as whether God can cease to exist and whether God is timeless or subject to an aging process. A study of the comments reveals several trends.

1. *God will live always because he is a spirit.* Randolph 17WISC-131__says: "God is a spirit. He will never die." The words of James 18WISC96__ are nearly identical: "God will always live because he is a spirit." "Jesus is a ghost," says Jane 18WAIS117A. "He can't die." "No. God is a soul and a soul can't die," remarked Alyce 18CAT13.4A. Mary 19WAIS116A fingerspelled that "God is immortal."

2. *God is eternal insofar as he has no end, but he did have a beginning.* The deaf who thus dilute eternity are included in the above 63%. Lorraine 17WISC121A believes that God will live forever, but he was born "when the sun began." The thoughts of Dora 16WISC104A are similar: "He can't die, but he began a long time ago, at the beginning of the earth." According to Ann 17__A, "Moses and the Jews were God before Jesus." "God the Father was born before Adam and Eve," says John 20WAIS114A.

3. *God is subject to an aging process which sometimes terminates in death.* "God can die," explains Denis 16WISC93__, "the same as people do." "God can get old and die," is the remark of Edna 16__ A Patrick 17WISC107__says; "God will die, maybe after millions of years." "God can die in the future," remarks Marilyn 18WAIS111A. "Maybe God is dead now. I go to church, ask God to forgive me, and he is never around there. I feel the same way after church as I did before."

Many of the 23% of the doubters limited their responses to "I don't know" and therefore are omitted from the categories of quotes. Other deaf gave statements with little elaboration, e.g., "God will never die," "God does not become older; he stays the same," and "God lives forever in heaven."

In contrast with the deaf, 80% of the control group responded that God cannot die and was not born, a few basing their statement on God's changelessness, as did Bruce, 18: "God can't die because he doesn't change." More typical is the remark of Frances, 17: "God was, is, and always will be."

Like some deaf, a portion of the control group hesitates on divine beginnings. Ritamarie, 16, speaks for them: "I've been thinking hard about this question. I don't suppose that God could have just leaped up out of nowhere. He had to have a beginning. And I believe he can age to a certain extent." Edward, 16, says: "God can't die. He was the only one who made the planets—but who made him I do not know."

When analyzed in the context of God's relationship with his people, a theology of the eternity of God surfaces. If God were temporal, his own covenant, which carries the promise of eternal life, would falter. His fidelity and his providence would lose their guarantee and the virtue of hope would lose its credibility. Offsetting this and bringing reassurance to the deaf is the pen of Second Isaiah: "The Lord is the eternal God. . . . He does not faint or grow weary" (Is. 40:28). Again: "You are my witnesses, says the Lord. I am God, yes, from eternity I am he; there is none who can deliver from my hand: who can countermand what I do?" (Is. 43:12-13). And Christ gathers all this to himself when he says: "I am the Alpha and the Omega, the one who is and who was and who is to come, the Almighty" (Rev. 1:8).

Some of the thought already examined underlies the deaf view of eternity. For instance, the God of the deaf is a person in the sense previously described and consequently labors under some of the limitations of the human person, including mortality. For some deaf, the concept of person excludes eternity—at least with regard to beginnings. A question lingering in the minds of some deaf students is: "Who made God?" If God was born, as the deaf explain, then he obviously had a beginning.

A further observation is in order. Although no deaf respondents said that God's having a name eliminates his eternity, indirect evidence suggests the distinct possibility that some deaf may recognize the implications of St. Justin's statement on names: "To the Father of all, who is unbegotten, no name is given; for anyone who has been given a name has received the name from someone older than himself."[101]

One can reduce the deaf from misconceptions of eternity by (1) purifying their understanding of "person" and then (2) developing the temporality of their own existence and contrasting it to God's and (3) giving the deaf youth illustrations of analogous timelessness in their own human experiences. Human memory and foresight, for instance, suspend time.[102] Sometimes mental concentration on work, prayer or hobbies or conversation with a loved one obliterates time, as these activities bring both the past and the future to bear upon the present.[103] Oftentimes the experiences that approach timelessness are the most enjoyable. Advancing from this, it would take little more to expose to the deaf the pure joy that awaits them in eternal life.

(h) *God's Presence*

When the Empress Eudoxia menacingly threatened St. John Chrysostom with exile, she was startled by his reply: "You will not frighten me, unless you are able to send me to some place where God is not."[104] Centuries before, God's presence strengthened David, "Even though I walk in the dark valley, I fear no evil; for you are at my side" (Ps. 23:4). Just recently the same psalm so vigorously uplifted certain American war prisoners deteriorating in Hanoi jails that it became known to them as "The P.O.W. Psalm." Divine presence can likewise stabilize vicissitudes in the lives of the deaf and raise them to new heights of contentment by acting as a deterrent to sin, by motivating the deaf to practice virtue and prayer, by keeping before their eyes the ultimate goal of their beatific vision, and by helping them to realize that even now God is their close companion who will never forget them or abandon them to that acute sense of loneliness so often felt by the deaf.

The abundant evidence of Scripture brings God to every place and to everyone. "Can a man hide in secret without my seeing him? Do I not fill both heaven and earth? says the Lord" (Jer. 23:24). Not only is God resplendent in the glory of a majestic king enthroned above, he is also present everywhere by his nature (Dt. 4:39; Pss. 102; 113; Am. 9:1ff.; Mt. 5:34-35). "Yet omnipresence," explains John Macquarrie, "is not to be taken objectively to mean that God is diffused through space like some all-pervasive ether, but that he is not tied to the factical situation that is a basic characteristic of our human 'being-there.' "[105]

The idea of presence has already appeared with such frequency throughout this entire exposition that the deaf viewpoint of divine presence may by now be apparent. Nevertheless, we are about to come directly to grips with the issue, and as a result there will be an exposure of nuances as well as confirmation of what was found before.

Two ideas previously analyzed are divine transcendence and immanence, ideas which overlap somewhat with our present question of divine presence. What we are about to find will substantiate what we learned previously, especially the deaf emphasis upon transcendence almost to the exclusion of immanence. An important exception to this proposition is the deaf adolescents' awareness that in or over all churches there hovers a divine presence—and this is their clearest consciousness of immanence. Yet it must be acknowledged that the deaf have lost the balance between transcendence and immanence and this loss influences their understanding of divine presence. To many deaf, divine omnipresence is mind-paralyzing for reasons which will unfold as this study progresses.

We turn now to the series of six drawings, beginning with Question 19a, and the accompanying questions, which were explained earlier. Questions 19g and h are follow-up questions inquiring whether God is in all churches or some churches and if he is in these churches at the same time or at different times.

A clear way to start our statistical inquiry is to arrange the charts as below. This will give a summary view and facilitate further discussion.

	Q. 19a		Q. 19b		Q. 19c		Q. 19d	
	GOD IN SPACE		GOD ON FARM		GOD IN CITY		GOD IN ROOM	
	Deaf	Control	Deaf	Control	Deaf		Deaf	Control
Yes	52.0	50.0	50.5	68.4	34.3	73.7	38.6	73.7
No	32.0	37.5	36.2	21.1	55.9	21.0	53.5	15.8
Don't Know	16.0	12.5	13.3	10.5	9.8	5.3	7.9	10.5

	Q. 19e		Q. 19f		Q. 19g		Q. 19h	
	GOD IN MAN		GOD IN CHURCH		ALL CHURCHES?		AT THE SAME TIME?	
	Deaf	Control	Deaf	Control	Deaf	Control	Deaf	Control
Yes	28.8	78.9	79.0	73.7	*All* 74.6	*All* 100	41.0	92.9
No	60.6	10.5	18.0	15.8	*Some* 25.4	*Some* 0	59.0	7.1
Don't Know	10.6	10.5	3.0	10.5	——	——	——	——

As seen in the table, 50.5% of the deaf affirm that God is in space. But as we move to earth, the percentages drop noticeably. Only 34.3% of the deaf say that God is on the farm, 37.3% that he is in the city, and 38.6% that he is in the living room. Question 19e asks the deaf if God dwells in the man, and 28.8% agree that he does. The percentages rise dramatically in Question 19f as 79% of the deaf say that God is in the church. In the follow-up questions, 74.6% of the deaf remark that God resides in all churches, but 59% say that he must take up these residencies at different times, since he must travel from one church to another. An overview of the statistics, then, shows that the God of the deaf, far from being indiscriminately everywhere, gives highest priority to two places: space and church.

An exploration of all the comments contributes to a better understanding of divine presence as seen by the deaf. Running through the responses are these trends:

1. *God is everywhere.* Although at first glance this group of deaf resolve the question correctly, further distinctions are in order. Subjected to follow-up questioning seeking the reasons behind their answers, some deaf acknowledged an exclusively authoritarian basis to their answers (i.e., "my teacher told me") or responded with a verbalism. Without wavering under further questioning, still other deaf exhibited an advanced comprehension. The final distinction to be made is that God can be successively anywhere but not simultaneously everywhere. This last distinction admittedly overlaps somewhat with category 4 below.

Here is some of what the deaf say. "Last year," asserts Mary Beth 19_A, "one nun taught me that God is everywhere and in everyone's heart. I don't know about this; I never feel anything." After commenting that God can be anyplace, Sandra 18WISC110A continues: "God can be in the man if the man accepts Christ. If not, then God is not in his heart." Daniel 17WISC111A says that despite God's failure to establish a residence in space, farm, city or living room, he can be in any one of these places "by his power"; furthermore, "Jesus' spirit or power, like love, can live in the heart of the man." Daniel's final remark is about the church. "Whether or not God can live in the church depends on the people. God can be there for only one person." The remarks of Michael 17WISC120A conclude category 1. God is in all the places depicted in the drawings, says Michael, "because he made them." Also: "If the man is sorry for his sins, God will come to him. I know that Jesus follows people. Jesus accepts their sorrow and lives in their heart. If a Russian becomes sorry, Jesus enters his heart, too. So Jesus must be able to be in many places at the same time." Moreover, Michael remarks that "God is in all churches—Catholic, Protestant and Jewish. God is everywhere so he must be in church."

2. *God is restricted to space or heaven, where his astroview covers the earth.* Explaining that a lack of air would suffocate God, a few deaf move heaven into the atmosphere. Le Roy 19_A says that "God is somewhere in space. We don't know where. God is above the church, watching it. But God is not in there." James 18CMMS103V remarks that God is in none of the places depicted in the drawings, but he adds: "God walks around in the sky—or he is sleeping." "God is there in space," says Timothy 17WISC100A, "but we can't see him. God looks down on the church, but he is not in it." "God is in heaven. He never comes down," is the comment of Carol 17CAT10.6A.

3. *God is in space (or the sky) and church, but in few other places.* According to some deaf in this and other categories, God, circumscribed in place and thereby handicapped in visual acuity, but intent on seeking his worshipers, travels from one church to another. Furthermore, en-

cumbered by the necessity to travel, God is in church only at specified times.

The deaf themselves elucidate their views. Patrick 17WISC107_, admitting that God is in heaven, but denying that he is or can be on the farm, city and living room, goes on to say that God is outside the man and is "in the church, but only on Sunday." Associating God with nature, William 17WISC89V explains that "God can be in the country, but not in the city." Also: "God is in the church only on Sunday." "God must stay up in the sky," says Anthony 17WISC86V, "except that Jesus comes down to church on Sunday during Mass." Patricia 18WAIS96A remarks that God can descend only to churches: "God sees, looks at the churches, picks one and goes there. Then he looks again, picks another one and goes there." David 17CAT8.0A doubts a divine presence in space and elsewhere, but he asserts: "He may be in the sky and he comes to church at the beginning of Mass, stays during Mass to see what the people are doing, then leaves."

4. *In addition to space, sky and church, God is to be found occasionally on the farm to observe plant growth, in the city to see what is happening, in the living room to care for the people, and behind or in the man to assist him in distress.* And through or in these sites he can quickly arrive or depart. Three samples of comments pertaining to each drawing in the series are given below:

Drawing	Comment ✗
Space	"Maybe God is walking around out there. I don't know because I never heard about it before."
Farm	"Yes. God is there. He travels all around the world and has many angels to help him."
City	"Yes. God is there because he watches the people to see who is good and bad."
Room	"Yes. God is in the room most of the time."
Man	"God is behind the man, not in him."
Church	"God is in the church."
	Q. In some or all churches?
	A. "In all churches."
	Q. At the same time or different times?
	A. "God is in many churches at different times. But if God is not in the church, the people don't know."
	Karen 16WISC117A ✗
Space	"God is somewhere in space."

Farm	"God can walk around on the farm. He wants to see if the plants are growing all right."
City	"God walks around the city, but you can't see him."
Room	"God could be in the room."
Man	"God knows what is inside the man, but he is not in the man. He can follow the man if he wants."
Church	"God is in church." Q. In some churches or all? A. "All." Q. Is God in all churches at the same time or different times? A. "Different times. He has to go from one church to another."

Debra 16WISC133A λ

Space	"Yes. God is in space."
Farm	"Yes. God is there to help the grass grow."
City	"No. God doesn't want to go there because there are too many robberies, too much crime."
Room	"If the people in the room believe in him, he will be there."
Man	"No. God is behind the man—if the man believes."
Church	"Yes, God goes. But he can't go to all of them. There are too many. God sends his saints to the church. If the name of the church is St. Joseph's, then St. Joseph is in that church."

John 20WAIS114A

A final remark must be made about those deaf who search for direct sensory experience. To them, lack of materialistic evidence is tantamount to lack of divine presence. Echoing the thought of the U.S.S.R. cosmonaut Gagarin, Betty 18WAIS117A says: "The Apollo spacecraft was out there and didn't see anything."

The statistical table exposes the most significant difference between the deaf and the control group; with the exception of church, a greater percentage of hearing young people place God in each locale. For instance, 68.4% of the control group place God in space, 73.7% place him on the farm, in the city and in the living room, and 78.9% place him in the man (contrasted with 28.8% of the deaf). But more deaf have God in church: 79% compared with 73.7% of the control group. However, to recall what was earlier analyzed, the deaf have only a vague awareness of eucharistic presence in church—a weakness only slightly less shared by the control group.

The control group, readily seeing God in the sequence of locales depicted in the drawings and readily acknowledging that God can be successively anywhere, intensifies its confusion when confronted with the concept of a simultaneous presence everywhere. Patti, 16, typifies this as ideas of an etherlike all-presence enter her mind: "God is everywhere. That means he must be gigantic, really enormous. Wow! I sometimes wonder if he can see everything or what." Here are samples of other thoughts: "God is everywhere all the time," "God is everywhere at once," and "God is always everywhere."

Some of the control group, however, retreated from simultaneous all-presence to the notion of a divine presence unlimited in extent, but restricted in the sense that God is confined to one place at a time. This segment resembles the deaf of category 4 and also recalls the earlier studied deaf viewpoint of a spirit-God flitting about the universe like a ghost. Thus Edward, 16, remarks: "He can go anywhere he wants. God can be on the farm, but he is not always necessarily on the farm."

Lastly there was a tendency among the hearing group to tie God's presence to people and their personal belief. God is expected to be in the midst of his believers or at least to come when addressed, but he is seldom found elsewhere. "If I were on the farm," says Steven, 17, "and I called him, he would be with me." Gerard, 18, says that God is absent from the room "when it is empty," and adds that God is probably "no more present in church than in the living room, but he may possibly be more present in the church because the people might believe and be more open to him."

We now pause to widen the discussion by including some related observations on the subject matter in connection with religious language, some Hebrew traditions and transcendence-immanence.

Considered abstractly, omnipresence eludes the deaf. To say that God is in all things everywhere or that God is free of spatial dimensions since he is simple and is present insofar as he is the source of being is to say little to the deaf. Though correct, expressions such as "God is everywhere," "he is present by his nature and power," and "he is present in the just by his grace" are equally debilitating. This is due not only to the language problem but also to the deaf student's comprehension of person.

As indicated earlier, God is indeed a person to the deaf. But instead of recognizing the philosophical "person," the deaf adolescents equate the term with "human being." Consequently, the mind of the deaf quickly endows such a person with a human nature and personality and thereby ushers in the restriction of necessarily being in only one place at a given time. If one can distill the notion of person, discard the physical residue, and retain the spiritual, one can proceed to attach a sensible meaning to omnipresence by speaking dialectically—placing divine presence in sharp contrast to a human presence which has to be in only one place at a time.

The deaf of categories 3 and 4 share an attenuated omnipresence in common with some early Hebrew traditions which depicted Yahweh as appearing locally and regionally—for example, "In whatever place I choose for the remembrance of my name I will come to you and bless you" (Ex. 20:24). Similarly Ezekiel portrays God coming down from the north along the road his people had traveled on their journey into captivity (Ez. 1:4ff.). Later Israelites freed Yahweh from his gross restrictions by allowing extensions or emanations, so to speak, of his personality so that, equipped with added powers, he could reach out into various areas and could increase his multi-presence even more by employing still other mediums of activity.[106]

The deaf forge another bond with the Hebrews. Some adolescents make God's presence in church and the room contingent upon the presence of people there worshiping him or at least believing in him. The Hebrew priestly tradition likewise restricts Yahweh's temple activity to cultic celebrations. Identifying religion with cult, the priests claimed that Yahweh was present only where his name was explicitly mentioned.[107] Some deaf similarly explain that God is in the living room (and in church) only when people are there, when believers are there, or when a crucifix is placed in the room.

Reactions to the farm drawing deserve a digressing comment. Although 56% of the deaf kept God away from the farm, others said that he sometimes comes down to inspect the plants as Yahweh had to come down to the city to examine the Tower of Babel (Gen. 11:5).

One would admittedly be hard pressed to link these farm tours with the plant epiphanies of ancient Near East religions. Nevertheless, some deaf credit God with a divine concern for the well-being of plants. Their willingness to associate divinity with agriculture can perhaps be a starting point for developing ideas on redemption. Perhaps the intrinsic symbol of the plant already wordlessly communicates health, healing, regenerative powers and a life cycle suggesting immortality. If this much is evident, it would take little to advance to the seed and its almost divinized energy, the subject of Jesus' classic parable on the grain of wheat. Like seed buried in the earth, the dead presently in embryo will grow into a new, more developed, more perfect life.[108] And so the ancient epiphany of agriculture, made existential, can underpin the hope of the deaf in their own redemption.

Similar to the farm in statistics but different in the reasoning behind them are the comments on a divine presence in the city. Some deaf prohibit God from entering the city because of the vast amount of vice and crime found there. God, they say, discerns the city as a den of iniquity and cannot associate himself with it, just as he ceases his vigil over the man who veers from virtue into sin. Curiously, these deaf resemble the prophet Habakkuk: "Too pure are your eyes to look upon evil, and the sight of misery you cannot endure" (Hb. 1:13).

We have already examined the deaf viewpoint on immanence, God's presence in all existent being. The deaf young people perceive God as working in the world, caring for crops while ignoring evil, and attending church, and to this extent they touch upon immanence. Yet a sense of divine warmth or intimacy terminating *in* them seems to evade numerous deaf. This is palpable in their understanding of God's relationship to the man (Question 19e). Prepared to follow and assist, God places himself behind the man, a vantage point from which his vigilance prompts him to block any adversity which may threaten the man and to guide the man occasionally.

But little mention was made of any thought beyond this—thoughts of divine activity *within* the man urging him to discard what estranges him from God, his neighbor, and himself and to embrace what God desires to give him, a new heart and a new spirit. (Jer. 31:32). The deaf undoubtedly understand the Lord speaking through Isaiah: "I the Lord, your God, hold your right hand; it is I who say to you, 'Fear not, I will help you' " (Is. 41:13). However, they hardly understand the Lord speaking through John: "Anyone who loves me will be true to my word, and my Father will love him; we will come to him and make our dwelling place with him" (Jn. 14:23).

The idea of teaching the deaf by contrast here bears repeating. Pedagogically, one way to break through the barriers that separate the deaf from the in-dwelling God is to recount in specific, concrete language (via total communication or other techniques) what divine in-dwelling did for David and what its absence did for Saul. One may wish to re-present the Lord's dramatic instructions to Samuel to have Jesse line up his sons so that from among them a king might be chosen (1 Sam. 16:1ff.). Beginning with the oldest, the Lord moved down the line and rejected them all, forcing Jesse to send for the youngest one, David, away tending sheep. The Lord then affirmed David as his choice, Samuel anointed him, and "from that day on, the Spirit of the Lord rushed upon David" (1 Sam. 16:13) and was largely responsible for his victory over Goliath (1 Sam. 17:46). On the other hand, jealousy evicted the spirit of the Lord from Saul and ushered in an evil spirit which shaped him into a brooding, melancholy man (1 Sam. 16:14; 18:10).

From the question of divine in-dwelling, we proceed to a final comment on God's presence in church, the deaf adolescents' clearest comprehension of immanence. To the deaf, such a presence is undiscriminating and largely overlooks the eucharistic presence in the tabernacle. Perhaps their concept can be refined by leading them back to the Old

Testament temple and Yahweh's presence in it. One may wish to dramatize the story of Ezekiel making meticulous measurements of the future temple (Ez. 40—42) and thus making it a fitting home for the Lord. And later, the deaf would learn, the God of Israel returned to it from the east (Ez. 43), and, seeing the glory of the Lord in the temple, Ezekiel fell prone (Ez. 43:4). And the voice of the Lord said to Ezekiel: "This is where my throne shall be, this is where I will set the soles of my feet; here I will dwell among the Israelites forever" (Ez. 43:7).

Perhaps in this and other ways, particularly by more effective teaching of the Eucharist as a permanent sacrament, the deaf will seldom have to remark with Jacob: "Truly, the Lord is in this spot, although I did not know it" (Gen. 28:16).

31
Relationship with God

This section ventures into two difficult areas. The overall objective is an attempt to determine the extent of the deaf adolescents' relationship with God: first, corporately as participants in the Church; second, privately as individuals at prayer in their own personal lives.

(a) The Church

Much contemporary Church writing concerns the Church as related to another theme. The Church and the third world, the Church and secular society, the Church and ecumenism, and the Church and politics are some examples. Instead of relating the Church to something else, the intention here is to gather deaf adolescents' concepts on the Church per se and to ascertain the degree to which they practice these by church attendance and activity during attendance. Accordingly, a series of questions were devised and they will now be examined individually. At the conclusion of this analysis, there will be related observations and further discussion.

Since all of the deaf and hearing alike identified the building in Question 21a as a church, one easily dismisses the question. It serves, however, as an introduction to Question 21b, a deeper question asking the deaf if they, as individuals, belong to Jesus. A total of 84% responded affirmatively. This high percentage becomes quite surprising when placed alongside the previously analyzed difficulty which the deaf have exhibited in acknowledging God's personal love for them as individuals (Question 14a).

Perhaps lurking within the minds of some deaf persons is a vague awareness of a unilateral relationship from humanity to the divine. This would mean that some deaf see themselves belonging to God, not as individuals, but as part of a larger solidarity or corporate entity (the Church). Or perhaps they see themselves in relation to God only insofar as all creatures automatically belong to God.

Such thinking is exemplified in at least some of the responses. For instance, Phyllis 19WAIS94V says: "All people belong to Jesus," and David 17WISC124A remarks that he belongs to Jesus "because I am a member of the Catholic Church." Paulette 18_A likewise says: "Yes, because I am a member of the Catholic Church."

Consequently, despite the high percentage of affirmative responses and because of the above-quoted reasoning coupled with the findings of Question 14a, it is still tenable to hold that God, as a relational being turned toward his people in a bilateral and personal affinity, is not well comprehended by the deaf.

Furthermore, responses to the same question expose a weakness previously analyzed: the identification of God as Father, Son and Holy Spirit. Lorraine 17WISC121A, for instance, says: "I belong to Jesus, but not to God, because Jesus helped people and died, but I don't know anything about God." On the other hand, Dora 16WISC104A is unsure about Jesus: "I don't know about Jesus, but I belong to God."

Continuing with the theme of the Church, we move over to Question 21c and analyze the issue of church attendance. A total of 56% of the deaf responded that they go to church. Answering negatively were 19%, while 25% said that they "sometimes" attend church.[109] Question 21d extracts more specific information from the deaf. Thus it is found that 53% attend church weekly, 19% attend monthly, 14% less often than monthly and 13% never go to church. Between the Catholic school deaf and secular school deaf there is no significant difference regarding the frequency of church attendance.

Question 21e underscores the importance of the family role in church attendance. A total of 95% of the weekly attenders go to church with either some member of the family or the entire family.[110] Note-worthy are those responses which reveal that some family members assist their deaf by fingerspelling in the pews or by bringing a notebook and pencil and writing a summary of the sermon and other key words as the liturgy unfolds. Family accompaniment to church diminishes somewhat with the control group. Only 68% of them go to church with their families and 27% go alone, whereas only 5% of the deaf young people attend church alone.

Question 21f asks the deaf if they attend only a church for the deaf, only a church for the hearing, or both. A total of 51% go only to a church for the hearing, 11% attend only a church for the deaf, and 38% attend both, alternating bi-monthly between the deaf church and hearing church, since the deaf church (as applicable to the 38%) serves the people only twice a month.

Those who attend the deaf church exclusively or both hearing and deaf church are further asked if the deaf church is Catholic (Question 21g). The rationale behind this question is the investigator's subjective suspicion that, given a choice, the deaf would prefer to attend any church with a deaf congregation, even if the nearby hearing church were of their own religious persuasion. Yet the statistics lend little support to such a suspicion, as 96% of those who go to a deaf church or both hearing and deaf church attend a Catholic deaf church.

Question 21h "What does the Mass mean to you?" was asked of only a limited number of students and the sampling was too small to be subjected to statistical analysis. The responses of the few, however, bear comment. The underlying factor in these responses was the tendency to equate the Mass with the overt actions of sitting, standing, kneeling, listening to sermons and coming forward for Holy Communion. The explanation of Lorraine 17WISC121A is typical: "Mass means all the people are together in church for a sermon and Holy Communion." Others moved beyond this as they struggled to explain the Mass in terms of Communion, sacrifice, and grace. Elaine 18CAT13.4A said: "Mass is the time to change the body and blood of Jesus." David 17CAT8.0A wrestled with "sacrifice" and explained: " 'Offer sacrifice' means that the people show God that they obey him and they are good." "Mass," says Charles 21RBE113_, "is the word for 'church.' The people pray together at the altar. They need grace. The priest works in the Mass to get grace for the people."

Inquiries on the Mass were also asked of the control group. When compared to the deaf, some control group members seem more effectively to set the Mass in its proper context. Joseph, 17, for instance, remarked that "Mass is a re-enactment of the Last Supper—the offering of Christ as the sacrifice of man to God." Approaching Joseph's response, Constance, 16, says: "That reminds me of the time when Jesus had the Last Supper before he was crucified."

Other control group responses, however, fail to reach this level. The Mass of David, 16, for example, is limited to an expression of belief: "It means showing that I believe in God." According to Patrick, 16, Mass is more intellectual than worshipful: "Mass? That's when God is closer to everybody. The people in church read and learn what he did in the past. Now God doesn't do anything anymore except judge people." In emphasizing Communion and readings, Frances, 17, resembles some deaf: "Mass means I can receive Communion and listen to the Scripture readings. The offertory and the other prayers don't mean much to me."

Question 21i asks the deaf to explain why hearing people go to church. Attributing an intellectual reason for church-going are a total of 22% of the deaf. These say that hearing people go to church primarily to learn by reading (the missalette) and listening to the sermon. Here are some samples of this view. "The priest tells the people about the Bible," says Robert 18CMMS104V, "and the people learn." Nearly identical are the words of Mark 18_A: "Because they want to know. They listen to what the priest says about the Bible." "The people want to know more about God," is the viewpoint of Ralph 18WISC107_.

A total of 38% of the deaf hold that hearing people go to church primarily to express contrition and offer prayers of petition. They voice their sorrow for past wrongdoing, ask for forgiveness, and pray for a favor or something they deem necessary to their well-being. Typical is the response of John 17WAIS96A: "People go to church to pray to God because they have sins." Karen 16WISC81A says: "Because they need to pray to Jesus. Sometimes people get sick; they want God to make them feel better. Parents worry about children and want them to grow up right. They ask Jesus to help the children." "The people are sorry," says Margaret 20MAT Adv.4.4A, "and they want Communion. They want a clean, white soul."

Finally, either faith, love or worship attracts people to church, accordiing to 30% of the deaf. For example, David 17WISC124A remarks: "The people believe in Jesus. They believe that Jesus is God." "The hearing people go to church to worship God," is the comment of Michael 17WISC120A. "They go," says James 18CMMS103V, "because they love God."

Question 21j asks the deaf churchgoers if anyone forces them to go. A total of 42% responded that someone, usually a school official or parent, coerces them; yet some of these spontaneously added that they would continue to go even if coercion ceased.

Question 21k inquires into the helpfulness of church-going. A total of 55% of the deaf affirm that in some way church is a help to them, while 31% answer negatively and 14% do not know. Control group percentages are similar, as 65% answer affirmatively, 20% negatively, and 15% do not know.

As previously seen, the deaf communicated freely and expanded their remarks. A study of these responses exposes several trends.

1. *Some deaf no longer attend church due to boredom, monotony, or utter lack of comprehension stemming from deafness.* Paulette 19RBE116_ says: "Church is same, same—talk, talk, talk. I don't know what it is all about. I stopped going." "I stopped going to church three years ago," explains Wayne 18WAIS98A. "It was too boring in church. I can't hear what they say." The comments of Daniel 17WISC111A include other factors: "I don't like the Catholic Church anymore. I don't learn much about God. And in church the same thing always happens; besides, the priest can't forgive me. I pray to God and he forgives me." "Church means nothing to me. I can't lip-read the priest. Church is for hearing people," is the view of Mark 18_A.

The same trend also appears in the control group where the sense of hearing does little to drive away monotony. Patti, 16, says: "I don't think church helps me, because the same thing happens each week, except for the Gospel." "Church bores me," observes Christina, 16. "It's always the same singing, kneeling, praying. I don't like it."

2. *Church helps because it makes people feel better.* According to the respondents, the term "feel better" could mean feeling forgiven, peaceful, free of weekday chores, or relieved that prayers for specific help have been answered. The deaf fail to further elucidate the term. Here are some samples.

Judy 18_A says: "Church helps me feel happy, to feel closer to

Jesus. I pray and God helps me to pass tests, to make safe trips." "Sometimes I have trouble with my friends," explains Melissa 17CAT10.6A. "I go to church, pray, and forget my troubles. I feel better." The problems of Julie 17MAT Adv.4.4V are likewise alleviated: "Sometimes I have trouble. I feel bad. I go to church, kneel down and pray, and then I feel better."

A segment of the control group likewise feels better. "Going to church," comments David, 16, "proves that I believe in God and it makes me feel better for going." When asked if church is helpful, Peter, 15, responded: "Church can't hurt me. When I hear the readings and the Gospel, it makes me feel a little better." Maureen, 17, observes that "people go to church for renewal. It makes you feel better. People feel closer to the church community."

3. *Church attendance can be advantageous insofar as God may physically see and thus identify the worshipers, distinguish them from non-church-goers and more readily answer their prayers and mark them for heaven.* (No one in the control group expressed this view.)

Thomas 19WISC106A explains that people go to church because "they want God to see them in church. Then, when they die, God will take them to heaven." "God looks at the churches," says William 18WISC121A, "to see who is inside. But he can't go in because the buildings are all over." "The people are in church because they want God to see them there and then God will know that they really want to go to heaven," is the observation of Kimberly 16CAT6.9A. David 17CAT8.0A remarks: "The people bless themselves with holy water and God sees it. That is like calling God and he comes down into the church right away and listens to the people. The holy water chases the devil away." William 20RBE85_explains his view: "God is in heaven and he looks down to see the people genuflect in church. He will open heaven for them. If he never sees them in church, he will not open heaven for them."

Staying with the issue of church helpfulness, some deaf establish a minor trend. Some, for instance, commented that although church signified almost nil, the lesser motives of habit, duty, routine or coercion compelled them to attend. Others justify their attendance on the basis of receiving Holy Communion. The main concern of the church, they say, is to distribute Holy Communion, a sacrament that whets the enthusiasm of the people and draws them to church, where their sins are forgiven and prayers answered.

Question 211 asks what the church-going deaf think about in church. Their thoughts are classified as relevant, irrelevant or both. Responses grouped under "relevant" include any thoughts connected with God or worship and any intellectual activity required for understanding the sermon or missalette, whereas "irrelevant" refers to thoughts utterly unrelated to God, worship, or religious matters. The term "both" means a mixture of relevant and irrelevant thoughts, with neither noticeably predominating. Relevant thoughts prevail in the minds of 35% of the deaf; mostly irrelevant thoughts occupy 18% of the deaf, and somewhat of a mixture of both belongs to 47%.

Here are some examples of relevant thinking. "I watch my father interpret. I receive Communion and I ask God to help me with my school work," is the response of David 17CAT8.0A. Joan 17CAT10.6A says: "My brother signs in church and I learn from him. I thank Jesus for a wonderful family and wonderful friends." "I pray," says Deborah 17_V, "for myself and for sick people. Sometimes I think about my problems. God sees me. He knows about my problems from my feelings."

The following illustrate irrelevancies. Richard 17_V stresses his dreams: "I dream about everything—my girlfriend, cars, baseball, school—everything." "I sleep," explains John 20WAIS114A. "I dream about sports and trips. I look at all the people, at the windows. Sometimes I try to lip-read the priest, but I can't." Windows, people and priest are objects of the gaze of Pearl 17_V: "I look at the windows. I look at all the people and the different kinds of clothes they wear. I look at the priest preaching, but I don't understand anything. I know how to pray a little bit."

The third category contains a combination of both. Michael 17WISC120A, for instance, says: "Before, I used to look at all the statues and windows and sometimes I still do. But now I have begun to think more about God in church." Yvonne 18WAIS95_ explains her plight: "I like church and sometimes I pray. But I can't understand anything. The people sing and I just look around. The priest talks and I don't know what he says. Sometimes I read the book (missalette), but the words are hard. I like to look at the windows."

A total of 28% of the control group admitted that in church their minds are filled primarily with irrelevancies. Asked what she thinks about in church, Maureen, 17, responded: "I plan what I'll do after church." The response of Joe, 17, is identical: "I think about what I'm going to do after church."

Those control group members entertaining both relevant and irrelevant thoughts number 72%.[111] Jeanne, 17, for example, says that she listens to the Gospel, "But not the whole Mass." David, 16, likewise says: "After the sermon I just sit there until after Communion." Sometimes Edward, 16, prays, but a portion of his time is wasted: "I don't think about much. I'm just there and I'm inclined to daydream. That's about it."

Question 21m inquires into the motivations behind genuflections in church. As we have already observed in the section on the Eucharist, a small 3% of the deaf said that people genuflect to revere or adore the presence of Jesus in the Eucharist, whereas a total of 25% responded that genuflection is meant to honor Jesus on the cross, which is on or above the altar. Far from concentrating on the cross, an additional 25% of the deaf expand divine presence to the entire church interior, a presence that must be acknowledged with a genuflection. Assigning other motives such as custom or habit are 19%, and 28% of the deaf do not know the motives for genuflecting. A total of 39% of the control group gave other reasons and 22% expressed ignorance.

Before moving on to related observations, another comment is in order. Something must be said of those deaf who infrequently or never attend church (27%) and others who go only because of coercion. Within this category are found many who believe in God but not in the Church and thereby touch upon one of the fundamental catechetical problems of our time, a problem common to deaf and hearing people alike. Far from seeing God as continuous with the Church, these deaf (and hearing) draw a line separating the two and hold that even if there is any such thing as a "group of believers" or "religious association," etc., it is quite apart from the Church, in the narrow sense. According to this group, all that is required to nourish and protect a living faith is the individual's personal relationship with God. Also intermingled in some of these responses is the Church's inability to assist: God can help, the Church cannot.

Here is some of what the deaf say. Robert 18MAT Adv.4.9V asserts that the Church can only advise and explain about God, and he adds: "Some people believe in the Church. I don't. People go to church to bless the baby (baptism), to get married. Or they get sick and nervous and then they pray to God for more life. God can help. The Church can't help. That is all." Shirley 17MAT Adv.4.2A explains that hearing people attend church because "those people believe in the Church. I don't. I think about God, not the Church." "God is satisfied," remarks Charles 21RBE113_, "if the people say they love him. It is not necessary to go to church for that." "I don't believe in the Church," says Eugene 19WAIS91V. "Other people believe in the priest. Me? I don't believe in the priest." Lisa 18WISC89_ gives her view: "I believe in God, but I don't believe in the priests, the nuns and the Church."

The control group voiced similar sentiments. Gerard, 18, believes in God, but he adds: "I don't consider myself a part of the Church." Christina, 16, says that we must keep the sabbath holy and emphasizes: "But you can keep it holy in other ways than going to church."

It is now time to open a wider discussion and make related observations on the broad issue of the deaf and the Church. From the reactions to the questions on the motives for church-going, the helpfulness of

Church, and thoughts while in church, it is safe to say that deaf and hearing both have made only a small penetration into the inner nature of the Church. The deaf are aware of a belonging or bond, however vague, between them and God. They are keenly aware of the church building as a sacred place into which God looks or comes down or is present and in which a reconciliation takes place between the sinner and God and in which favors may be obtained in answer to prayer. Since the deaf have a grip on these elements, they may be used as starting points leading the deaf in the direction of an improved theological understanding of the Church.

But if the deaf are to be oriented in the right direction, careful attention must be paid to the kind of religious language used, for the issue of religious language, as we have already seen in this work, constantly plagues the deaf. Nearly all attempts to describe the inner nature of the Church have, unfortunately for the deaf, depended heavily upon figurative language. Such descriptions can hardly be avoided, since the Church is a mystery and consequently transcends definition and eludes efforts to package it into a precise concept. Therefore, analogies and other figures of speech have customarily described the Church through the centuries as "the community of salvation," "the extension of the incarnation,"[112] "the Mysterium Lunae,"[113] "the body of Christ" and numerous other figures.

While emphasizing the "people of God" aspect of the Church, the Second Vatican Council presents other biblical metaphors which largely fall into four groups: the Church is the flock of Christ, the vineyard of God, the temple of the Holy Spirit and the spouse of the Immaculate Lamb. These images are drawn from four basic areas of human living: sheep-herding, agriculture, buildings and matrimony.[114]

As far as the deaf are concerned, if a metaphor must be used, a suitable one for pedagogical purposes would be the church building, since the deaf already clutch the concept of a divine presence there. One may wish to begin by stressing to the deaf the holiness of the altar and recall to them Abraham's travel habits; he immediately built an altar and worshiped whenever he stopped (Gen. 13:4, 18). An expansion from the altar to the entire building can deepen the deaf understanding of the Church as the edifice of God (1 Cor. 3:9). One name given to this building is "the house of God" (1 Tim. 3:15), and anyone who goes there becomes a member of God's own family—the household of God in the Spirit (Eph. 2:19-22); consequently, the deaf are no longer strangers to God.

Pursuing the same thought further, the deaf must prepare themselves to face the consequences of God's visits to them in church. The Lord used to say "I have chosen you" whenever he visited the men of the Old Testament.[115] God says likewise to the deaf in church, echoing the words of Christ: "It was not you who chose me; it was I who chose you" (Jn. 15:16).

But the Lord hardly expects the initiative to remain with himself, for inherent in his choosing is a challenge. He does not say "I choose you" without simultaneously saying: "Choose!" In his farewell address, Joshua begged the Israelites to discard false deities and choose the Lord, and he ended the speech with his own witness: "As for me and my household, we will serve the Lord" (Jos. 24:15). This simple but powerful para-liturgical scene can be recounted for the deaf and made existential by insisting that they too are to freely choose the Lord, as did Joshua. It is only a short step from here to a description of the Church as a gathering of those people who choose the Lord.

Before moving ahead to present a description of the Church as befitting the deaf, we here pause to study a distinct but related idea. As seen earlier, some deaf conceive of the Church primarily as the place where reconciliation takes place and prayers are answered. Maximum advantage can be taken of this embryonic understanding, and it can be developed by bringing before the deaf the Pharisee and the tax collector as they prayed in the temple (Lk. 18:10-14)—the one proud, the other humble. Speaking of the tax collector, the humble one, Jesus says: "Believe me, this man went home from the temple justified but the other did not" (Lk. 18:14). Professor Jeremias explains that the term "to be justified" means "to find God's good pleasure," which in turn means that God is disposed to hear prayer. In other words, Luke 18:14 may even be translated as: "Believe me, this man went home from the temple as one whose prayer God had heard, and not the other."[116] But before God hears the prayer of the deaf, it must be pointed out to them that they must enter the church with reverential humility, as did the tax collector. An aspect of the Church, then, may be portrayed to the deaf as the place, especially when filled with the Christian assembly, within which God acts.

Shifting over from the place aspect to the people aspect of the Church enables one to work out a broader description of the Church that would be meaningful to the deaf. Given the findings of this study, it is advisable to start with a discriminating choice of religious language. Metaphors and other figures of speech, for example, must be used sparingly and only after they have been meticulously taught. A description appropriate for the deaf can unfold in several ways, but it here unfolds with the emphasis upon the idea of the people of God. The Church is a community (large family) of brothers and sisters, made so by baptism and held so by the remaining sacraments, chosen by a God who intensely loves them and asks them to return that love both to himself and to one another and who commands them to spread such love and belief throughout the world using the Gospel of Christ as the criterion. Although it keeps abstruse and figurative language to a minimum, the description and some of its elements still require dissection and attention.

1. "Community (large family) of brothers and sisters": Unless explained, these terms may be construed as meaning "family" in the narrow sense and "brothers and sisters" in the congenital sense.

2. "Made so by baptism and held so by the remaining sacraments": This, of course, presupposes a basic knowledge of the unifying power of baptism, joining people together after the manner of kindred.

3. "Love": Much light must be thrown on this supremely significant but elusive word. Love as the basis of community is no mere emotion or romantic fantasy. Rather, the kind of love referred to here is that selfless and active concern for the growth of another that is concurrently directed to and beats with the heart of God.[117] It is furthermore a covenant love issuing from God and calling for obedience and order. The specific examples of Calcutta's Mother Teresa at prayer and work and of the early Christians loving one another will edify the deaf.

4. "Using the Gospel of Christ as the criterion": As Church members, the deaf should become living illustrations of the Sermon on the Mount and shun the enemies within man—selfishness, arrogance, anger, jealousy, lust, laziness, etc., as well as the enemies without—tyranny, conflict, hatred, poverty, racism and social injustice. Such a declaration of war co-exists with the peaceful embrace of humility, courage, discipline, and concern as necessary accompaniments of love. In this way will the deaf come to think of themselves as men with a mission, as living parts of the Church.

Our study of the inner nature of the Church makes no pretense of being adequate. It is only a beginning. The all-important Old Testament theme of covenant love, for instance, needs to be amplified. Two other vital elements previously left untouched must also be remembered. First, the community of brothers and sisters is compassionately and extensively but not exclusively involved with world poverty, world justice and world development as it passes through on pilgrimage, intent on raising sinful humanity to God's kingdom. The Church is therefore closely related to eschatology.[118] Second, the most mysterious (sign) aspect of the community is its identification with Christ who in turn is identified with the kingdom. The Church, then, is joined to Christology, and before one attempts to present this aspect he should recall the doctrine of the person of Christ as understood by the deaf.

Only after attention is directed to what the Church really is can the deaf be expected to give their allegiance to its most obvious part—the organizational part. Knowledge of the inner reality of the Church authenticates the duty, law and authority which the Church asks of its members and which, to the uninitiated, seem to comprise its essence.

(b) *Group and Private Prayer*

Just as food is vital for nourishing the life of the body, so prayer is essential for nourishing the worshiper's life with God. Consequently, what prayer is to the deaf adolescent and how he prays is of utmost interest to anyone concerned with leading him to God. One is tempted to begin by going straight to the heart of the issue and examining the deaf students' understanding of the clichés that prayer is the opening of the heart to God, or conversation with God, or raising the mind to God. But before fathoming these, it is prudent to pause and reintroduce some basic preliminaries already analyzed, for the prayer of the deaf is necessarily conditioned by some of our earlier findings.

As we have seen, the deaf have constructed a finite God, bent over with excessive anthropomorphism. In itself, anthropomorphism is praiseworthy insofar as it moves the deaf close to the personhood of God, an accomplishment that abstruse theological language can hardly claim. Yet *excessive* anthropomorphism presents God with an atrophied divinity or no divinity and without his infinite personality and therefore reduces him to slightly super-human proportions. Although this study has already exposed corollaries flowing from such a God, a resume is now opportune.

First is the failure of numerous deaf to place the transcendence-immanence relationship in proper perspective. The deaf teenagers' emphasis on transcendence at the expense of immanence removes the deity far from mundane affairs and positions the deaf in the awkward posture of praying to a distant God. But as we have already studied, some of the deaf assign acute powers of seeing (and hearing) to the deity, powers consistent with the deaf viewpoint of God as a celestial being and powers which are necessary equipment for such a God to scan enormous distances. This thought pattern applied to pre-Christian sky gods as they receded from the life of man. One wonders if similar thoughts occupy the mind of the deaf and if this would weaken or nullify prayer as communication, for communication is possible because God is immanent, and immanent in every being,[119] and his self-communication from within prompts our response.

Second, one may remember that the deaf acknowledge a collectively universal love of God for mankind—a love which weakens or even breaks down completely at the personal level. In view of a weakened divine love for the individual, the deaf may instinctively pose the question as to whether God would *desire* to communicate on a personal basis and whether such a communication is worthwhile. Unless strengthened with the idea of divine love for the individual and divine knowledge of the individual, the deaf will lack a foundation upon which to build communication.

Third, we have earlier seen the deaf view of divine providence. Although basically benign, God's providence enters the personal life of the individual usually when there is suffering, disharmony or death. To increase the efficacy of prayer, it becomes important to elevate the deaf to a more positive understanding of the nature and extent of providence and divine action in their lives.

Fourth, we recall that some deaf have lowered divine power to the super-human or human level, while others have removed all power from God, reasoning that God, precisely as a spirit, can possess no power whatsoever. Such thoughts paralyze prayer and produce only an inadequate comprehension, unless the deaf are made to realize that prayer originates in God's holy power, something that reaches within them. Once God desires to begin a prayer, his power carries his self-communication to the deaf, and whatever they subsequently say is characterized as a response.

All of these prerequisites to prayer should be placed alongside the responses and trends which immediately follow. Thus taking everything into consideration, the comments of the deaf are illuminated more clearly.

Question 21a asks to whom the prayer "Our Father" is addressed. A total of 93% of the deaf say that the prayer is addressed to God: 100% from the Catholic schools and 91% from the secular schools. Mentioning that prayer is addressed to someone else are 7% of the deaf. All of the control group respond that God is the recipient of the prayer. Although the general tendency among the deaf is that the prayer is addressed to God, the same confusion concerning the identification of the deity that was seen previously again surfaces. Some deaf insist that the people are praying to Jesus and are unsure of Jesus' relation with the Father.

Question 22b is an open question and inquires into the reasons behind the converse with God. The responses fall into five categories—petition, contrition, love, other reasons, and "don't know."

According to 37% of the deaf respondents, the man, woman, and child are engaged in prayer of petition, a view shared by 13% of the control group. Many of these deaf say quite simply that the three people are asking God to help them, they want something from God, they wish to allay illness, or they are praying for a recently deceased friend or relative. "They are asking God to help them," is the explanation of Paul 17WISC108A. Patricia 18WAIS96A says: "These people have problems."

A total of 14% of the deaf and 6% of the control group say that the people are praying to express sorrow for sin. John 20WAIS114A, for instance, says that the people are talking to God "to forgive their sins." "The people have sins," comments Robert 17WISC105A, "and they want God to forgive them."

In the view of 18% of the deaf and 50% of the control group, love of God is the basis of the prayer. Michael 18WAIS112V says that the three are praying "because they love God." The view of Adrien, 18, typifies this portion of the control group: "The people are praying to show him that they really love him and that they are thinking about him and to tell him how happy they are and maybe thank him for something."

Finally, 32% of the deaf and 6% of the control group are ignorant of the motivations for the prayer, explaining that they have no idea why the three people are praying.

Question 22c asks if God knows what the three people are saying. Responding that he knows are 94% of the deaf and 100% of the control group.

Following through on Question 22c, Question 22d queries the deaf as to how God knows. A total of 50% of the deaf (and 26% of the control group) hold that physical hearing is the basis of God's knowledge of the prayer. Some deaf maintain that God's extraordinarily acute hearing equips him to hear prayer from the atmosphere or even outer space. According to other deaf, however, God must descend since his hearing is only slightly superior or equal to the hearing of human beings. A few deaf also raise the issue as to whether God can decipher the simultaneous talk of a crowd or group of worshipers.

Here is a sampling. "People can't hear far away," explains Linda 18RBE109, "but God can hear far away." Benjamin 18_A says that "God can hear from heaven." To Richard 17_V the deity is more restricted: "God can hear. But if he is too far away, he can't." "God knows what they say. He follows them and then he can hear," is the view of Elizabeth 17_V. As understood by Dean 20WAIS121_, God's hearing has its shortcomings: "I told you before. The Church is too small, the world is too big. There are too many churches. God can't listen to everybody." Frances, 17, a member of the control group, puts it this way: "God knows everything and he hears everything in an auditory way."

Explaining that God's knowledge of the prayer is derived from his physical sight is another category of Question 22d—20% of the deaf and 5% of the control group. God as a celestial being appears again, as the deaf respond that God studies faces and speech-reads from afar. For some deaf, however, the restrictions of physical sight compel him to descend before he can comprehend the content of the prayer.

Here are some examples. Shirley 17MAT Adv.4.2A says that "God comes down to the people to see what they are talking about. Maybe God can hear them, too, but I doubt it." "God is always watching," comments Kimberly 16CAT6.9A. "He sees what the people are doing. Even if he doesn't understand the prayer, he knows if they are good or bad. If they are good, he will bless them." "God knows. He watches their faces and he knows their feelings. God can read their lips," is the view of Robert 20WAIS102A.

Continuing with Question 22d, we arrive at the group which assigns omniscience as the rationale for divine knowledge of the prayer. Included in this category are 58% of the control group and 12% of the deaf, a noticeable statistical difference indicating the less materialistic approach of the control group. Joanne 17WISC93_ speaks for the 12% of the deaf as she says: "God knows everything."

In the control group, Sarah, 16, used the identical words: "He knows everything." "He knows all of it," explains Jeanne, 17. "You don't even have to say the words. He knows what you are thinking." "He knows what they say by what's going on in their minds. There is nothing he doesn't know" responds Bruce, 18.

Finally, 8% of the deaf and 5% of the control group gave other reasons as the basis for God's knowledge of the prayer, while 10% of the deaf and 5% of the control group did not know.

Question 22e asks the deaf if God answers the people. The pre-testing uncovered a serious flaw in the formulation of this question, a flaw concerning the interpretation which the deaf adolescents put upon the word "answer." Their understanding of the term would obscure accurate feedback; nevertheless, the term was deliberately retained because of the light it throws upon the issue of religious language, specifically literalism.

Our power to correctly communicate the thought contents of our minds to the minds of others and to receive into our own minds the thoughts that are theirs depends upon our ability to name the reality with a word (or sign) that enables the recipient to identify the same reality in his mind. If the word identifies a reality other than the intended one, correct communication has failed to occur,[120] and to a noticeable degree this is what happened when the word "answer" (which was signed in total communication) arrived at the eyes of the deaf recipients. They decoded this word into the narrowest thought. In the context of Question 22e, most of the deaf understood the term in a most literal sense. To them, "answer" meant a direct and immediate response, usually by voice or by granting the desired material benefit, such as the curing of illness and the like. The following statistics and quotes support and illustrate this observation.

Only 5% of the deaf, compared with 55% of the control group, responded that God always answers prayers. A total of 27% of the deaf stated that he sometimes answers, and 69% of the deaf, along with 5% of the control group, said that he *never* answers prayers.

Robert 18MAT Adv.4.9V reflects some of the above thinking in his comment: "God does not answer. He listens—that is all The people pray and leave. They don't stay and wait for an answer." Divine silence disappoints Dora 16WISC104A: "He never answers. That is the trouble. God never says anything. If people believe, then God should talk to them. If God talks, then I will believe more." "God never answers," complains Julie 17MAT Adv.4.4V. "Before, Jesus talked. The people saw him; they learned. He helped them. But now it is different. I pray, pray—and nothing happens." To Andrew 16MAT Inter.3.7V, God listens and approves: "The people talk. God listens. He hears. He says O.K. That is all." Joanne 17WISC93_ discerns an indirect answer: "God never answers. The people ask for faith and God gives them faith. But God does not talk to them."

Unhampered by the term "answer," the control group reflect a higher spiritual comprehension. They detect the hand of God at work in a variety of subtle ways. Christine, 18, for instance, says that God always answers "in little, good things that happen to you. It doesn't have to come in one lump sum." According to Sarah, 16, God "always answers in lots of ways. Sometimes you feel better. Sometimes he helps you to understand the people around you." Intellectual illumination satisfies Sheila, 16: "God always answers by making things obvious to them that were not obvious before."

What the deaf really think regarding Question 22e is better obtained from the reconstructed follow-up Question 22f: "Can God help these people?" Discarding the term "answer" clarifies the issue for the deaf. The question is inaccurately posed for prayer purposes, although it does reveal somewhat indirectly the deaf view on prayer efficacy and God's ability to act. The statistics here change significantly. A total of 90% of the deaf state that God can help them in some way, which can be considered as tantamount to receiving divine responses to prayer. (Control group statistics on Question 22f are nearly identical with the deaf.) So far as the deaf are concerned, one of several ways that God emerges from obscurity and involves himself in mundane affairs is by manipulating human emotions to make people "feel better." For example, Marilyn 18WAIS111A explains that the people "pray, pray—and then God makes them feel happy." "God can help," says Charles 21RBE113_. "Maybe the people will feel good, will feel something in their body." "God can help them feel better," is the explanation of Alan 17MAT Adv.5.5A.

Another way in which God helps is by satisfying the deaf with quick and specific results, usually a material advantage. For Paula 17WAIS108_ the benefit is employment: "The people pray for work and then they find a job. So God helped them." Steve 18CAT7.3A turns to accidents: "God can help, but he can't do everything himself. He will send an angel to warn the people not to get into that car because it will get in an accident." "I prayed to win the basketball game," says John 17WAIS96A, "and we won. God helped." Audrey 18WAIS102_ reflects a similar view: "I pray for a passing mark. God answers when I pass."

Question 22g intentionally reinstates the word "answer" to further explore the trail of literalism. It asks the deaf if God answers with his voice, and 21% of the deaf expect God to respond to prayer with a spoken voice, a view shared by none of the control group.[121] Consequently, due to their lack of hearing, the 21% would logically be separated from their God. Under follow-up questioning, however, some of them proposed that "God could put words in the minds of the deaf" or otherwise detour around the quandary. Inquiring into whether God then speaks only to hearing people, Question 22h is a logical follow-through of Question 22g. A total of 16% of the deaf acknowledged that God indeed talks only to hearing people, and "talk" is again understood in its narrowest sense.

Pursuing the subject further and inquiring into *how* God "talks" to the deaf, we now move over to Question 22i. The word "talk" is here clarified by the investigator to mean "communicate." But even with the clarification, 17% of the deaf fall short of a spiritual interpretation and still insist that God communicates mechanistically—with a voice or sign-language. Divine communication baffles William 17WISC89V: "God can sign, but we can't see him." Paul 17WISC108A says that God does no talking or signing; instead, he "writes for the priests and the priests explain it to the people on Sunday." Anthony 17WISC86V explains that human beings are ill-equipped to receive divine communication: "God can talk back to the people, but the people can't hear God. God hears the people, but the people can't hear God." William 20RBE85_ holds similar views: "God talks and the people can't hear because God is too far away. But Jesus is right behind them. Jesus can talk to the people and they can hear. But not me: I'm deaf."

Bursting through the mechanistic restrictions and arriving at a more spiritual and interiorized understanding of divine communication are 33% of the deaf, compared with 72% of the control group. Instead of presenting an anthropomorphic God speaking as one man to another, these deaf respond to Question 22i with traces of auto-suggestion, dreams, and interior talking, all of which have a divine origin. Here are some illustrations. Joan 16MAT Adv.3.5V says that "God can answer the people in dreams or in their minds." "God communicates only with good people," explains Shirley 17MAT Adv.4.2A, "and maybe God works on their brain, or he speaks to the good people's heart." "God sends words to the mind of the deaf," is the view of Charles 18WISC121_. James 18WISC96_ thinks similarly: "God talks in my mind."

Finally, a total of 42% of the deaf (21% from the Catholic schools and 49% from the secular schools) simply do not know how God communicates with the deaf, even after a preliminary clarification of the word "talk" was given by the investigator.

Scattered throughout the spectrum of Question 22 are insightful remarks of the deaf which are numerically insufficient to constitute separate categories, but are nevertheless summarized and listed below with an accompanying quotation.

(1) Great distance forbids any communication:
    "Jesus can't sign to me. He is too far up." (Gary 19WAIS105V)
(2) God begins communications only at the time of death.
    "Jesus waits for the deaf to die. Then he communicates with them. Now—nothing." (David 17WAIS109__)
(3) Only a few privileged people receive communication from God.
    "God does not answer most people. He answers a few people —the pope, some priests, some people who really believe in him." (Joseph 19MAT Adv.4.2V)

An inquiry into the prayer activity of the kneeling boy, Question 23 divulges much of what we have already learned throughout this study, especially on literalism and a restricted divine knowledge. Therefore, little need be said beyond what was previously analyzed.

Nearly all the respondents agree that the boy is praying (Question 23a), that he is speaking in some way (Question 23b), and that he is speaking to God (Question 23c) or Jesus. But the deaf succumb to literalism and excessive anthropomorphism in Question 23d, as 36% of them (24% from the Catholic schools and 39% from the secular schools) and none of the control group say that in prayer the boy must use his voice. Nevertheless, some of the 36% moderated their view when they further remarked that a low voice suffices.

The restrictions which we have already seen the deaf place upon divine knowledge appear again in Question 23e, asking the deaf if God knows sign-language. Claiming that God knows the sign-language are 65% of the deaf (84% from the Catholic schools and 58% from the secular schools), while 17% of the deaf say that he is ignorant of sign-language and 18% are in doubt. None of the control group ascribe ignorance to God, 10% have doubts, and 90% affirm that God knows sign-language.

Curiously, the deaf teenagers explain alternatives which enable Jesus to circumvent his ignorance of sign-language. According to Richard 19MAT Adv.3.0V, Jesus enlists the aid of the deceased deaf: "The deaf die and they go to heaven. Jesus meets them and asks them to help. They write for him and Jesus understands." The thoughts of John 20WAIS114A are similar: "No, Jesus doesn't understand. But the old priests who used to sign to the deaf died and now maybe they interpret for Jesus." Mary Lou 18WISC89__ assigns this duty to the angels: "One of the angels interprets for God." "God does not know signs," explains

Patricia 18WAIS96A, "but he watches your face. If you look sad, he knows something is wrong."

Question 23f asks, "Do you ever pray?" That 86% of the deaf answered affirmatively is indeed surprising, considering their mechanistic technique ascending to a finite God. But a closer study reveals several shortcomings. Among the 86% are those who (a) say only rote and stereotyped formulas, (b) pray seldom and usually to escape distress, and (c) pray only at specified times (bedtime, mealtime and in church).

As in previous areas of this study, the remarks of the deaf can be grouped into categories and allow an enlarged understanding of their view of prayer.

1. *It can be said that the main motives for the boy's prayer are contrition and petition, although some deaf mention praise and love.* The petition is usually for a specific material benefit. Judy 18WISC97_ says: "The boy is praying because he used bad words and got in trouble. Now he wants God to forgive him." Commenting that she prayed for help at bedtime when things had gone wrong that day, Rita 18_A was then asked if she prayed when things had gone well. Her answer: "No." According to Andrew 16MAT Inter.3.7V, the boy is praying "to ask God to forgive his sins."

2. *Some of the prayer can be characterized as a formula taking place at specific times and under the direction of a prayer leader, usually a nun in Catholic school or a priest signing Mass on Sundays.* George 17_V, for instance, prays in common: "I say school prayers at lunch. Sometimes I pray before bed and I follow the priest's signs in church." The activity of Michael 17WISC116A prevents prayer, except in church: "I pray each Sunday in church. I don't pray on other days because I have to go to school. I don't have time." Admitting that she never prays at home or in church, Linda 18RBE109_ added: "I only pray in school with the sister. I follow the sister. That is all." After responding that he says the words "Hail Mary" each night before bed, Richard 19MAT Adv.3.0V was asked if he knew the remainder of the prayer and responded "No."

3. *A trend that appears both among the 14% of those who do not pray and among a few of the 86% of the deaf who do pray is the feeling that they have outgrown prayer.* To them, perhaps prayer is associated with childhood and is nowhere to be found among maturing adolescents. "Before, when I was small, I used to pray," says Edna 18CMMS99V, "but now I've stopped." The thoughts of Raymond 17WAIS112A are identical: "Before, I prayed many times. Now I've stopped." Judith 17CMMS103V gives the reasoning behind her cessation: "I don't pray

anymore. I pray, pray. What for? Nothing happens. Nobody is looking at me."

It must be pointed out, however, that some deaf have achieved a deeper understanding of prayer and accompany their understanding with an edifying prayer life. Such is Mary Ann 18CAT13.4A, a devotee of the rosary: "The boy is praying for favors, to ask God to forgive his sins or maybe to adore him. I pray the rosary every night during Lent." Asked if he ever prayed, Leroy 19_A responded: "Yes. I say words in my mind. I say: 'Bless the food. Keep peace. Forgive my sins.'" Dorothy 20CNE98A comprehends the idea of spontaneous prayer: "Yes, I pray. Sometimes when I walk along the hall I say, 'O my Jesus, I love you. I am sorry for all my sins.'"

Two observations are pertinent when comparing the deaf to the control group. The first concerns the place of prayer, and the second concerns prayer technique. Much of the prayer of the deaf happens largely in two places: at bedside and in church. Some members of the control group share this view. Like the deaf, David, 16, prays before bed: "Whenever we have a softball game, I pray that we win it." "I pray at night before bed," says Constance, 16, "and in church. I talk to God about my school work."

Regarding the second observation, we said earlier that 72% of the control group have nothing in common with mechanistic restrictions which complicate prayer technique. These hearing young people achieve a spiritual understanding of prayer and see a divine presence with or within them. The prayer of Joan, 18, arises from her awareness of God's presence within her: "I pray spontaneously during the day—anytime—because God is within me." "Anytime, anyplace," says Frances, 17, "I carry on a conversation with God. He is with me."

Although we made prefacing remarks on prayer prerequisites, some further observations bear comment.

First is the relationship between omniscience and mental prayer. If we remember that, at least to some deaf, omniscience means all-seeing, then the question arises as to whether God can *see* into the mind of the individual (cf. Question 15d). Inability to see implies that God must remain external to the mind and therefore excluded from mental prayer, assuming that mental prayer is thought of as sub-vocal, interior speech. Alongside this must be placed the following question: Given a basic desire to pray, can the deaf, because of restricted verbal ability, perform the exercise of mental prayer? And should not the "low verbal" deaf be encouraged to pray mentally with the use of interior sign-language phantasms rather than an interior flow of sub-vocal speech? This, of course, presumes a divine penetration to the mind as well as a divine comprehension of sign-language—two accomplishments which only some deaf assign to God and which, therefore, the teacher must not take for granted.

Mental prayer is the most common form of private, personal prayer and is distinguished from vocal prayer, the most common form of public, liturgical prayer. Those deaf who pray only when they "follow the sign-language of the priest in church" or "follow the sister at mealtimes" may possibly be unaware of the interior activity of mental prayer, an impoverishment which would rob them of the riches of prayer at an ideal time—the reception of the Eucharist.

Second, the cliché that prayer is "conversation with God" falls down badly in the face of those deaf who object to such conversation on the grounds that "I don't know God" or "I never met God." These deaf youth must be made to understand that prayer is no ordinary conversation or communication.[122] Ordinary communication between human beings presupposes a shared pool of ideas or a common background; it also presumes that if one is speaking, the other party will talk back, sustaining the conversation with his own contributions. But as far as the deaf and hearing alike are concerned, one may legitimately raise the question of what common ideas are shared with a transcendent God and whether and how God "talks back." To many deaf and hearing adolescents the answer is obviously negative on both counts.

And yet a discourse is possible not because of shared ideas or background or the efforts of the deaf, but because God's love for them impels him to reach them. But even the divine initiative may miss its mark and go unrecognized without that rebirth or conversion experience elaborated earlier in this work. A change of heart ignites true prayer. If, as the fourth Gospel emphasizes, rebirth is the one way to God, it is likewise the one way to that genuine prayer which separates a real Christian from a conventional one whose prayer is largely limited.

Acknowledging that prayer follows upon rebirth and that the beginnings of prayer require a recognition of divine presence, we may now introduce the issue of conceptualizing for the deaf a God whom many of them see as geographically distant. That it is possible for even an ordinary person to make immediate contact with such a God and vice versa is a pedagogical point that needs attention. Old Testament prophetic language can here illuminate the mind of the deaf with its "messenger style," characterized with the preface "Thus says the Lord . . ."[123] where the verb "says" refers to physical speaking. This would be a start, but more work must be done to cultivate a religious language that communicates direct contact with God.

Another means of bringing a distant God near is to distinguish between spatial presence and personal presence.[124] The implication that there are so many units of measurements—yards, miles, light years—separating God from the deaf, a notion that is part of the deaf understanding of God as a celestial being, is the meaning of spatial presence. The responses have revealed enough of this. However, personal presence is thought of in terms not of distance but of love, for nearness is a concomitant of love. Who can separate a mother from her infant? Who can separate St. Paul from the love of Christ Jesus? On the other hand, two lovers soon find themselves "keeping their distance" after their love deteriorates, and the ensuing silence signals the eventual end of their relationship. Deaf recognition of the nearness of God, then, calls for a mutual interaction: a loving God seeks the deaf and the deaf, in turn, lovingly seek God. Far from happening automatically, this process requires the time and cooperation of the deaf. Abundant scriptural evidence can reassure the deaf that God's love thrusts him into the maelstrom of human affairs and makes him very near to each one, especially when we call upon him.[125]

Third, something should be said of the basic attitude toward God which prayer implies. As we have seen, more deaf adolescents associate prayer with petition than with contrition, love, or other motives, a position different from the control group.[126] Petitionary prayer is praiseworthy to the extent that it acknowledges that God is oriented toward us, is for us, and can alleviate distress. But those deaf who beg God to help them win a basketball tournament, etc., unveil a petition entangled with egocentric desires. These deaf should be led to see that in responding to prayer of petition, God refrains from manipulation. An understanding of the will of God, especially as it relates to their own handicap and affects their own lives, which they are to subordinate to it, can enrich their prayer.

Egocentric left-overs can be further lessened by expanding petitions to include the community at large and by appealing to the deaf person to commit himself, if possible, to whatever his prayer is trying to bring about. For example, instead of just praying for better school grades, let him accompany his prayer with more efficient study habits; instead of just praying for the removal of employment discrimination against the deaf, let him do something about it by becoming a better worker and thus pave the way for other deaf to enter the plant. Joining commitment to prayer is what St. Ignatius Loyola meant when he said: "Pray as if everything depended on prayer, and work as if everything depended on work."

Staying with the same theme of basic attitudes implied by prayer, another observation should be made. We saw earlier that to the deaf (and hearing) the term "person" means "human being," a view which leads the deaf to minimize divinity and make God simply a person among persons or a sort of super-person. Unless he is seen as the creator and sustainer of all reality and as the awe-inspiring "mysterium tremendum" to be adored for his own sake, there will be little sense of dependence upon him and therefore a minimal basis for praying to him. Furthermore, until existentially meaningful symbols of atonement and justification are developed and conveyed to the deaf, there will likewise be a weakened underpinning for their prayer, since God shattered his silence and spoke with supreme eloquence on the cross. From here he intends his Word for even the deaf to hear, and from the cross he expects to receive not only the petitions of the deaf, but also their praise, thanksgiving, love and adoration.

Deliberately withheld until now because of its relationship to Questions 24 to 27 is an essential prerequisite for prayers: compassion mixed with fraternal kindness. The prophet Isaiah states it clearly: "Sharing your bread with the hungry, sheltering the oppressed and the homeless, clothing the naked when you see them and not turning your back on your own. . . . Then you shall call and the Lord will answer, you shall cry for help and he will say: Here I am!" (Is. 58:7-9).

Brotherly love and compassion occupy Questions 24 to 27 and conclude our investigation. Some of the findings, however, have already surfaced in previous questions or been used before, and therefore what is non-essential or repetitious is omitted.[127] Love and compassion were inserted at the suggestion of deaf adults who believed that some deaf "isolates" (those deaf people who refuse to socialize with other deaf) withdrew from the deaf community, (i.e., social and church groups) because the deaf, in general, have "hard hearts." But the responses to Questions 24 to 27 allay these suspicions as the deaf adolescents reveal unequivocally that fraternal love and compassion are found as much among themselves as anyone else.

Some material in the responses deserves discussion. Whereas nearly all of the deaf love their parents, only 52% of them love their houseparents at the residential schools and 27% "sometimes" love them. Only occasional follow-up questions were asked here, and therefore it is risky to present the reasoning behind the percentages. The one factor that did appear, however, was discipline. In the residential school setting, the task of correcting and disciplining errant behavior often falls to the houseparents—a task which is unlikely to endear them to the deaf student. Hence it seems safe to say that these adolescents interpret the word "love" to mean "like."

An observation worthy of note concerns the black man of Question 25. A total of 68% of the deaf love the black man, but only 42% believe that the black man loves them, thus reflecting a willingness to give love coupled with an uncertainty of receiving love.

Statistics on the love of the deaf adolescent for hearing people are these: 63% say they love the hearing, and 35% explain that they sometimes love, depending upon the individual. Reasons most often given for a selective love or no love center upon frustration in communication which manifests itself in (1) the deaf person's difficulty in speech reading which often produces a stress situation, (2) the hearing person's lack of interest in and patience for communicating with the deaf, and (3) the deaf person's shyness and, in some cases, even fear of socializing with hearing people because, as Randy 17WISC131—says, "I can't talk to them." Someone once accurately remarked that it is in this situation— social involvement with the hearing—that a deaf person feels his deafness the most.

Lastly, Question 27 reveals that there is room for compassion in the lives of the overwhelming majority of both the deaf (94%) and hearing (95%) adolescents. By having compassion on the helpless—the kitten, accident victim, puzzled student, fight victim and elderly lady—the deaf adolescent exhibits the beginnings of a real fraternal love, and by making the needs of these helpless ones as important as his own, he draws close to the heart of love. Thus would he fulfill the prophet Isaiah's requirement for prayer.

IV
Conclusion and Recommendations

At this juncture our original intention had been to bring together the attributes we have studied and thereby reconstruct a unified God of the deaf adolescent and compare him with the orthodox God of revelation. However, since the reader is now in a position to do this for himself, it was decided to change the original intention and direct the conclusion and recommendations into different avenues. Reflection compels us to first take a brief look backward and then a longer, exploratory look forward into tracts that will most effectively build upon what we have been learning throughout this study, tracts that will capitalize upon the strengths of the deaf and illuminate a deeper awareness of God.

32
Review

A brief look over the ground we have covered up to now suggests four areas which were discussed before but need extended treatment beyond this study: (1) personal faith, (2) the deaf understanding of the transcendence-immanence relationship, (3) the deaf conception of God's universal love for mankind as weakening or failing at the individual level, and (4) anthropomorphism and its implications.

With regard to personal faith, the route that the deaf (and hearing) travel from baptism to a personal act of faith should be studied, and if it is found to lead elsewhere it should be redirected to culminate in the act of faith, which may be expressed, perhaps, in a para-liturgical ceremony of renewing baptismal promises. It is crucial that Christianity be understood not as idle information but as knowledge demanding a decision, knowledge remaining not external but becoming internal to the individual. It is the personal act of faith that internalizes what was previously external knowledge and ushers the deaf and hearing into the world of the sacred. This faith then expresses itself while it strengthens and concretizes itself in a liturgy of Ameslan, bodily postures, gestures and song.

Transcendence-immanence, the second point, is significant because any imbalance between the two can have serious repercussions. The deaf accent on transcendence (as they understand the term) leaves them with a sky-god limited in location and knowledge and remote from the mundane. If the suggestions presented earlier for awakening immanence fail, it becomes all the more necessary to stress the employment of intermediaries: the Blessed Virgin, the saints, and angels.

The third point, the question of love, is central to Christianity; therefore, further investigation should be made to uncover the causes of a weakened divine love for the individual—whether the cause, perhaps, is in a defective pedagogy, or whether it pertains to a wider difficulty with their reasoning from the more universal to the less universal (deductive argumentation), or whether it is due mainly to the restrictions they place upon the person of God and the confusion of "person" with "human being."

The fourth point concerns the deaf idea of an anthropomorphic God, someone much like ourselves. A review of the responses reveals a God with human shape and human feelings, a God performing specific actions and giving specific commands and prohibitions, a God who visits the churches and listens to prayers. As one advances to the stage of classical theism, he may disparage anthropomorphism and discard first the human shape, then the human feelings, and finally the activities, and he is left holding a pure abstraction or an all-encompassing and formless spirit. Perhaps it was the theistically-taught deaf who, in the interviews, described God as "nothing." While it is true that pedagogy must purify some of the grosser anthropomorphic elements and that the God of the deaf is less than "the whole show" and that the deaf rarely pay him "metaphysical compliments" and call him "infinite," nevertheless he is *living* and *acting*.[1] Yet the advantages of having a living and acting God can be lessened if the deaf humanize God to the extent that he becomes so much like one of ourselves that the deaf can manipulate or exploit him. To offset the danger of a diminished divinity and to preserve the right kind of anthropomorphism, we should first stress God as "holy" and then turn to the incarnation, for Jesus—at once God and man—offers the clearest evidence of God to the deaf. To attempt to raise the deaf to the level of classical theism would be to throw them into the clutches of a figurative religious language abounding with metaphor, analogy, allegory, paradox and slanted usages. Such a language would entangle them in utter confusion, even if it were presented in Siglish.

We have completed our backward look and are now ready to turn around and open up vistas that originate in and are continuous with what the deaf have been telling us throughout the body of responses, vistas that develop and culminate into the following categories: (1) basic and early Christianity, (2) myth, and (3) symbol. Since all three are of utmost significance in deepening the deaf understanding of God and religion in general, they are now separately examined.

33
Earliest Christianity

A comprehensive examination of the responses leaves no doubt that some deaf have a simple and beautiful faith unencumbered by the numerous non-essentials which seem to often distract the minds of the more educated Christians. To take the deaf into the depths of dogma is to approach them with content and language style that retard rather than promote religious belief and living. However, since deaf and hearing people alike need to understand before they believe, it becomes essential to lay out a most appropriate foundation. This can best be done by bringing scholarship and a creative imagination to bear upon the belief and life of earliest Christianity of the period of approximately 30-150 A.D., before the onset of the great Christological and Trinitarian controversies and the complexities they spawned.

One of the finest sources for imparting early Christianity, and one which the deaf easily comprehend because of the literary directness and simplicity of its language, is the Gospel of Mark. The Jesus of Mark fulfills the need for a concrete picture of Jesus at work performing miracles and preaching his way of life. In Mark's Gospel, Jesus is "the Son of God who is endowed with divine power and divine knowledge, but he is also the one-time Jewish teacher and prophet with human feelings. . . . In this way, Mark has for all time set the tone for the popular view and for the theological conception of the earthly Jesus."[2] Interested mainly in missionary activity, Mark presents details of Jesus' life which were of the highest importance to the early Church and therefore gives us a "mirror of the faith in Jesus of the Gentile missionary Church."[3] Other source material reaching back into the earliest period include the Johannine Epistles and several uncanonical books such as *The Teaching of the Twelve Apostles (The Didache)* and *The Epistle of Barnabas.*

An adequate catechesis would surely follow if the deaf are presented with early and essential truths. A brief line up would include the following:

(a) A Pauline theology of conversion. This theme and how it differs from the contemporary position of one who is born into his faith should be elucidated. Enough has already been said about this and there is no need to reiterate. Here it suffices to recall that this was essential to the experience of the early Church.

(b) Jesus' death as the inauguration of a new relationship between God and the Christian. Men are now children of God, whereas previously they had been "God's enemies" (Rom. 5:10). Included within the new relationship are the theological concepts of covenant, reconciliation, justification and election. One way to express that we now enjoy God's good pleasure and a closeness unknown before the time of Jesus is to dramatize what happened in the temple at the moment Jesus died: "At that moment the curtain in the sanctuary was torn in two from top to bottom" (Mk. 15:38). This can signify that God is no longer confined to the temple, but that he broke out, so to speak, and is now with us. And this nullifies the mentality that urges us to acquire the attitude of the high priest, keep our distance, and approach the holy of holies but once a year. On the contrary, from now on we are encouraged to join Jesus as he calls the first person of the Blessed Trinity "Abba," an Aramaic word connoting warmth, security and intimacy, a word which was informal and familiar and which a child would use in speaking with his father —a word, therefore, which the Jewish mind had previously regarded as unthinkable to use in prayer.[4]

(c) A theme that is in the nucleus of early Christianity and therefore basic to any catechesis is the sacrificial death of Christ. Several observations have already been made about the crucifixion and they need not be repeated now. The question arising here is how to impart to the deaf the vicarious nature of Jesus' death. Evidence in the responses demonstrates that many deaf fail to move beyond Calvary and either blame no one for Jesus' death or impute guilt only to the king and soldiers, those immediately and physically responsible for Jesus' death. But to stretch the meaning of the crucifixion to *our* sins is to require the deaf to expand their understanding beyond the physical Calvary and enter the area of time and divine foreknowledge.

Through an effective use of symbols, the deaf can be taught that at one point in time (B.C.) the crucifixion was something in the future that corresponded with the already existing divine plan—and we contemporaries are part of that plan. St. Thomas gives the example of a line of men, one behind the other, looking straight ahead and walking toward a hill. An individual man in the line cannot see the men behind him, but an observer on the hill can see the whole line at once.[5] Similarly, we see only piecemeal and in succession, but God sees all at once.[6] And God foresaw the sufferings of his Son as the Suffering Servant of Isaiah 53: "But he was pierced for our offenses, crushed for our sins" (Is. 53:5). The atoning power of Jesus' death derives from his conformity to the divine will, from his patient and voluntary endurances of the suffering, and from his own innocence.[7] Nevertheless, to enlighten the deaf, modern symbols of atonement and time should be worked out.

(d) Also pertaining to bed-rock Christianity is the resurrection of Jesus. There will be no repetition of what was earlier discussed, but more should be said on making the resurrection more meaningful for the deaf. It would be good to make known the Pauline idea that the resurrection and ascension are one and that, accordingly, the appearances to the disciples are those of an already ascended Christ; however, it would be better to make known the Lucan idea (in the kerygmatic speeches of

Acts) that the ascension happened after forty (a sacred number) days of the continued earthly life of Christ. Peter's sermon (Acts 10:40 ff.), which describes Jesus eating and drinking and therefore restores his former corporeal body, and the doubting Thomas incident (Jn. 20:27) have impressed the deaf. At any rate, one can circumvent the complications of interpreting the resurrection by appealing to the earliest traditions and by the use of simple but meaningful expressions such as "Jesus lives" and "Because Christ lives, we shall also live." What is important, especially for those deaf who look backward toward a predominantly historical Jesus, is to stress that the resurrection does not conclude the ministry of Jesus and make it a thing of the past, but that it allows Jesus' work to continue now in the Church—work which includes his healing, his teaching, his breaking the rule of Satan, and his promises of eternal life. In short, the resurrection enables what Jesus stood for to continue.[8]

(e) Earliest Christology grappled with the central question: "Who is Jesus of Nazareth?" Interestingly, the views of numerous deaf coincide with earliest Christology as they explained that sonship subordinates Jesus to the Father and that Jesus *became* Messiah after his exaltation, as expressed in Acts 2:36; 13:33. The earliest community perceived Jesus as a recipient of revelation from the Father, who alone fully comprehended Jesus' mission—a mission which Jesus unfolds to men.[9] Between Jesus and the Father existed a unique relationship of mutual knowledge. Yet only after his death was Jesus exalted and enthroned in the full office of Messiah.[10] Limited as this conception appears, it was the highest attribution of divinity that the earliest community seemed capable of bestowing upon Jesus.[11] All of this is called "Adoptionist Christology," and it is the kind which the deaf frequently describe in their responses.

Since many deaf adolescents already share this kind of thinking, it would perhaps be an apt point of departure from which the deaf could advance along the route of the early Church as it developed its thinking on the person of Jesus, beginning with Jesus himself, finding God in him, and finally seeing him as a divine person. Although earliest thought regarded Jesus' exaltation and enthronement as happening after his death, his designation as future king took place at his baptism in the Jordan. Thus, Jesus was chosen by God, dedicated to God and anointed as king, but for a while he mingled incognito among the people—except for his partial recognition by demons, disciples and others like the centurion at the cross (Mk. 15:39). However, the turning point came with those sayings of Jesus in which he referred to himself in a unique Son-relation to the Father (Mt. 11:27), and this gave birth to the idea of divine sonship and bestowed upon him the right to be addressed as Son of God (Mt. 14:33). The sonship development was of the highest significance and later drew from the Gospels the notion of Jesus as "a divine 'Son' living on earth for a time."[12] Subsequently, the idea of divine sonship outgrew and enveloped the idea of heavenly exaltation and spread backward into his earthly life,[13] culminating to mean Jesus' participation in the divine essence as illustrated at the transfiguration (Mk. 9:2-8).

All of the preceding was most superficial and brief and was meant only to highlight the route of the early Church as it progressed toward a fuller understanding of Jesus. This procedure is sometimes called Christology "from below," since it begins with Jesus the man and works upward, so to speak, toward his divinity.[14] The method of Christology "from below" is more suitable for the purpose of illuminating the divinity of Christ for the deaf. The method of Christology "from above," on the other hand, is less suitable since it presupposes the divinity of Christ and therefore, pedagogically at least, begs the question. The important task is to present an orderly array of activity and reasons indicating how Jesus' historical appearance opens out into a recognition of his divinity. Even though this procedure begins with the man Jesus, his unity and relationship with God become central. Accordingly, it becomes important to recall all that the deaf have revealed throughout this study about their conception of God. It would likewise be profitable to study what the deaf describe as "spirit," since some of the most primitive attempts to express God's presence in Jesus were characterized by the concept of spirit.[15]

But even after clarification, divinity needs a closely related partner: salvation. Unless the two are joined, Jesus would remain incomplete in the minds of deaf and hearing people alike. Who Jesus is pertains to him as God; what he does pertains to him as Savior. How can the deaf deepen their understanding of what Jesus did and does for them? How can Jesus be made existentially significant for the deaf? Relevant here are some of what was said earlier about the sacrificial death on the cross and the development of a meaningful symbol of time. Also relevant are observations demonstrating for the deaf how sin operates in contemporary society and what sin can do to both the individual and society— how sin, for instance, begins with selfishness and stagnation, leans toward brutality, and works itself out into destruction and death. Standing in sharp contrast to this are Jesus' teachings and obedient life and death which reverse the tendencies of sin and ultimately enable the Christian to be delivered from his archenemy, death.[16]

(f) The doctrine of Christ's return and judgment is basic even though it expresses itself very early in divergent traditions containing inconsistent elements. Yet common features are discernible. First are the cosmic events—earthquakes, famines and pestilences described in the seal-visions of Revelation 6; alongside this are the great tribulations predicted in Daniel 12:1. During these awesome events the elect will be spared, although severe tests await the disciples, and they are warned that they must persevere to the end (Mk. 8:34-38) to be saved. The sign that the end is imminent is the "abomination of desolation" (Dan. 9:27; 11:31; 12:11). Up to now the Messiah has not yet come. When he does come, he will appear suddenly and in regal glory (Lk. 23:42), gather his elect (Mk. 13:27, 2 Thes. 2:1), and acknowledge those who remained faithful to him (Lk. 12:8).[17]

The question is what to do with the 2,000-year interval that has come between us and the expectations of the earliest Christians. Pannenberg remarks that the amount of time elapsing between Jesus' earthly life and his return is unimportant.[18] What is important with regard to the coming judgment is the present attitude of men toward Jesus (Mk. 8:38). Inherent in these observations is a realized eschatology along with a futuristic eschatology for the individual, the community and the cosmos.[19]

(g) Much of the remainder of bed-rock Christianity concerns vital concepts earlier discussed: (a) the founding of the Church of God as a gathering of brothers and sisters; (b) the sacraments, especially baptism and the Eucharist; (c) the exaltation of love—accompanied with a joy that originates in confidence in Christ—as an outward activity stemming from faith.[20]

34
Myth

Even though we have concluded that the content of basic Christianity as understood by the earliest Christians is the kind best suited for the deaf, we are still faced with the issue of communicating—whether by Ameslan, Siglish, Rochester, Oralism, the printed word, or other technique—religious language to the concrete mind of the deaf. Throughout this study we have seen how language deficiency works and how it alters the deaf conception of God. Specifically, we have seen that figurative language, so common in religious discourse, is a nearly indigestible item on the language menu of the deaf adolescent. The question becomes how to use what the deaf give us to the greatest advantage.

Approaches to an answer lead into an area of utmost importance. As we observed once before, this study uncovers a parallel between the mythological thinking of ancient man, some Hebrew traditions and the similar thinking of numerous deaf adolescents. The abundance of evidence already presented justifies the drawing of this parallel. Furthermore, when the works of Goldman, Piaget and Jung are brought abreast of this study, they extend the parallel to the thinking found in young children and in dreams.[21]

Jung remarks that religious myth, far from being an infantile phantasm, is one of man's greatest achievements.[22] It is rooted in the psyche and therefore can never become obsolete. Jung concludes that the mythmakers of the past thought in much the same way as we still think in dreams.[23] When the question arises as to where the mind's aptitude for such symbolic thought originates, Jung distinguishes between the directed and adapted thinking and the subjective (or non-directed), which is actuated by inner motives. Directed thinking is a conscious phenomenon which happens, for example, when the contents entering the mind are channeled into the construction of the objective world picture—for instance, concentrating on a geometry problem or discursive reasoning toward the conclusion of a syllogism. On the other hand, subjective or non-directed thinking is, in the main, subjectively motivated and produces a world picture different from that of directed thinking. Non-directed thinking is fantasy-thinking. Fantasy-products directly engaging the conscious mind are daydreams.

These prefacing remarks enable us now to make two important observations. (1) Non-directed or fantasy thinking brings directed thinking into contact with the oldest layers of the human mind, layers buried beneath the threshold of consciousness.[24] Jung explains that it is in this area, through non-directed thinking, that myth originates. (2) It seems that the deaf are at no disadvantage in this non-directed part of the mind since it functions without syntactical language. Therefore, as far as a style of religious or pre-religious discourse is concerned, the myth can be a most effective bearer of divine revelation to the deaf.[25]

The monumental research of Jean Piaget is well known to educators. He has elaborated, among other things, a theory that intelligence develops in a sequence of stages related to age. These stages begin with the sensory-motor period and end in the formal operational period (usually twelve to fifteen years of age). Formal operations, Piaget says, are manifested in propositional and hypothetical thinking. It is the second and final stage of operational intelligence which "reflects" on concrete operations through the elaboration of formal group structures. In popular language, this means, among other things, that the adolescent can reflect upon his own thoughts, reason by inference, generalize, and reason about contrary-to-fact propositions. Another characteristic of formal operational thought is that it makes possible the understanding of metaphor.[26]

In an unintentional but noticeable way, Piaget's experiments on the formal operational stage throw light on our study. Anecdotal observations made throughout the interviews (and outside this study) lead the investigator to the subjective opinion that many of the deaf interviewees inadequately handle contrary-to-fact propositions; moreover, one can say with a strength greater than subjective opinion that due to the frequent recurrence of literalism, the deaf lack a full comprehension of metaphor. Both weaknesses are indications casting doubt on whether the deaf adolescents have arrived at the stage of formal operations—at least in the religious area. If this much is true, the deaf adolescent remains in Piaget's concrete operational level, making direct use of visual and sensory data and moving little beyond it. In other words, the deaf adolescent is still thinking non-reflectively—and this is another reason for the use of myth. For myth, which needs no accompanying necessity to reflect, lays out before the deaf the ultimate questions of the meaning of life and relationship with the divine. Myth touches the spiritual dimensions in man even before reflective thought processes (formal operations) are awakened and begin a formulation of its contents.[27]

In addition to the preceding psychological observations, two other factors, discussed interchangeably, make myth valuable for the deaf. (1) The language of myth communicates with an evocative power unknown to abstract or alternate language. (2) The language of myth is a bridge over the troubled waters of literalism. Regarding the latter, John Macquarrie mentions that "at the mythological level, the distinction of literal and figurative, of symbol and what is symbolized, has not yet been made."[28] For modern man, proud of his language precision and philosophy-based systematic theologies, the literal and the figurative are hardly compatible with each other; but for ancient man and the deaf adolescent, bereft of such systematic ways of thought, the two merge and present an account of factual reality having nothing in common with figurative language. "Myths," says John Knox, "presume to say not what things are like (they might be like any number of things), but what they actually are and how they became to be."[29] Figures of speech can have variety, even when the same object is being described, but myths tend to be exclusive.[30]

Staying with the same subject, one more observation is in order. We said before that at the mythical level there is no distinction between the literal and the figurative and that consequently the myth is a bridge over literalism. But the question is raised as to how figures of speech (e.g., personification) used in telling myth are to be regarded. Again in the early stages of myth a lack of distinction is to be maintained. To the ancient Greek, referring to Eos (Aurora) was the only adequate way of speaking of the dawn, just as referring to Helios was the way of speaking of the sun.[31]

The myth, then, imaginatively and concretely describes something which is affirmed to have taken place in objective reality. The story or narrative is inseparable from and shares in its own truth. Accordingly, the language problem with the deaf is eased to the extent that we are confronting one consistent figure, so to speak, which is not really a figure insofar as its function is not to make comparisons, but to directly describe what the act or event actually is.[32] Imagery and thought unite.

Since the word "myth" labors under heavy abuse and ambiguity and under the stigma of "untruth," "fairy tale," "tall story" and the like, we pause to examine the term, at least as far as it fits our purposes. It is clear from the entire body of responses that when the deaf adolescents describe the other-worldly, they do so with terms (signs and words) that are this-worldly. We have seen the deaf speak of God as "resting," "eating," and "talking to the people who died yesterday" as they construct a finite, anthropomorphic God with a language derived from human experience. And this fits Rudolf Bultmann's explanation of myth as "the use of imagery to express the other-worldly in terms of this world and the divine in terms of human life, the other side in terms of this side."[33] Understood in this way, myth is applicable to much of Scripture and tradition since in this sense it is "a human story of a divine action."[34]

Sometimes, however, myth is more closely associated with what it meant to ancient man, who stands on common ground with the deaf. Like the deaf, the ancients "would not have admitted that anything could be abstracted from the concrete imaginative forms which they left us."[35] The myth, furthermore, is not allegory since its imagery and thought are one.[36] When we wish to analyze an event, we follow logical and scientific thought procedures; when the ancients wished to analyze an event, they told a myth—and they did this seriously. Therefore, it is a mistake to disparage myth as fantasy or fairy tale. "True myth," says Henri Frankfort, "presents its images and its imaginary actors, not with the playfulness of fantasy, but with a compelling authority. It perpetuates the revelation of a 'Thou.' "[37]

Henri Frankfort summarizes the character of myth in these words: "Myth is a form of poetry which transcends poetry in that it proclaims a truth; a form of reasoning which transcends reasoning in that it wants to bring about the truth it proclaims; a form of action, of ritual behavior, which does not find its fulfillment within the act, but must proclaim and elaborate a poetic form of truth."[38]

John Macquarrie summarizes the meaning of myth according to its form, events, and persons.[39] The *form* of the myth is narrative, especially appropriate for the deaf since its graphic language easily adapts itself to Ameslan or Siglish. On paper it could easily be imparted by pictorial sequence accompanied with a minimum of printed words. Moreover, the myth lends itself to drama, a mode of communication which delights the deaf. The ancients were likewise dramatizers of much of their myth. A famous example was the annual New Year's Day festival of the Babylonians, who re-enacted the victory of Marduk over the powers of chaos, a victory originally won on the first New Year's Day, when the world was created.[40]

The *events* narrated in myth reach into the deepest recesses of man's being and describe the phenomena of the surrounding world, which ancient man perceived as a "Thou"—"life confronting life."[41] The events are frequently miracles and wonders concerning creation or beginnings and are equipped with a mystique that puts them beyond scientific verification. Therefore, the events of myth can be a prelude bringing the deaf to the vestibule of mystery.[42]

Lastly, the *persons* of myth have human characteristics—they eat and drink for their sustenance, they fight and so on. But they are no ordinary people: they are gods or spirits or demons inhabiting a world described as an atmospheric heaven or a subterranean hell or a remote island to the west.

A brilliant writer in the field of mythology, Mircea Eliade describes myth in these words: "Myth narrates a sacred history; it relates an event that took place in primordial time, the fabled time of the 'beginnings.' " In other words, myth tells how, through the deeds of supernatural beings, a reality came into existence, be it the whole of reality, the cosmos, or only a fragment of reality—an island, a species of plant, a particular kind of human behavior, an institution.[43] It must be emphasized that myth tells not of an imaginary but of a real happening. Man, says the myth, is what he is because of supernatural intervention.[44]

As far as the deaf are concerned, the myth can be an effective communicator of the sacred, the super-sensible, the other-worldly as this-worldly and touching their own personal lives and awakening them to the reality of God. Our greatest interest, then, is in the myth as a way of theological discourse for the deaf. Although mythology, strictly speaking, is only a pre-theology, the vividness of its communication enables the deaf to stand on a firm spiritual base from which a more systematic catechesis can grow. When the deaf adolescents describe God anthropomorphically, as we have seen them do throughout this study, they are already within mythology or mythopoeic thought, to use Henri Frankfort's term.[45] Therefore, it would be a pedagogical mistake to correct the deaf and say that God does not really act or feel like a man because he is not a man. For when this is done, the teacher brings upon himself the responsibility of communicating the person of God to the deaf (whether by Ameslan, Siglish, Oral or other) in an alternate language—the language of philosophical theology with vocabulary and expressions the deaf fail to share, or even the language of straight Scripture where oblique usages are often found.

It is quite possible to present to the deaf a God worthy of their worship and allegiance with an anthropomorphic language derived from human life, a language evocative of impressions that to a pre-eminent degree speak of God's mercy, love, wisdom, strength and loyalty, and a language which makes no distinction between the literal and figurative, the univocal and analogical. Anthropomorphic language is consistent with the biblical doctrine that man is created in the divine image. More important, it is myth-thinking and it is how the mind of the deaf works when it tries to apprehend and describe the being and character of God. Myth-thinking, then, is a legitimate form of the religious thinking of the deaf.

Myth can be effective as a communicative preliminary to presenting a Christ who is much more than a man only and thereby purify some of the grosser anthropomorphisms. One may begin, for instance, by going back to the origin of the hero who, far from being associated with detached fantasy, really lies unformulated in the depths of the unconscious.[46] This being true, consider a presentation of Gilgamesh, Mithras or other primordial heroes: it becomes an appeal to all that is best in the human figure and latent in human longings. Whatever the feats of the hero, they approach divinity and can transport the deaf through the barriers that separate them from God and mystery. The route of rationalistic theology toward the same goal, at least as far as the deaf are concerned, is more devious and may still leave the deaf describing God as "nothing." Employing the principle of teaching the deaf by comparison and contrast, one may then compare Jesus to these hero figures and demonstrate how he surpasses them and therefore must be more than an historical man, a Julius Caesar. Such an approach reaches for specific images embedded in the mind, images that are universal and soul-gripping and psychologically relative to what Jesus did and does. Thus can the deaf contact a contemporary Jesus and experience an irresistible attraction that comes from the feeling of being part of him, especially through prayer and the sacraments.

Two questions now present themselves: (1) Besides clarifying the person and work of Christ, how can myth, as a pre-theological and pedagogical technique, provide a matrix for more accurate deaf insights into Christianity? (2) How much of the Old and New Testament is myth in the sense that Bultmann has used the word?

1. Religious faith revolves around those central and perennially important ideas which alone give life a meaning and inner strength.[47] Jung claims that these dominant ideas are already embedded in the unconscious.[48] Myth can draw them out into the open, so to speak, out into the conscious area of the mind where they can be identified and ventilated and thereby elevate the concrete mind of the deaf adolescent to more profound spiritual realms.

As an illustration, consider the concrete theme of the tree both as a pedagogical preface to the crucifixion of Christ and as a symbol of mother and rebirth. From remotest times, trees have had a religious significance, as we have already seen in Question 12a. Famous among these were the tree of life and the tree of paradise. The hanging of Attis (in effigy) on a pine tree and a whole series of hanged gods in Germanic hanging sacrifices[49] can effectively prepare the mind of the deaf to more clearly understand the hanging of Christ on the cross. The cross is at once a tree of life and a tree of death—a coffin. "Just as the myths tell us that human beings were descended from trees, so there were burial customs in which people were buried in hollow tree trunks, whence the German 'Totenbaum,' 'tree of death,' for coffin, which is still in use today."[50] If we remember that the tree is predominantly a mother symbol, then the meaning of this mode of burial becomes clear: the dead are delivered back to the mother for rebirth.[51]

For a second illustration, consider the dominant idea of rebirth. The New Testament conversation between Jesus and Nicodemus (Jn. 3:4ff.) might as well be a conversation between Jesus and a deaf person. From the cast of Nicodemus' mind, one could easily imagine him as deaf. Jesus' statement that no one can enter God's kingdom without being born again of water and the Spirit would be as incomprehensible to the deaf as it was to Nicodemus.

But here again, the mythological meaning of water and spirit can serve as a matrix. It is basic to myth that water has a maternal significance since life comes from water, and therefore to be born of water means to be born of the mother's womb. Pedagogically, birth by the spirit can follow the Egyptian myth of the vultures: they were female only and the wind fertilized them.[52] Accordingly, to be born of the spirit means to be born of the fructifying breath of the wind.

On the concrete level, a bewildered Nicodemus knows that he cannot impregnate his mother and cause himself to be born again, but Jesus insists that Nicodemus elevate himself by allowing himself to be impregnated in some extraordinary way by a spiritual being.[53] It is noteworthy that Jesus found Nicodemus' crudity unacceptable. Tactfully, patiently —almost as though Nicodemus had expressed no crudity at all—Jesus went over the entire explanation again, underlining for Nicodemus the importance of learning to think symbolically.

Carl Jung has an observation pertinent to the Nicodemus episode: "The reason why Jesus' words have such great suggestive power is that they express the symbolic truths which are rooted in the very structure of the human psyche."[54] Stressed by Jesus himself, the myth of water enables the deaf adolescent to replace water with the mother and spirit with the father and raises him to a new level of birth into the larger family of brothers and sisters with God as his Father.

2. We now turn to the second question regarding the amount of myth (as the word is used by Bultmann) in the Old and New Testaments. The question is large and complex even for the Scripture scholar, and we can here do no more than give a superficial overview as it fits our purposes.[55] Again, we are talking about myth as a narration of a primordial event as recounted in cult. Although the narrative imagery originates in the imagination, the intention is not to tell baseless fantasy but to recount what really happened in story form. The myth-maker, then, struggles mightily to describe a real contact with God or a real divine action. In this sense, the creation account of Genesis 1, the fall of man, the exodus, and the eschatologically narrated "last things" are among those events which may be interpreted as myth.

Since the publication of Rudolph Bultmann's famous essay in 1941,[56] controversy has raged around the term "demythologize." This, Bultmann says, is simply a hermeneutical way of interpreting the truth behind the myth. The New Testament message of salvation, for instance, is clothed in mythological images. Bultmann, in his "demythologizing," seeks to remove the clothing and interpret these images in straight and objective language according to their proper sense. This is necessary because the mythological clothing of the New Testament period is out of step with modern fashions, and therefore modern man may be inclined to reject the message itself. What modern physics, for example, has taught man about the universe makes his acceptance of New Testament cosmology impossible. As far as the deaf are concerned, it seems that "demythologizing" is desirable to the extent that it can discard archaic and unnecessary elements which would interfere with the message of the myth. The implication is that "demythologizing" can existentially interpret myth.

Even in a scientific age myth will be retained if Jung is correct in saying that it is an inherent part of the psyche. That the deaf have preserved it is evident throughout this study. It follows that the most prudent course of action is to accept what the deaf give us and use this mode of discourse to deliver to them a wide range of religious thought.

35
Symbol

We have just concluded a brief discussion of myth as a pre-theological language and as a form of thought communicating effectively to the deaf. But one cannot speak of myth without speaking of symbol, for symbol pursues the interpretation of myth. Like "myth," the word "symbol" is much maligned and misunderstood. In this work, the word "symbol" does not mean "that which is empty of any real content,"[57] e.g., the Eucharist as a mere reminder of Christ's real presence. Insofar as the symbol—especially what was earlier referred to as an intrinsic symbol—is a wordless message carrier conveying information about the spiritual, it is most valuable for the deaf. Ancient man, with whom the deaf have often made contact in this study, failed to distinguish between the symbol itself and that which it symbolized. It seems that the deaf similarly look upon the symbol.

Lest some misunderstanding arise, it should be stated from the outset that we are not speaking primarily of symbols used as metaphor or analogy, for these would only confuse the deaf. We communicate little in telling a deaf adolescent that Jesus is a door or a vine or the light of the world. In the latter example, the deaf person would immediately think of physical illumination and would, without prior preparation, fail to transfer these properties to the person of Christ. The concept "light," in this context, is proxy for another concept which is nameless and therefore forces "light" to work harder as it takes on a wider meaning.[58] In this expression, "light" intervenes to symbolize the brightness of Jesus' teaching and life. By now it is obvious that the literalism we have encountered forbids the easy use of this kind of symbol with deaf adolescents.

The symbol that tells us something about what it symbolizes is the kind most appropriate for the deaf. It has, as we described earlier, a built-in relationship with what is symbolized and therefore communicates with its own power, without or with minimal support from words. Consequently, it is unnecessary to get behind the intrinsic symbol to understand it. The symbol itself suffices. Among the intrinsic symbols that can easily become intelligible and valuable to the deaf are blood, bones, smoke, fire, bread, wine, water, seashells, trees, wind, tying and binding, height, light, darkness, and time.

Consider blood. Despite their scant Scripture knowledge, some deaf attributed expiatory power to blood, nearly repeating the words of Leviticus 17:11: "Since the life of a living body is in its blood, I have made you put it on the altar, so that atonement may thereby be made for your own lives, because it is the blood, as the seat of life, that makes atonement." And the blood of Christ constantly cleanses us from our sins (1

Jn. 1:17). The original meaning was that the blood holds the secret of life and is itself life. It belongs to Yahweh, the originator of life, and that is why it is given back to him. Beginning with its role in Old Testament ritual, the symbol of blood can work its way toward the crucifixion and the Mass.

Consider bones. Among nomadic shepherds and hunters of central and northern Asia, a widespread custom prescribes that not one bone of animals sacrificed in cult shall be broken, and this originates from the idea that bones are considered a support for the soul.[59] Modern Arabs likewise refrain from breaking the bones of the sacrificed victim and thereby assure not only the victim's survival or rebirth but their own.[60] Certain biblical passages designate the bones as an essential part of man and "the seat of his principle of life."[61]

Consider smoke. The Greek derivative of the English verb "to sacrifice" or "to slaughter" also houses the meaning of "blazing" or "flaring up."[62] This refers to the sacrificial fires which consumed the gifts offered to the gods. The primitive idea was that the food offering nourished the gods and the smoke carried the food up to their heavenly abode. Later, the food was regarded as a spiritualized food offering.[63] In Old Testament holocausts the entire victim was burned and its smoke ascended to Yahweh.[64] Just as smoke carried the offering to Yahweh, so now holy smoke, or incense, raises the prayers of the deaf to God. Related to the idea of smoke as ascending is the more common concept of smoke as shrouding the actual presence (i.e., the glory or external manifestation of this holiness) of Yahweh in the temple (Is. 6:4; 1 Kgs. 8:10-13).

Consider light and darkness.[65] From antiquity men have welcomed light and shunned darkness, and modern technology testifies that this is still true, as it puts the electric light to work to eliminate as much darkness as possible. Acting this way has always been natural to man, a fact which becomes obvious when we analyze what light and darkness can do. Light, for instance, reveals, dusk highlights, and darkness conceals. Light brings reassurance, dusk brings insecurity, and darkness brings fear. Light means certitude, dusk means doubt, and darkness means ignorance. Light is associated with good and darkness with evil. During the day good men pursue their business with honesty and openness and they do not mind being seen, but during the night evil men pursue their business with stealth and they resent being seen.[66] Thus does modern English slang rightly coin the term "underworld" for evil activity. Ancient religions, therefore, naturally connected their gods with light and demons with darkness, a connection which carries over into the Old and New Testaments and culminates in the first letter of John: "God is light; in him there is no darkness" (1 Jn. 1:5). While it is true that "God is light" is a metaphor, it is also true that with some preparation the concepts of goodness, true knowledge, reassurance, wonder and openness all coalesce in the imagination as a simple unity and bring us close to a literal statement.

As a final example of the intrinsic symbol, consider binding and tying. Knots, strings, cords, nets and ties have always assimilated themselves into religion, although they have also entangled themselves in superstition, an undesirable area which one does well to avoid with deaf and hearing alike. For example, knots and bonds defended against disease, witchcraft, demons and death.[67] But we also meet nets in the Old Testament, where their usage is acceptable. Job, for instance, says: "Know then that God has dealt unfairly with me and compassed me round with his net" (Jb. 19:6). Furthermore, the early Christian spoke of God as the "master of the bonds."[68] All of this, of course, is a concrete base upon which to build a firm and specific concept of the deaf person's relationship with God.

The instrument of communication used in the above examples is not so much the theological concept as the symbol which, if it is not already intrinsic, can quickly become so with easy and concrete pedagogy. The more important point is that even after the deaf clearly understand these symbols there is something more to be done: the symbols are not to be left floundering in isolation but are to be drawn together and weaved into a matrix out of which can develop a clearer comprehension of the person and activity of God. Height, for instance, fits in with the deaf adolescents' conception of the sky-god and can arouse a sense of awe at God's majesty which is raised far above the mundane.[69] Height can also be used in conjunction with the enthronement psalms to bring out the exaltation of Jesus at the right hand of the Father. Tying and binding introduces the deaf to the God who "spreads my net over him, and he shall be taken into my share. I will bring him to Babylon" (Ez. 12:13). Of still greater significance, tying and binding leads to the God who binds with a covenant.

Another value of these and other intrinsic symbols is that they are transformers that can accelerate the deaf to the circuit of their relationship with God through the sacraments. We are already at the roots of the sacramental principle, for instance, when the intrinsic symbols— water, oil, bread, wine—are put to work in washing, rubbing, eating and drinking. To wash away dirt is familiar to everyone, and it is a short step from here to washing away sins, although, linguistically, we still have only partially evaded the metaphor. But if the soul is conceived of as a white, ethereal entity—a concept which some deaf used in this study —then it becomes easier to imagine sin as making it "dirty." In this way It becomes less figurative to imagine water as cleansing the soul. Similarly, if one starts with the Egyptian custom of leaving bread at a tomb with the understanding that it sustains the life of the spirit of the deceased, it is only a short pedagogical step from here to the eating of "holy bread" to gain eternal life. All of this is evocative and specific: it communicates in a form of thought and religious language comprehensible to the deaf by reducing dominant religious thought to concrete common denominators which fit the human condition of deafness.

Besides, it all rests on the theological principle that not only humanity but also lower creation shares in the redemption of Christ and that the chemical elements—the material "stuff" of this world—have already begun to participate in the new creation (Rom. 8:19-21). At the ascension, Christ departed in the sense that we can no longer see and touch his physical body. Yet his departure puts no distance between him and us, since he decrees that we are now to see and touch him in the material elements. When the risen Jesus commanded an excited Mary Magdalene not to touch him (Jn. 20:17), he was telling her that he had inaugurated a new way of contacting him: the old order of sight and touch had given way to the new order of faith and sacrament.[70]

Our study began with no hypotheses to justify, but with the intention to discover what the deaf adolescent thinks about his God and to discuss the theological meaning of his thoughts. The honesty and openness of the deaf adolescents and the control group made possible the valid and scientific achievement of our objectives. As we moved into the conclusion, it was decided to forge ahead to explore the meaning of the responses as a whole. Thus did we arrive into the simplicity of earliest Christianity, intrinsic symbol, and myth, but we could do no more than superficially survey these. The affinity of the deaf with the Hebrews and other ancients and the linguistic deficiency and literalism of the deaf combine to urge a further investigation into the use of the mythopoeic and symbolic form of thought, along with a simplicity of language structure to bring the deaf closer to God. If these are indeed interpretative keys opening the minds of the deaf to God, then this conclusion may well become an introduction calling for that research which would strengthen the spiritual lives of the deaf.

36
Specific Recommendations

Belief in God

(a) To offset the effects of positivism, the deaf should be introduced into the realm of mystery. Using not the concept but the image as instruments of communication, the teacher confronts the deaf youth with epiphanies and theophanies, events which allow the mind of the deaf to wonder *at*, not wonder *why* or *how*.

(b) Maximum appeal should be made to the sense of sight, especially through non-abstract religious art, photography of holy sites and of recent saints, and visual evidence of unusual but authentic phenomena such as the Shroud of Turin.

(c) Teachers can ill afford to by-pass the personal act of faith as they probe to locate the position of the deaf adolescent as he travels from unbelief (or conventional belief) toward belief. Having discovered the adolescent's lack of personal faith, the teacher reverts to evangelization.

Teachers sometimes talk to deaf (or hearing) teenagers as if they already possessed personal faith, whereas they may not. Faith-communication directed at someone without faith makes little sense even if it is conceptually understood.

Christology

(a) Throughout this study, one notices tensions that come from attempts to relate the deaf to a post-Pauline Chalcedonian Christ. Rather than teach them ideas which grew out of later conflict, it would be more effective pedagogically to bring the deaf youth back to earliest New Testament Christology and then guide them along the route of the early Church as it developed its thinking on the person of Christ.

(b) Creative ways should be generated to assist the deaf to know God in the humanity of Christ, according to the procedure of John's Gospel.

(c) Once an understanding of the person of Christ has been attained, resourceful ways should be found to relate his person to his work, but this relationship should not permit soteriology to swallow up Christology.

(d) Some theologians charge that much of the Church's contemporary preaching and teaching (directed to the hearing population) has so sharply focused on the divinity of Christ that his humanity has become badly blurred. The resulting hollowness or unreality of Jesus' manhood makes him irrelevant to us. When, for instance, Jesus wept over Jerusalem, he shed crocodile tears since he foresaw what would happen. Hence, for hearing people the contemporary task is to refocus the humanity of Jesus.

But for the deaf there is far less likelihood of the appearance of such distortions, since the deaf readily understand and accept the humanity of Jesus without attaching unreal appendages to it. One realistic portrait of a masculine Jesus, for instance, sufficiently carries to the deaf the reality of Jesus' manhood.

The challenge with some of the deaf seems to lie in the opposite direction if we attempt to pin their faith on Jesus alone without reference to the triune God. Under these conditions, which presume acute difficulty in teaching the Father and Holy Spirit to some deaf youngsters (especially the low verbal deaf), the individual's faith would have to rest on Christ alone—on his divinity, not his humanity, even though humanity serves the valuable functions of revealing divinity and modeling.

Therefore it is recommended that, for this kind of deaf person, creative ways be found to communicate the divinity of Jesus, his uniqueness, his stature as someone of cosmic significance, and his ability to lift the deaf above the transitoriness of everyday life, answer their prayers, and fulfill their destiny.

Experimentation Leading to Catechetical Books

To provide opportunities to receive feedback from deaf adolescents, it is suggested that a small number of experimental centers be provisionally established in various parts of the United States. Staffed by a catechist competent in the use of total communication, these centers would present teaching which relies upon the suggestions and findings of this study—the intrinsic symbol, myth, Hebrew religious language, and earliest Christianity. Where possible, the teacher would begin with pre-Christian practices (e.g., god-eating among the Aztecs) and work toward the Christian truth (e.g., the Eucharist).

Having completed such a presentation, the catechist would carefully record the reactions, the conceptual understanding and the attitudes of the adolescents. All of this would then be correlated and used to plan, invent, combine and advance religious ideas fitted to the human condition of deafness, ideas for a series of catechetical books, or materials designed specifically for the deaf.

Furthermore, to overcome the weaknesses of once-a-week religion, materials which require no explanation from a teacher should be placed in the hands of the deaf for their perusal during free time. Such material may follow the comic book format or a format employing a sequence of drawings to carry the message with minimum support from words. Pictures in a sequence may flow into one another so that the flow itself carries the movement of the story.

(a) Consider the value of grooming witnesses (or models) from the "leading crowd" in school society and thus using the power of the "leading crowd" and of the peer group to the maximum.

(b) Consider the importance of male influence, especially for boys.

(c) Perhaps Christianity can be put to work systematically within the school by:

- directing the adolescents to perform specific acts of charity and tying this to the life of Christ.
- having the adolescents extend their sympathy (and possibly almsgiving) to a family in distress.
- asking them to give a hearty welcome to new pupils, often homesick and uneasy in their new surroundings.
- attaching a Christian meaning to activities uppermost in the mind of any student, activities such as the school prom, athletic contests, and graduation.

(d) Middle schoolers (approximate age 9—14) aspire to membership in upper school (approximate age 15—19) society. Therefore upper schoolers, whom the younger children closely observe and imitate, are potent models for the younger ones and should be encouraged to involve themselves with and perform organized patterns of Christian activity for the younger group. Besides inducing Christian performance, the older peer model (or witness) assists in blunting the notion that religion is something to be outgrown and left behind with childhood.

Relationship with God

(a) Excessive anthropomorphism transforms the God of the deaf into someone much like ourselves, even though he may be positioned in the sky. Therefore it is recommended that deaf youth often be reminded of God's uniqueness in what he knows (omniscience), how he loves (providence for both the community and individual), what he can do (omnipotence), and what he deserves (adoration).

(b) To offset over-emphasis on divine transcendence (remoteness), it is suggested that a special effort be made to bring the Blessed Virgin, saints, and angels into the lives of deaf teenagers—including patron saints and guardian angels who direct their attention to the individual, and stigmata saints who are visible Christ-figures. A study should be made of how ancient Mesopotamians and Romans brought deities into their lives, for the Church later adapted this kind of process for its cult of saints.

(c) Due to the language deficiency of deaf youth and to their mechanistic conception of prayer, it is suggested that (1) short, spontaneous (ejaculatory) prayers be emphasized with the deaf, and that (2) the deaf be taught to talk to God as they would to their deaf friends, i.e., God understands prayer devoid of English syntax: Ameslan phantasms in the imagination reach God without the accompaniment or addition of subvocal speech.

(d) To divest the deaf of a spirit of self-sufficiency and to help them understand that gratitude to God is the whole point of human existence, it is recommended that a thorough presentation of creatureliness be made.

A few deaf and hearing teenagers remarked that their own interior feelings led them to God. An excellent way to understand that we are creatures is to look first at ourselves and later at the works of nature. We have interior knowledge of ourselves only, and we can analyze and experience our own spirit, but we cannot experience nature, to which we must remain extrinsic. Therefore our experiences of ourselves—our inadequacies, our dependency on others and on nature, our inability to self-generate life on this planet—teach us about our creatureliness and turn us toward another, toward God.

It is a short step from here to the realization that everything is a gift and that we cheapen the gift when we fail to give thanks.

In conjunction with this, creation can be thought of as an on-going process. Alerted to what God is still giving us, the deaf and hearing youth alike are disposed to thank him continuously.

Religious Language

(a) It is suggested that numerous theological concepts, especially those derived from classical theism, be largely avoided and replaced with the intrinsic symbol, concrete biblical imagery, the language of some Hebrew traditions, and the mythological mode of pre-theological discourse—all of which are instruments of communication paving the way for a *creative* religious language.

(b) Since anthropomorphism puts a face on God, teachers should willingly speak anthropomorphically, especially to the "low-verbal" and "average" deaf youth.

Found throughout the Old Testament and often wrongly characterized as "childish" or "primitive," anthropomorphism harmonizes with the expressions of numerous deaf youth. Therefore further study should be done to determine how the right kind of anthropomorphism can best serve the deaf.

(c) Consider the use of mime to teach religious metaphors.

(d) To assist deaf youth with their language deficiency, an illustrated wordbook of religious vocabulary should be devised. It would list and clarify often used but half-understood terms such as grace, sacrament, salvation, sacrifice, covenant, and the like.

By illuminating liturgical terms and the recurring words of the missalette, the wordbook would support those deaf youth who attend only a hearing church and therefore draw their understanding largely from reading.

(e) The latest theology has abandoned dualistic or compartmentalized religious language which had rested on Greek philosophy and which had traditionally divided man into body and soul, mind and heart, or intellect and will, and the like; theology now accepts integrated language which rests on existential philosophy and which reunifies man and sees him only in his totality and unity. At Mass, for instance, church-goers used to say: "Lord, I am not worthy to receive you, but only say the word and *my soul* shall be healed." Now they say: ". . . but only say the word and *I* shall be healed."

One has to ask if dualistic religious language is a clearer instrument of communication for the deaf. This question, it seems, is one that deserves further thought.

(f) Deaf youth can hardly get away from their "ball-and-chain," literalism. Although the myth-symbol-Hebrew language approach may alleviate the problem of literalism, the assumption that it ever lurks nearby is a valid premise for the teacher to work from. It is an important premise, since literalism sometimes appears unexpectedly, as it did, for instance, in various parts of this study.

One should stand ready, therefore, (1) to perform surgery on obliquely used words, phrases, and larger expressions upon which deaf youth may put a literalistic interpretation, and (2) to never assume that deaf youth, on their own initiative, will connect a religious truth (e.g., a parable) with their own life. Both the performance of surgery and the building of bridges that lead straight into the personal life of the deaf remain as components of any effort to communicate religious truth to the deaf.

Soteriology

Rooted in the New Testament, taught by St. Irenaeus, and introduced to the modern generation by Gustaf Aulén in his *Christus Victor*, the classic view of the atonement—it is suggested—suits deaf youth better than alternate views. Briefly, the classic view has Christ victorious over demonic powers. Locked in cosmic battle with demons, Christ culminates the struggle with his victory on the cross, a victory over sin, death, and powers that enslave man, and a victory that logically concludes his entire life of self-giving love.

What makes the classic view apt for the deaf is (1) its dramatic quality, and (2) its existential quality. It is dramatic insofar as Christ, in his kingly office, fights against and conquers evil powers. Such a conflict can be set in a mythological mode of discourse, besides fitting exactly the principle of teaching the deaf by comparison and contrast. It is existential insofar as it demonstrates divine work in the world today to the deaf. To the first Christians, an idol was a demon. An idol, then and now, obliterates the presence of God and enslaves and destroys the man who embraces it. Our own society abounds with idols—preoccupation with materialistic success, fascination with the machine, forms of pseudo-love, compulsion to consume, the credit card as a new sacrament. These idols, some of which can be narrowed to school society, can unmake the personality of the deaf, enslave them, and doom them to lifelong superficiality and separation from God.

From these Christ stands ready to free the deaf and turn them toward himself and their neighbors if the deaf accept the cross and begin a life of self-giving love. From the cross both the deaf and Jesus triumph over their archenemies—separateness, selfishness, superficiality, and the most fearsome of all enemies, death. For the deaf, a lifetime of self-giving love issuing from the cross blooms into permanent life with God, as it did for Jesus.

The psychological processes of love and hate that built up to the crucifixion still operate, and they can be applied to the life of the deaf adolescent. William Golding has captured these processes in his novel *Lord of the Flies* in which he shows what the defects of human nature can do among a group of boys marooned on an island. The boy "Piggy," struggling to manifest the beginnings of selfless caring, is killed because of the rampant and uncorrected hatred patterns of his peers who, like "Piggy" himself, were bereft of adult guidance.

The Sacraments

The teaching of the sacraments to the deaf assumes added significance when it is realized that sacraments make a special appeal to the sense of sight. And the communicative power of sacramental action may more intensely convey a sense of divine presence than would verbal (or signed) communication alone. Therefore creative ways should be found to make the sacraments more clearly understood by the deaf. We now turn to the suggestion of one such way.

Teaching the meaning of sacraments may begin both with pre-Christian ritual and practices and with the work of the intrinsic symbol. Water washing, oil healing, Eucharist unifying—all can be exalted into sacred realms, an exaltation understandable to the mind of the deaf partly because, on the natural level, the meaning is already built into the action. Consider this further.

A daily habit like eating draws partakers together, something that is lost sight of in the speed of a technological society. Closer than the relationship among eaters, however, is the relationship between the eater and the eaten: identification. And when this happens we have arrived at a sacramental principle which skirts philosophy but travels straight to the mind of the deaf. To illustrate: hostile Indians demonstrated a profound sacramental intuition when they excised the heart of St. John De Brebeuf and drank its blood. To these Indians, courage is in the blood. And the saint's courage under their prolonged torture had so amazed the Indians that when he succumbed, they scrambled to drink his blood and thereby partake of his courage.

Accordingly, it is recommended that the two strands of sacramental intuition found in non-Christian thought and the intrinsic symbol put to work both be weaved into the thread of a Christian sacramental theology for the deaf.

May these suggestions, carried through to fulfillment, lead deaf youth to

PRAISE, ADORE, AND LOVE
HIM FOREVER,
AMEN.

Appendix I
The Birth of a Notion

By Michael Mleko
Condensed from *The Gothic*

John J. Stoff, Jr. had an idea. He closed his eyes and imagined his brain lying before him. Then, like Alice, he shrank in size with bewildering rapidity until he was smaller than the smallest of brain cells. He stepped into the vast and intricate mechanism that was his brain.

Before him lay a complicated maze of nerve chutes and passageways, each of which was carefully labeled—"Auditory Department," "Memory Storeroom," "Odors, Inc.," "Ideal Shipping Department," "Humor Control," "Taste Laboratories," "Word Shellac Factory," "Conscience Stamp and Die Shop," "Nerve Conduit Control," and many others of a like nature. John J. decided on the "Sense Communication Exchange" passage. He entered the well-lighted tunnel marked "Sight." He had scarcely gone a few feet when a physico-chemical impulse, composed of electrons and deutrons bearing an image of a long-eared quadruped imprinted on its sensitive surface, shot past him, almost knocking him over with its rush. Ah, thought John J., here is the beginning of an idea. He hastened after it to see how it would be developed.

The tunnel which the impulse had taken led to the "Crossways" where it had been sidetracked into one labeled "Memory Storerooms." He followed the nerve impulse to the storeroom. Here the impulse was shot through a condenser, ejected at an opening, and automatically tabulated and filed in the "A" file of the memory. John J. wondered if that would be the end of that idea. A clicking noise behind caused him to turn around in time to avoid being knocked over by an incoming sound-wave from the "Auditory Department." This impulse sounded exactly like a bray, and it, too, was condensed, tabulated and classified under the "B's" and cross-filed with the "A's." No sooner than both were filed away, a whirring noise resulted and a split second later came a click—and out issued an idea in skeleton form. In the filing and tabulating process the two impulses had taken on all the former impressions stored away in the memory.

John J. had no more time to analyze the idea, because it shot into a nerve tube marked "Special Delivery." Just as it shot away, he managed to grab hold of one of the floating ribs of the skeleton. Away they went up a spiral tube to the third floor, where he and the idea were ejected into a large room labeled "Word Shellac Factory." Here a curious process took place. The skeleton idea was first given a coating of verbs.

John J. watched the proceedings with interest. To make a verb, two separate ones were taken, fractured, and compounded to form a whole by as neat a process of grafting as even a politician could invent. The idea was meanwhile moving slowly on a line much as a car frame in an automobile factory. After one coat of verbs came a sanding-down operation of subjects and objects. These were added to give body to the idea, and lastly came a high polish of adjectives and adverbs. The idea was almost a finished product. It had now to pass the supreme test of the "Word Shellac Factory" before being okayed and allowed to proceed. It was fed into a tester stamped "Fortuitous Concourse of Words Examiner." It passed the test successfully on the first attempt.

Unfortunately, John J. had followed the idea into the tester. He came out stamped "Poor Effort." The ever-developing idea was now put through the categories of space and time and came out possessing regular dimensions. John J. was wiser this time. He did not attempt to go through that process, but contented himself with waiting for the idea, already a very complicated structure of neutrons, electrons, protons, and deutrons, of a physico-chemical nature, which was then side-tracked by an order-bearing impulse from the "Nerve Conduit Control Center" to the small tube on the right. The explanatory-attracto-retractive impulse that followed the order showed that the passageway just ahead was clogged by another idea struggling for existence. Accordingly, John J.'s idea was forced to go through still another process because the nerve tube into which it had been sidetracked led to the "Conscience Stamp and Die Shop." Here the idea was stopped for a second before two huge attractive forces on the magnetic principle. One was marked "Evil" and the other "Good." The struggle of these two forces for the possession of the idea was nip and tuck, but gradually the "Good" principle won out. Irresistibly the idea was drawn to it where two plates were clamped about it, giving it the form of a "Good" idea.

The process of idea formation was now complete. It was shot down a tube at breathtaking speed and ended up in the "Ideal Shipping Department" which for some reason had no carrying charges. Here the idea was carefully packed, labeled, and set aside to be called into being at the order of the Ego (the Boss).

John J. Stoff, Jr. was satisfied. He had seen what no other mortal man had seen—the birth of an idea. Stepping out of his brain, he regained his true proportions as rapidly as he had previously lost them. He then called forth the idea whose formation he had witnessed. It came at once: "I am a long-eared quadruped, braying my head off, a poor effort and a poor excuse of a man, yet I consider myself good." (*Catholic Digest*, May 1937)

Now consider what would happen if John J. were pre-lingually deaf

—if the "Auditory Department" were permanently closed. The idea would develop minus its sound-unit. The long-eared quadruped would become brayless—or brayless as a hearing John J. would understand the term.

But where the "Auditory Department" is closed, the idea detours around it and arrives at the "Analogy Department" which automatically substitutes for the shut down "Auditory Department." On reaching the "Analogy Department" the developing idea is given a new set of instructions: observe the movements of the quadruped's mouth and head and you will understand something of what braying means. Then later, in the "Word Shellac Factory," the idea receives a hand sign: the thumb touching the right side of the forehead with the remaining four fingers drawn together and pointing upward. And farther along, it receives a coat of finger-spelling: d-o-n-k-e-y. Unfortunately, in the "Word Shellac Factory" irrelevant and unnecessary words, especially nouns, often inundate the idea, while relevant and necessary words—especially adverbs, adjectives and pronouns—are withheld or delayed.

Furthermore, staying with a deaf John J., the tunnel marked "Sight" will be dimly lighted when imageless ideas like "prestige" or "tradition" or "equality" pass through. For these, a confused "Analogy Department" will have no orderly set of instructions and will hurry them off to the "Word Shellac Factory," where they will be left to flounder.

The above is, of course, a popular presentation based on philosophical premises. Scholastic philosophy has much to say on concept formation and abstraction, although it communicates with terminology ill-suited to modern man. Interested readers are invited to pursue the following more technical presentation which lies close to the heart of the idea formation.

Suppose someone lacks the external sense of hearing. His apprehension of the external world passing through the internal senses, i.e., the "Sense Communication Exchange" passage which in more technical language is known as the central sense, will sometimes be lacking one dimension, and this must certainly affect the synthesizing process of the central sense and, therefore, the intellect's formation of the concept. Undoubtedly, some concepts will be deficient. The concept "bird," for instance, will be dissociated from chirping, singing, mate calling and the like. The concept "orchestra" will be associated with conductor, musicians, instruments and vibrations, but dissociated from the agreeable, melodious sound we call music. The concepts "tree," "field," "sun" or "moon," on the other hand, will remain perfectly intact in the mind of a deaf person, since it is unnecessary to hear "tree," "field," "sun" or "moon."

We now come to a new plateau—the higher plateau of intellectual knowledge. We know that we have within us a power to know immaterial things and also concrete individual substances in an immaterial way. We call this power of knowing immaterial things and material things in an immaterial way *the intellect*, an inorganic faculty through which things are apprehended insofar as they are immaterial. There are ways of proving that the intellect is a spiritual faculty and not a sense faculty, but these are irrelevant to our purpose here. We are, however, interested in intellectual knowledge—knowledge of the intellect. Intellectual knowledge appears in three phases—ideas (or concepts), judgments and inferences. An "idea" is an intellectual representation of a thing. My idea of a thing is very different from my sense perception of that same thing. For example, as I walk along, I see a man. His skin is white. He is six feet two inches in height with black hair and black eyes. He is slim but muscular, and a slight limp gives him a somewhat halting walk. He wears a cap, a brown suit, a gray topcoat, blue socks and black oxfords. This is a picture of an individual human being as he meets the eye and is perceived as a unit—a composite.

But my idea of man is that he is a bodily, living, sentient, rational substance. In other words, this man is a rational animal. The sense perceives this man in all of his concrete individuality, with all of the particular traits and characteristics which make him to be *this* man and which differentiate him from every other human being. However, my idea of man apprehends him in those essential attributes which he has in common with all other human beings: he is bodily, he is living and he is a rational animal. So this leaves aside all of the individualizing marks (accidentals) which are peculiar to himself. Sense perception, therefore, represents a man in the concrete, whereas the idea of man represents him in the abstract.

A deaf person's sense perception of this man will be deficient. The deaf person, for example, since he cannot hear the man's voice, misses certain aspects of the man's personality. The goodness and kindness or perhaps the bitterness or sadness of the man, which hearing people know from his voice, is not captured or captured only analogously (e.g., observing facial expressions and gestures) by the deaf person. There is no doubt that the deaf person's sense perception of the man, representing him in the concrete, will be, in some instances, defective.

But the deaf person's abstract and universal concept (idea) of man need not be defective. It is just as obvious to the deaf person that man is a bodily, living, sentient and rational animal, although the deaf person may not have the words to express this. Flowing from this, consider a new question: Is there a necessary connection between idea and sense perception? Will the deaf person's idea be derived from his sense perception?

Those experienced with the deaf have remarked how they tend to describe things in terms of singular concrete cases instead of giving general and universal meanings to words. Numerous studies have confirmed this. Those who have observed the art work of deaf children and adolescents have commented on the exactness of detail. This author once drew a picture of a bus. A background item and not intended to be the center of the drawing, the bus lacked a door handle. A deaf adolescent, viewing this drawing, immediately added the door handle. It seems that he failed to see the secondary role of the bus to the picture as a whole.

It has been said, as private judgments based on anecdotal information, that hearing is a bland sense, a stabilizing, neutral sense, giving balance to the other external senses and enabling a deeper penetration of the concept. And it is the key sense enabling the human person to derive the substance of the reality. It has also been said that because the sense of hearing is lacking, the deaf person will tend to place too much emphasis upon the accidentals. In other words, the deaf person, instead of quickly fathoming the substance of man as a rational animal (as bodily, living and sentient), will focus too sharply on the accidentals of the man—that he is white, that he is six feet two inches in height, that he has black hair and black eyes, that he is slim but muscular and that he has a slight limp. He will focus too much attention on the fact that the man is wearing a cap, a brown suit, and a gray topcoat.

Now if some ideas are defectively formed by the intellect of the deaf person, then when he compares ideas, the comparison may be sometimes defective. The intellect, for instance, consciously apprehends and compares the ideas "tree" and "plant" and it finds that they agree. Then it pronounces this agreement in the form of a judgment: "The tree is a plant." But when the intellect compares the ideas "tree" and "animal" and sees that they do not agree, it makes the judgment that "the tree is not an animal." If the intellect's affirmation or denial in the judgment is correctly made, i.e., corresponds to the way the things are in reality, it is a true judgment; but if it is incorrectly made, it is a false judgment. Judgments, therefore, contain truth or error.

But what about those sense perceptions that require hearing? What about those concepts that require hearing—concepts such as singing, shouting, loudness, and softness? If these concepts are incorrectly formed due to a deficient sense perception, the judgments then may be incorrectly formed because the deaf person will have insufficient evidence to make a correct affirmation or denial. The deaf person then will sometimes have difficulty in his judgments about reality as it actually is in itself. So we see that the deaf person may sometimes have difficulty in making judgments which are derived from direct experience through sense perceptions, since, in the case of some concept formations, one sense (hearing) will be lacking. The deaf person, obviously, will have no trouble making the judgment that "the lady walking along the street has a package under her arm" or that "the boy is running" or that "I have a pain in my tooth." The deaf person, however, will have some difficulty making the judgment that "the bird is singing" or that "Joan is a good pianist."

A corollary to the discussion is the question: "Do we derive concepts from words?" One school of thought holds that the human intellect is incapable of attaining any ideas by its own power. This view maintains that without verbal instruction men can have only sense perceptions like the animals, since ideas in the intellect are taught by words.

We can make a criticism of this school of thought. The first ideas we have cannot be due to human speech, for words are arbitrary or conventional signs of concepts. The same sound may mean different things. The same thing may be signified by different words. A word may be intelligible to one person but not to another. Conventional signs have value or signification only if a person already has an idea of the thing and can perceive its relation to the sign. Furthermore, we are aware from experience that we do not know things merely by hearing words. We are aware of seeking words to express ideas, not vice versa. Helen Keller never saw or heard words, yet she could derive ideas from other sense experiences. Consequently, the deaf person can and does possess intellectual ideas.

An idea is necessarily universal and abstract; therefore, it is incorrect to say that a deaf person cannot abstract. There is a principle in Scholastic philosophy that says: "Nothing is in the intellect that was not previously, in some manner, in the senses." Merely because a person is lacking one sense does not mean that he has nothing in his intellect. Sense and intellect, sense perceptions and concepts do exist in a close relationship, even though there is a great difference between them, between sense knowledge and intellectual knowledge. Things in nature are always individual and concrete, and the sense perception of these things depicts them in this concreteness and in this individuality. Thus the percept or image has a content which is singular, individual and concrete. When I see, hear or touch a man, for instance, it will always be a definite man with a specific size, shape, color, age, sex, weight, and so forth; but not so to the intellect. It directly apprehends that which pertains to man as man. This would be just as true of the intellect of a deaf person as of a hearing person.

The intellectually derived sense experience retains in the deaf person only that which all men have in common—that which makes a man to be what he is precisely as a member of the class of men, leaving aside all of the individual characteristics. A deaf person may not have the words "rational, sentient, living, corporeal substance," but this is, indeed, his intellectual perception of man. Intellectual ideas, therefore, by their very nature are not singular, individual and concrete, but universal and abstract. If we are to deny abstraction to a deaf person, we deny the deaf person's possession of ideas, and this, of course, is contrary to all experience.

It has been observed, however, that hearing is a key sense leading the person on the journey from concreteness of his sense perception through symbolization and into abstraction. Therefore, it may be correct to acknowledge that the deaf person has difficulty in abstracting, but not a basic inability to abstract. It seems more correct, however, to say that a lack of hearing may lead a deaf person to place too much emphasis on the accidentals (size, shape, color, etc.) and, perhaps, may signify greater difficulty in perceiving the substance of the thing. The abstractive function of the mind enables the person to penetrate beneath the accidentals to the substance of the thing. This function reveals, as Aristotle said, "what a thing is."

There are three grades of abstraction which must be considered: physical, mathematical and metaphysical. The person's sense perception reveals *this* chestnut tree or *this* pine tree or *that* oak tree. The intellect, however, can strip these trees of their individual sizes, colors, shapes, etc., and penetrate to what all trees are: "woody perennial plants having a single main stem or trunk arising from the soil, their tops consisting of branches and foliage." This is the universal concept or idea of "tree." This is the first grade of abstraction and is sometimes called "physical" abstraction. There is no evidence indicating that a deaf person would have any difficulty in forming the universal idea "tree." There would, of course, be difficulty in physical abstraction where the concept has a hearing dimension and thus would be known only analogously by the deaf person, e.g., lion, dog, orchestra, jet engine, etc.

The second grade of abstraction concerns itself with the magnitude, extension and quantity present in bodies. It is called mathematical abstraction and encompasses the abstract ideas of "point," "line," "square," "plane," etc. The commendable mathematical performance of numerous deaf students is testimony that the deaf do arrive successfully at the second grade of abstraction.

Finally, the highest degree of abstraction considers objects purified of all matter. The knowledge here is of that which is beyond sensible nature, or of being as being. Immaterial qualities such as beauty, goodness, etc., come under this degree. It is precisely in this area that the deaf seem to experience their greatest difficulty. Knowing immaterial things or qualities in an immaterial way—concepts such as justice, prestige, humanity, duty, equality, capitalism, tradition, etc.—is a special challenge for the deaf. These concepts are not initially grasped as a material thing. A study in this area comparing the deaf and the blind— with the hypothesis that the blind have considerably less difficulty comprehending immaterial things in an immaterial way—should be most interesting.

A summary, conclusion, and related observations may be noted as follows:

● It is an over-simplification to say that the deaf person has great difficulty abstracting, since the act of abstraction is an operation belonging to the nature of the intellect.

● It is precisely in the realm of the highest degree of abstraction that the deaf person's difficulty is most acute.

● This difficulty is due to the nature of the handicap and not to extrinsic factors such as retarded vocabulary development, faulty teaching, etc.

● Since ability to abstract in the third degree is a condition for knowing substance, it seems correct to say that the deaf person is too greatly preoccupied with or attached to accidentals.

● The deaf person can learn some concepts by *analogy*. Perhaps more attention should be devoted to this in the educational process.

● Traveling by an entirely different route, we reach one of Vernon's conclusions: There is no relationship between concept formation and level of verbal language development.

● Scholastic philosophy can contribute toward clarifying current ambiguity surrounding the term "abstraction" as found in literature describing the cognitive processes of the deaf.

Appendix II
Language Deficiency

Some of what was already said in Appendix I bears directly upon the question of language deficiency. From the outset it is advantageous to keep in mind that for a deaf child, English is a foreign language. Even after years of unflinching effort, many deaf adults (with normal intelligence) must still grope for the written word, as the following letter from a deaf adult to this writer indicates:

Dear Rev. Anthony:
It was pleasant and cool weather. I am sorry of myself. Because It make me homesick with my ankle pain. but every day I drank some Pill White + Blue from Genral Hospital. I shall go to the hospital on January 9. 1974 and clinic. I do not stay lay on bed in the hospital. Might I am learned change of my age time. I thank you. Very much. God will keep see your teacher in school training tuesday night. Ok alright say me?

Your dear sincely
E.J.

This syntax, of course, diverges widely from the written language of hearing people. Peculiarities like those in E.J.'s letter are characteristic of the deaf and have been coined "deafisms" or "deafy language." Researchers studying these have issued various classifying procedures to pinpoint error types. Some of these are Omitted Words, Wrong Use of Words, Wrong Tense, Excessive Use of Words, Sentence Length, Number of Erroneous Words per Given Number of Words, and so on.

In the conclusion of his unpublished doctoral thesis, *A Linguistic Analysis of the Written Language of the Deaf* (Vol. I), Arthur N. Gunderson, Jr. states the following:

Deafness affected written language in three ways. It depressed certain aspects of language, elevated some, and distorted others; for a few functions, it had no effect. It uniformly depressed pronouns, tense endings and syntactical phenomena, but elevated spelling and punctuation. It distorted the usual ratio of added to omitted words. In handwriting, finally, it had no effect. These observations give a preliminary delineation to the concept of 'deafisms.'

The most influential and consequential language problem found among the deaf was the omission of necessary words. This was followed in importance by the tendency to perseverate on an alinguistic level of mere naming. A third problem of consequence was

the addition of unnecessary words, and together, these three consti-
tuted 84% of the language problem of the deaf.

Continued exposure to language undoubtedly alleviates deficiencies;
yet, as their education nears completion, many deaf adolescents still
wrestle with severe language problems. As a rule of thumb it is said that
the English mastery of most deaf adults is at about the fifth grade level.

Appendix III
SURVEY FORM FOR
THE RELIGION TEACHER*

1. Do you have a full-time occupation or profession with deaf people? (If so, please identify this occupation)_____

2. As a religious worker with the deaf, are you a part-time volunteer or a full-time worker? _____

3. For how many years have you been teaching religion to the deaf?

4. What communication method do you use in religion class? (e.g., strict oral, total communication, etc.)_____

5. How often do you have catechetical instruction? _____
Are your classes held during or after school hours? _____
How long is each class?_____

6. Do you have a liturgy for the deaf? (If so, please briefly describe)

7. Your own preparation for teaching religion is:
C.C.D. certificate _____
College credits in religion_____
Degree in religious education or theology _____
Others_____

8. Is your hearing profoundly impaired, somewhat impaired (i.e., hard of hearing) or normal? _____

SURVEY FORM FOR SCHOOL

Name of School_____
Date _____
1. Name of pupil to be tested _____
2. Date of birth _____
3. Sex _____
4. Number of years at the school _____
5. Names of previous schools attended and length of time at each school _____
_____
_____
_____

6. Cause of deafness _____
7. Age at onset of deafness _____
8. Performance I.Q. _____Name of Test _____
9. Is this pupil in the academic or vocational program? _____
10. School attainments, honors, etc. _____

*This form is to be given only to the religion teachers of the pupils to be interviewed.

11. The official method of communication at the school is: _____
12. This pupil
_____(a) has no obvious emotional maladjustments;
_____(b) has some difficulty getting along with others;
_____(c) has some difficulty getting along with himself.
13. Are the pupil's parents hearing or deaf? _____
Are there any family difficulties—i.e., divorce, etc.?_____
Comment:

_____

_____

Appendix IV
Statistical Charts

Belief In God

			Catholic		Secular		Deaf		Control	
#	Question	Answer	N	%	N	%	N	%	N	%
1a	Is God real?	Yes	25	71	79	75	104		20	
		No			3		5			
		Don't Know			26		20			

NOTE: These totals represent subjects selected *because* of their affirmative answer. Thus, they constitute a selected group which is then studied further.

#	Question	Answer	N	%	N	%	N	%	N	%
1b	How do you know? (Basis of Belief)	**Creation**	**14**	**58.3**	**29**	**41.4**	**43**	**45.7**	**2**	**9.1**
		Revelation	**4**	**16.7**	**13**	**18.6**	**17**	**18.1**	**4**	**18.2**
		Human Authority	**4**	**16.7**	**16**	**22.9**	**20**	**21.3**	**4**	**18.2**
		Natural Reasons & other	2	8.3	12	17.1	14	14.9	12	54.5
1c	What is the source of your belief?**	**Catechist**	**21**	**84.0**	**46**	**74.2**	**67**	**77.0**	**5**	**26.3**
		Parents	**1**	**4.0**	**5**	**8.1**	**6**	**6.9**	**6**	**31.6**
		Bible	**3**	**12.0**	**8**	**12.9**	**11**	**12.6**	**3**	**15.8**
		Other	**0**	**0**	**3**	**4.8**	**3**	**3.4**	**5**	**26.3**
2a	Do you want proof?	**Yes**	**1**	**4.5**	**19**	**29.2**	**20**	**23.0**	**3**	**16.7**
		No	**21**	**95.5**	**24**	**36.9**	**45**	**51.7**	**15**	**83.3**
		Don't Know	**0**	**0**	**22**	**33.8**	**22**	**25.3**	**0**	**0**
2b	Do you want to see God?	Yes	11	45.8	44	63.8	55	59.1	11	61.1
		No	3	12.5	12	17.4	15	16.1	7	38.9
		Other	10	41.7	13	18.8	23	24.7	0	0
3	Who is God?	**Whole Trinity**	**10**	**41.7**	**10**	**12.8**	**20**	**19.6**	**5**	**25.0**
		Part Trinity	**9**	**37.5**	**31**	**39.7**	**40**	**39.2**	**6**	**30.0**
		Part & others	**2**	**8.3**	**20**	**25.6**	**22**	**21.6**	**1**	**5.0**
		Others	**1**	**4.2**	**9**	**11.5**	**10**	**9.8**	**5**	**25.0**
		Don't Know	**2**	**8.3**	**8**	**10.3**	**10**	**9.8**	**3**	**15.0**

*"Catholic" refers to Catholic deaf youth enrolled in the Catholic schools. "Secular" refers to Catholic deaf youth enrolled in secular schools. "Deaf" refers to the statistical totals from the "Catholic" and "Secular" columns. "Control" refers to the group of teenagers with normal hearing.

**Bold type indicates a notable difference between the deaf and control group or between Catholic school deaf and secular school deaf.

#	Question	Answer	Catholic		Secular		Deaf		Control	
			N	%	N	%	N	%	N	%
5	Who is this baby in the picture of the Nativity?	Jesus	25	100	76	96.2	101	97.1	20	100
		Not Jesus	0	0	3	3.8	3	2.9	0	0
5b	If the baby is Jesus, is he God?	Yes	18	72.0	39	51.3	57	56.4	10	52.6
		No	6	24.0	21	27.6	27	26.7	9	47.4
		Don't Know	1	4.0	16	21.1	17	16.8	0	0
6	Whose portrait is this?	Jesus	25	100	77	97.5	102	98.1	20	100
		Not Jesus	0	0	2	2.5	2	1.9	0	0
7a	Whose portrait is this?	Mary	25	100	75	98.7	100	99.0	20	100
		Not Mary	0	0	1	1.3	1	1.0	0	0
7b	Is Mary God?	Yes	1	4.0	15	19.7	16	15.8	0	0
		No	23	92.0	50	65.8	73	72.3	20	100
		Don't Know	1	4.0	11	14.5	12	11.9	0	0
8a	Did the crucifixion happen?	Yes	24	100	74	93.7	98	95.1	20	100
		No	0	0	0	0	0	0	0	0
		Don't Know	0	0	5	6.3	5	4.9	0	0
8b	**What is the reason for your belief about the crucifixion?**	**Literal**	**6**	**24.0**	**52**	**65.8**	**58**	**55.8**	**1**	**5.0**
		Non-Literal	**14**	**56.0**	**16**	**20.3**	**30**	**28.8**	**19**	**95.0**
		Doubtful	**5**	**20.0**	**11**	**13.9**	**16**	**15.4**	**0**	**0**
9a	Did the resurrection happen?	Yes	24	96.0	75	94.9	99	95.2	19	95.0
		No	0	0	0	0	0	0	1	5.0
		Don't Know	1	4.0	4	5.1	5	4.8	0	0
9b	Did Jesus' body rise or only his soul?	Full	22	91.7	53	67.1	75	72.8	14	73.7
		Partial	0	0	19	24.0	19	18.4	3	15.8
		None	0	0	0	0	0	0	1	5.3
		Doubtful	2	8.3	7	8.9	9	8.7	1	5.3
		None & Doubtful	2	8.3	7	8.9	9	8.7	2	10.5
10	Do you believe the Eucharist is Jesus?	Belief	15	62.5	20	28.6	35	37.2	7	35.0
		Non-Belief	5	20.8	37	52.8	42	44.7	11	55.0
		Don't Know	4	16.7	13	18.6	17	18.1	2	10.0

#	Question	Answer	Catholic		Secular		Deaf		Control	
			N	%	N	%	N	%	N	%
11a	Is there life	Yes	24	96.0	76	96.2	100	96.2	16	80.0
	beyond the	No	0	0	0	0	0	0	3	15.0
	grave?	Doubtful	1	4.0	3	3.8	4	3.8	1	5.0
11b	Is heaven real?	Yes	17	68.0	64	81.0	81	77.9	15	75.0
		No	1	4.0	3	3.8	4	3.8	3	15.0
		Doubtful	7	28.0	12	15.2	19	18.3	2	10.0
11c	**Is hell real?**	**Yes**	**14**	**56.0**	**25**	**32.1**	**39**	**37.9**	**15**	**75.0**
		No	**6**	**24.0**	**33**	**42.3**	**39**	**37.9**	**3**	**15.0**
		Doubtful	**5**	**20.0**	**20**	**25.6**	**25**	**24.3**	**2**	**10.0**
11d	**Where is**	**Place**	**21**	**84.0**	**68**	**83.9**	**89**	**84.0**	**3**	**16.7**
	heaven?	**State**	**1**	**4.0**	**5**	**6.2**	**6**	**5.7**	**8**	**44.4**
		Don't Know	**3**	**12.0**	**8**	**9.9**	**11**	**10.4**	**7**	**38.9**
11e	Is God in	Yes	23	92.0	75	94.9	98	94.2	16	94.1
	heaven?	No	1	4.0	2	2.5	3	2.9	0	0
		Don't Know	1	4.0	2	2.5	3	2.9	1	5.9
11f	**What does God**	**Observes**	**20**	**64.5**	**69**	**66.3**	**89**	**65.9**	**6**	**33.3**
	do?*	**Intervenes**	**10**	**32.3**	**32**	**30.8**	**42**	**31.1**	**10**	**55.6**
		Don't Know	**1**	**3.2**	**3**	**2.9**	**4**	**3.0**	**2**	**11.1**
11g	Does God know what is	Yes	22	88.0	60	78.9	82	81.2	17	89.5
	happening on	No	1	4.0	2	2.6	3	3.0	0	0
	earth?	Don't Know	2	8.0	14	18.4	16	15.8	2	10.5
12a	Is the tree	Yes	0	0	0	0	0	0	1	5.3
	God?	No	22	88.0	69	94.5	91	92.9	17	89.5
		Don't Know	3	12.0	4	5.5	7	7.1	1	5.3
12c	Are the	Yes	0	0	4	5.1	4	3.9	2	10.5
	children God?	No	22	88.0	73	93.6	95	92.2	16	84.2
		Don't Know	3	12.0	1	1.3	4	3.9	1	5.3
12d	Is the angel	Yes	0	0	22	28.6	22	21.6	1	5.3
	God?	No	23	92.0	53	68.8	76	74.5	17	89.5
		Don't Know	2	8.0	2	2.6	4	3.9	1	5.3
12e	Is the Blessed	Yes	1	4.0	23	28.7	24	22.9	1	5.3
	Virgin God?	No	24	96.0	55	68.7	79	75.2	18	94.7
		Don't Know	0	0	2	2.5	2	1.9	0	0

*Some subjects answered in more than one category, thus accounting for greater frequencies. Likewise for Question 21i.

#	Question	Answer	Catholic N	Catholic %	Secular N	Secular %	Deaf N	Deaf %	Control N	Control %
12f	Is Jesus God?	Yes	19	76.0	41	52.6	60	58.2	12	63.1
		No	4	16.0	25	32.0	29	28.2	3	15.8
		Don't Know	2	8.0	12	15.4	14	13.6	4	21.1
13a	Is God fantasy?	Yes	0	0	0	0	0	0	3	15.8
		No	25	100	72	94.7	97	96.0	16	84.2
		Don't Know	0	0	4	5.3	4	4.0	0	0
13b	Is God	Yes	0	0	0	0	0	0	3	15.8
	Superman?	No	24	96.0	73	96.1	97	96.0	16	84.2
		Don't Know	1	4.0	3	3.9	4	4.0	0	0
13c	Are God and	Yes	0	0	0	0	0	0	3	15.8
	the Flying Nun	No	25	100	72	94.7	97	96.0	16	84.2
	same?	Don't Know	0	0	4	5.3	4	4.0	0	0
13d	Are God and	Yes	0	0	0	0	0	0	3	15.8
	the bishop the	No	24	96.0	73	96.1	97	96.0	16	84.2
	same?	Don't Know	1	4.0	3	3.9	4	4.0	0	0
13e	Are God, Jesus,	Yes	15	60.0	13	17.1	28	27.7	7	36.8
	and the Host	No	4	16.0	40	52.6	44	43.6	10	52.6
	the same?	Don't Know	6	24.0	23	30.3	29	28.7	2	10.5
14a	How do you	<1	10	40.0	29	37.7	39	38.2	9	45.0
	rank God with	1-5	8	32.0	31	40.2	39	38.2	5	25.0
	those who have	>5	1	4.0	2	2.6	3	2.9	2	10.0
	been wonderful	?	6	24.0	15	19.5	21	20.6	4	20.0
	to you?									
14b	Is God angry	Always	0	0	1	1.3	1	1.0	0	0
	like this man?	Sometimes	12	48.0	33	42.3	45	43.7	9	45.0
		Never	9	36.0	38	48.7	47	45.6	9	45.0
		Don't Know	4	16.0	6	7.7	10	9.7	2	10.0
14c	Does God	Often	0	0	5	6.2	5	4.7	0	0
	punish people?	Sometimes	16	59.3	50	62.5	66	61.7	10	58.8
		Other	7	25.9	9	11.3	16	14.9	2	11.8
		Never	4	14.8	16	20.0	20	18.7	5	29.4
14d	Who told you	Parents	3	15.0	5	9.2	8	10.8	2	
	that God	Teacher	16	80.0	36	66.7	52	70.3	2	
	punishes people?	Other	1	5.0	13	24.1	14	18.9	1	

#	Question	Answer	Catholic N	Catholic %	Secular N	Secular %	Deaf N	Deaf %	Control N	Control %
14e	Are you afraid of God?	Yes	5	20.0	20	27.8	25	25.8	4	20.0
		Sometimes	1	4.0	0	0	1	1.0	6	30.0
		No	16	64.0	48	66.7	64	66.0	9	45.0
		Don't Know	3	12.0	4	5.5	7	7.2	1	5.0
15a	Does God know that 2 + 2 = 4?	Yes	25	100.0	66	83.5	91	87.5	18	94.7
		No	0	0	5	6.3	5	4.8	0	0
		Don't Know	0	0	8	10.1	8	7.7	1	5.3
15b	Does God know more than the teacher?	Yes	22	88.0	59	76.6	81	79.4	18	94.7
		No	2	8.0	16	20.8	18	17.6	0	0
		Don't Know	1	4.0	2	2.6	3	2.9	1	5.3
15c	Does God know more than Nixon?	Yes	23	92.0	62	79.5	85	82.5	17	89.5
		No	0	0	14	17.9	14	13.6	1	5.3
		Don't Know	2	8.0	2	2.6	4	3.9	1	5.3
15d	Does God know more than the baseball player?	Yes	20	80.0	49	63.6	69	67.6	18	94.7
		No	2	8.0	20	26.0	22	21.6	0	0
		Don't Know	3	12.0	8	10.4	11	10.8	1	5.3
15e	Does God know the most?	Yes	22	88.0	55	72.4	77	76.2	18	94.7
		No	1	4.0	13	17.1	14	13.9	0	0
		Don't Know	2	8.0	8	10.5	10	9.9	1	5.3
15f	Does God know you?	Yes	22	88.0	56	70.0	78	74.3	17	89.5
		No	2	8.0	13	16.3	15	14.3	1	5.3
		Don't Know	1	4.0	11	13.7	12	11.4	1	5.3
15g	Does God know your name?	Yes	17	68.0	52	65.0	69	65.7	16	84.2
		No	5	20.0	13	16.3	18	17.1	2	10.5
		Don't Know	3	12.0	15	18.7	18	17.1	1	5.3
15h	Does God know your address?	Yes	16	64.0	42	52.5	58	55.2	16	84.2
		No	6	24.0	20	25.0	26	24.8	2	10.5
		Don't Know	3	12.0	18	22.5	21	20.0	1	5.3
16a	Is God stronger than the boy?	Yes	22	88.0	67	88.2	89	88.1	18	94.7
		No	2	8.0	7	9.2	9	8.9	0	0
		Don't Know	1	4.0	2	2.6	3	3.0	1	5.3
16b	Is God stronger than the weightlifter?	Yes	19	76.0	58	75.3	77	75.5	18	94.7
		No	6	24.0	17	22.1	23	22.5	1	5.3
		Don't Know	0	0	2	2.6	2	2.0	0	0
16c	Is God stronger than a train?	Yes	19	76.0	51	65.4	70	68.0	18	94.7
		No	6	24.0	24	30.8	30	29.1	1	5.3
		Don't Know	0	0	3	3.8	3	2.9	0	0

#	Question	Answer	Catholic		Secular		Deaf		Control	
			N	%	N	%	N	%	N	%
16d	**Is God stronger**	**Yes**	**19**	**76.0**	**48**	**61.5**	**67**	**65.0**	**18**	**94.7**
	than a rocket?	**No**	**5**	**20.0**	**28**	**35.9**	**33**	**32.0**	**1**	**5.3**
		Don't Know	**1**	**4.0**	**2**	**2.6**	**3**	**2.9**	**0**	**0**
16e	Is God stronger	Yes	19	76.0	48	65.8	67	68.4	17	89.5
	than divine	No	5	20.0	23	31.5	28	28.6	2	10.5
	power?	Don't Know	1	4.0	2	2.7	3	3.1	0	0
17a	Can God die?	Yes	2	8.0	13	16.5	15	14.4	0	0
		No	21	84.0	44	55.7	65	62.5	16	80.0
		Don't Know	2	8.0	22	27.8	24	23.1	4	20.0
17b	**Was God born?**	**Yes**	**4**		**2**		**6**	**54.5**	**1**	**6.7**
		No	**4**		**1**		**5**	**45.4**	**14**	**93.3**
18	Do you identify	Row A	7	31.8	32	43.8	39	41.1	5	29.4
	Christ with Row	Row B	11	50.0	33	45.2	44	46.3	12	70.6
	A; B; Both?	Both	4	18.2	8	11.0	12	12.6	0	0
19a	Is God in deep	Yes	13	52.0	40	50.0	53	50.5	13	68.4
	space?	No	8	32.0	30	37.5	38	36.2	4	21.1
		Don't Know	4	16.0	10	12.5	14	13.3	2	10.5
19b	**Is God on the**	**Yes**	**13**	**52.0**	**22**	**28.6**	**35**	**34.3**	**14**	**73.7**
	farm?	**No**	**10**	**40.0**	**47**	**61.0**	**57**	**55.9**	**4**	**21.0**
		Don't Know	**2**	**8.0**	**8**	**10.4**	**10**	**9.8**	**1**	**5.3**
19c	**Is God in the**	**Yes**	**15**	**60.0**	**23**	**24.9**	**38**	**37.3**	**14**	**73.7**
	city?	**No**	**7**	**28.0**	**47**	**61.0**	**54**	**52.9**	**4**	**21.0**
		Don't Know	**3**	**12.0**	**7**	**9.1**	**10**	**9.8**	**1**	**5.3**
19d	**Is God in the**	**Yes**	**14**	**56.0**	**25**	**32.9**	**39**	**38.6**	**14**	**73.7**
	living room?	**No**	**8**	**32.0**	**46**	**60.5**	**54**	**53.5**	**3**	**15.8**
		Don't Know	**3**	**12.0**	**5**	**6.6**	**8**	**7.9**	**2**	**10.5**
19e	**Is God in the**	**Yes**	**9**	**36.0**	**21**	**26.6**	**30**	**28.8**	**15**	**78.9**
	man?	**No**	**12**	**48.0**	**51**	**64.5**	**63**	**60.6**	**2**	**10.5**
		Don't Know	**4**	**16.0**	**7**	**8.9**	**11**	**10.6**	**2**	**10.5**
19f	Is God in the	Yes	20	80.0	59	78.7	79	79.0	14	73.7
	church?	No	4	16.0	14	18.7	18	18.0	3	15.8
		Don't Know	1	4.0	2	2.7	3	3.0	2	10.5
19g	**Is God in all**	**All**	**9**	**60.0**	**41**	**78.8**	**50**	**74.6**	**14**	**100**
	churches or	**Some**	**6**	**40.0**	**11**	**21.2**	**17**	**25.4**	**0**	**0**
	some churches?									

#	Question	Answer	Catholic		Secular		Deaf		Control	
			N	%	N	%	N	%	N	%
19h	Is God in the church at the same time or at different times?	Same	9	69.2	16	33.3	25	41.0	13	92.9
		Different	4	30.8	32	66.7	36	59.0	1	7.1
21a	Is this building the church?	Yes	25	100	79	100	104	100	18	100
		No	0	0	0	0	0	0	0	0
21b	Do you belong to Jesus?	Yes	22	88.0	64	83.1	86	84.3	16	84.2
		No	2	8.0	3	3.9	5	4.9	3	15.8
		Don't Know	1	4.0	10	13.0	11	10.8	0	0
21c	Do you go to church?	Yes	16	64.0	42	53.2	58	55.8	18	94.7
		Sometimes	3	12.0	23	29.1	26	25.0	1	5.3
		No	6	24.0	1	17.7	20	19.2	0	0
21d	Do you go to church each week, etc.?	Weekly	16	61.5	39	50.6	55	53.4	19	95.0
		Monthly	3	11.5	17	22.1	20	19.4	0	0
		Less	3	11.5	12	15.6	15	14.6	1	5.0
		Never	4	15.4	9	11.7	13	12.6	0	0
21e	With whom do you go to church?	Family	11	91.7	29	96.7	40	95.2	15	68.2
		Other	0	0	0	0	0	0	1	4.5
		Alone	1	8.3	1	3.3	2	4.8	6	27.3
21f	Do you go to church for the hearing, deaf or alternately both?	Hearing	8	36.4	39	55.7	47	51.1	20	100
		Deaf	4	18.2	6	8.6	10	10.9	0	0
		Both	10	45.4	25	35.7	35	38.0	0	0
21g	If you attend a church for the deaf, is the church Catholic or non-Catholic?	Catholic	14	100	28	93.3	42	95.5		
		Non-Catholic	0	0	2	6.7	2	4.5		
21h	What does Mass mean to to you?	Clear	3	20.0	1	13.0	4	17.4	5	29.4
		Confused	7	46.7	5	62.0	12	52.2	7	41.2
		None	5	33.3	2	25.0	7	30.4	5	29.4
21i	Why do hearing people go to church?	Listen and learn	5	17.9	21	23.1	26	21.8	3	13.6
		Contrition	2	7.1	11	12.1	13	10.9	0	0
		Petition	8	28.6	24	26.4	32	26.9	3	13.6
		Faith—Love—Worship—	9	32.1	27	29.7	36	30.3	8	36.4
		Other	3	10.7	6	6.6	9	7.6	8	36.4

#	Question	Answer	Catholic N	Catholic %	Secular N	Secular %	Deaf N	Deaf %	Control N	Control %
21j	Does anyone force you to go to church?	Yes	8	36.4	31	44.3	39	42.4	8	42.1
		No	14	63.6	39	55.7	53	57.6	11	57.9
21k	Is church helpful?	Yes	12	54.5	40	55.6	52	55.3	13	65.0
		No	7	31.8	22	30.5	29	30.9	4	20.0
		Don't Know	3	13.6	10	13.9	13	13.8	3	15.0
21l	What do you think about in church?	Relevant	10	47.6	20	ˉ31.3	30	35.3	0	0
		Irrelevant	2	9.5	13	20.3	15	17.6	5	27.8
		Both	9	42.9	31	48.4	40	47.1	13	72.2
21m	Why do people geneflect in church?	Eucharist	2	9.5	1	1.5	3	3.4	2	11.1
		Cross	7	33.3	15	22.1	22	24.7	0	0
		General Presence, etc.,	6	28.6	16	23.5	22	24.7	5	27.8
		Other	5	23.8	12	17.6	17	19.1	7	38.9
		Don't Know	1	4.8	24	35.3	25	28.1	4	22.2
22a	To whom are these people talking?	God	25	100	71	91.0	96	93.2	20	100
		Other	0	0	7	9.0	7	6.8	0	0
22b	Why are the people talking to God?	Petition	15	57.7	20	29.0	35	36.8	2	12.5
		Contrition	1	3.8	12	17.4	13	13.7	1	6.2
		Love	5	19.2	12	17.4	17	17.9	8	50.0
		Other	0	0	0	0	0	0	4	25.0
		Don't Know	5	19.2	25	36.2	30	31.6	1	6.2
22c	Does God know what they are saying?	Yes	23	92.0	72	94.7	95	94.0	20	100
		No	0	0	2	2.6	2	2.0	0	0
		Don't Know	2	8.0	2	2.6	4	4.0	0	0
22d	How does God know?	Hears	9	32.1	48	56.5	57	50.4	5	26.3
		Sees	7	25.0	15	17.6	22	19.5	1	5.3
		Knows All	2	7.1	12	14.1	14	12.4	11	57.9
		Other	6	21.4	3	3.5	9	8.0	1	5.3
		Don't Know	4	14.3	7	8.2	11	9.7	1	5.3
22e	Does God answer them?	Always	1	4.0	4	5.3	5	5.0	11	55.0
		Sometimes and Other	8	32.0	18	23.7	26	25.7	8	40.0
		Never	16	64.0	54	71.0	70	69.3	1	5.0

#	Question	Answer	Catholic		Secular		Deaf		Control	
			N	%	N	%	N	%	N	%
22f	Can God help these people?	Yes	21	95.5	64	87.7	85	89.5	17	85.0
		No	0	0	4	5.5	4	4.2	1	5.0
		Don't Know	1	4.5	5	6.8	6	6.3	2	10.0
21g	Does God answer with his voice?	Yes	6	27.3	11	19.0	17	21.3	0	0
		No	16	72.7	47	81.0	63	78.8	20	100
22h	Does God talk only to the hearing people	Yes	3	12.5	12	17.4	15	16.1	0	0
		No	21	87.5	57	82.6	6	83.9	20	100
22i	How does God talk to the deaf?	Physically	5	20.8	11	15.5	16	16.8	0	0
		Spiritually	9	37.5	22	31.0	31	32.6	13	72.2
		Other	5	20.8	3	4.2	8	8.4	0	0
		Don't Know	5	20.8	35	49.3	40	42.1	5	27.8
23a	What is the boy doing?	Praying	24	96.0	74	100.0	98	99.0	20	100.0
		Other	1	4.0	0	0	1	1.0	0	0
23b	Is he speaking to anyone?	Yes	24	96.0	74	100.0	98	99.0	20	100.0
		No	1	4.0	0	0	1	1.0	0	0
23c	To whom is the boy speaking?	God	24	100.0	74	100.0	98	100.0	19	95.0
		Nobody	0	0	0	0	0	0	1	5.0
23d	Must the boy use his voice?	Yes	5	23.8	28	39.4	33	35.9	0	0
		No	15	71.4	43	60.6	58	63.0	20	100.0
		Don't Know	1	4.8	0	0	1	1.1	0	0
23e	Does God know signs?	Yes	21	84.0	43	58.1	64	64.6	18	90.0
		No	3	12.0	14	18.9	17	17.2	0	0
		Don't Know	1	4.0	17	23.0	18	18.2	2	10.0
23f	Do you ever pray?	Yes	21	84.0	65	86.7	86	86.0	17	85.0
		No	4	16.0	10	13.3	14	14.0	3	15.0
23g	Does God answer you?	Yes	6	25.0	13	15.5	19	17.6	10	71.4
		No	18	75.0	46	54.8	64	59.3	3	21.4
		Don't Know	0	0	25	29.8	25	23.1	1	7.1
24a	Do you have love for your mother and father?	Yes	24	100.0	68	98.6	92	98.9	14	100.0
		Sometimes	0	0	1	1.4	1	1.1	0	0
		No	0	0	0	0	0	0	0	0

#	Question	Answer	Catholic		Secular		Deaf		Control	
			N	%	N	%	N	%	N	%
24b	Do your parents have love for you?	Yes	24	100.0	67	97.1	91	97.8	14	100.0
		Sometimes	0	0	2	2.9	2	2.2	0	0
		No	0	0	0	0	0	0	0	0
24c	Does God love your parents?	Yes	21	87.5	60	84.5	81	85.3	13	100.0
		Sometimes	0	0	5	7.0	5	5.3	0	0
		No	0	0	1	1.4	1	1.1	0	0
		Don't Know	3	12.5	5	7.0	8	8.4	0	0
24d	Do you love your house parents?	Yes	19	79.2	23	40.4	42	51.9	—	—
		Sometimes	5	20.8	17	29.8	22	27.2	—	—
		No	0	0	17	29.8	17	21.0	—	—
25a	Do you have love for the black man?	Yes	14	66.7	38	69.1	52	68.4	13	92.9
		Sometimes	6	28.6	8	14.5	14	18.4	1	7.1
		No	1	4.8	9	16.4	10	13.2	0	0
25b	Does the black man love you?	Yes	6	28.6	26	47.3	32	42.1	5	35.7
		Sometimes	13	61.9	18	32.7	31	40.8	9	64.3
		No	2	9.5	11	20.0	13	17.1	0	0
25c	Does God love the black man	Yes	19	95.0	49	90.7	68	91.9	11	100
		No	1	5.0	5	9.3	6	9.1	0	0
		Sometimes	0	0	0	0	0	0	0	0
26a	Do you forgive the driver?	Yes	22	100	65	100	87	100	—	—
		No	0	0	0	0	0	0	—	—
26b	Do you have love for hearing people?	Yes	13	56.5	44	64.7	57	62.6	—	—
		Sometimes	10	43.5	22	32.4	32	35.2	—	—
		No	0	0	2	2.9	2	2.2	—	—
26c	Does God have love for the hearing strangers?	Yes	21	95.5	66	97.0	87	96.7	—	—
		Sometimes	0	0	1	1.5	1	1.1	—	—
		No	0	0	0	0	0	0	—	—
		Don't Know	1	4.5	1	1.5	2	2.2	—	—
26d	Do the boy and girl love each other?	Yes	23	100	67	98.5	90	98.9	13	100
		No	0	0	1	1.5	1	1.1	0	0
26e	Does God love you like this?	Yes	12	52.2	31	47.7	43	48.9	8	61.5
		Sometimes	1	4.3	2	3.1	3	3.4	0	0
		No	0	0	10	15.4	10	11.4	5	38.5
		Don't Know	10	43.5	22	33.8	32	36.4	0	0

#	Question	Answer	Catholic N	Catholic %	Secular N	Secular %	Deaf N	Deaf %	Control N	Control %
26f	Does God love	Deaf	1	4.0	4	5.4	5	5.1	0	0
	the deaf or	Hearing	0	0	4	5.4	4	4.0	0	0
	hearing people	Equal	24	96.0	66	89.2	90	90.9	11	78.6
	more?	Don't Know	0	0	0	0	0	0	1	7.1
		Doesn't Matter		0	0	0	0	0	0	2	14.3
27a	Would you make	Yes	15	71.4	56	87.5	71	83.5	16	100
	effort to help	No	6	28.6	8	12.5	14	16.5	0	0
	the kitten?									
27b	Would you help	Yes	18	85.7	63	96.9	81	94.2	17	100
	the accident	No	3	14.3	2	3.1	5	5.8	0	0
	victim?									
27c	Would you help	Yes	18		62		80		17	
	help with the	No	2		3		5		0	
	homework?									
27d	Would you stop	Yes	17	81.0	64	98.5	81	94.2	16	94.1
	the fight?	No	4	19.0	1	1.5	5	5.8	1	5.9
27e	Would you help	Yes	18	90.0	65	100	83	97.6	17	100
	the old lady?	No	2	10.0	0	0	2	2.4	0	0

Appendix V
Interview Form

<u>BELIEF IN GOD</u>   Comments

1a. Is God real?
     Yes ____ No ____ Don't know ____   _____

1b. How do you know?
and My Cathechist told me ____   _____
1c. My parents told me ____   _____
     The Bible is proof ____
     The church teaches me ____   _____
     Other ____

2a. (If the person does not believe)
     Do you want proof?
     Yes ____ No ____ Don't know ____

     (If the person does believe)
     Do you have proof?
     Yes ____ No ____ Don't know ____

2b. What proof?
     The Bible ____
     Tangible evidence (e.g. -
          a photo of Jesus) ____   What proof?
     Contemporary miracles ____
     Other ____   _____

2c. Do you want to see God, touch God
          or meet God?   _____
     Yes ____ No ____ Don't know ____   _____

3.   Who is God?
     Jesus alone ____   _____
     Jesus and the Father ____
     Jesus, Father, Spirit ____   _____
     Nobody ____

4.   Please draw a picture of God.[1]   _____

[1]Question 4 was asked only in the pre-testing.

INTERVIEW FORM

2

BELIEF IN GOD

Comments

5. NATIVITY SCENE (identify the picture)

5a. Who is this baby?   Jesus ___
                         Not Jesus ___

5b. If Jesus, is this God?
    Yes ___ No ___ Don't know ___

6. JESUS PORTRAIT

   Who is this?   Jesus ___
                   Not Jesus ___
                   If not Jesus, who? ___

7. DRAWING OF THE BLESSED VIRGIN MARY

7a. Who is this?
    Mary ___
    If not Mary, who? ___

7b. Mary-God-same?
    Yes ___ No ___ Don't know ___

8. CRUCIFIXION

8a. Did this really happen?
    Yes ___ No ___ Don't know ___

8b. Why did Jesus die? ___

Whose fault is this? Anyone else? ___

Did Jesus die to forgive sins? ___

INTERVIEW FORM

BELIEF IN GOD

Comments

9. THE RESURRECTION (identify picture)

9a. Did this really happen?
    Yes _____ No _____ Don't know _____
9b. Did Jesus' Body rise or only His Soul?

10. THE HOST

    What is this? Bread _____
                   Holy Bread _____
                   Jesus _____
                   Other _____

    In church, can the priest say words to
    change the bread? Yes _____ No _____

11. THE GRAVE

    Is this the end? Yes _____ No _____
    If no, what happens?

11a. Is there more life? Yes _____ No _____
11b. Is heaven real? Yes _____ No _____
11c. Is hell real? Yes _____ No _____
11d. Where is heaven?

11e. Is God in heaven? Yes _____ No _____
11f. What does God do in heaven?

11g. Does God know what is happening on earth?
     Yes _____ No _____

INTERVIEW FORM

GOD'S NATURE AND ATTRIBUTES

IDENTIFYING GOD

	Yes	No	Don't Know	Not Sure	Comments

12.

12a. The tree is God
12b. The city is God
12c. The children are God
12d. The angel is God
12e. The Blessed Virgin is God
12f. Jesus is God

GOD: REAL OR FANTASY

	Yes	No	Don't Know	Not Sure

13.

13a. God-fantasy characters-same
13b. God-superman-same
13c. God-flying nun-same
13d. God-bishop-same
13e. God-Jesus-Host-same

QUALITIES OF GOD'S CHARACTER

14a. List the persons who have been most wonderful to you.

What number would you give God?

14b. God is angry like this man   Why?
Always ___
Sometimes ___
Never ___

14c. Does God punish people?
Often ___
Sometimes ___
Never ___

INTERVIEW FORM

QUALITIES OF GOD'S CHARACTER

Comments

14d. Who told you that God punishes people?

Parents _____
Teacher _____
Other _____

14e. Are you afraid of God?

GOD'S OMNISCIENCE

15. Does God know more than ----?

	Yes	No	Don't Know	Not Sure
15a. $2 + 2 = 4$				
15b. Teacher				
15c. President Nixon				
15d. Baseball				
15e. The Most				
15f. Does God know you?				

15g. Does God know your name?

15h. Does God know your address?

GOD'S OMNIPOTENCE

16. Is God stronger than ----?

	Yes	No	Don't Know	Not Sure
16a. Boy				
16b. Weightlifter				
16c. Train				
16d. Rocket				
16e. Divine power				

INTERVIEW FORM

GOD'S ETERNITY

17. Phrasing the question:
     Old man dead in 2 years.
     Will God die in 2 years?
     Will God die in 20 years?
     40 years?
     Abbreviated form:
     Can God die?

	Yes	No	Don't Know	Not Sure	Comments
17a. | | | | | |
Old man (2 years) | | | | | |
Middle age man (20 years) | | | | | |
Young lady (40 years) | | | | | |
Boy (60 years) | | | | | |
God will live always | | | | | |
Infant (80 years) | | | | | |
God will still be living after the lifetime of the infant. | | | | | |

17b. How old is Jesus? _____

Was God born? _____

GOD'S LIVING PRESENCE

18. Christ is with Row A only _____
     Christ is with Row B only _____
     Christ is with both _____

INTERVIEW FORM

GOD'S OMNIPRESENCE

19.

	Is God in deep space ----?			
	Yes	No	Don't Know	Not Sure
19a. Deep space				
19b. Farm				
19c. City				
19d. Living Room				
19e. In-Dwelling				
19f. Church				
19g. Is God in all churches or some churches?				
19h. Is God in the churches at the same time – or at different times?				

(Q. 20 is omitted, although the accompanying drawings are retained in the Introduction.)

RELATIONSHIP WITH GOD: GROUP AND INDIVIDUAL

21a. Is this building the church?
Yes ___ No ___ Don't know ___

21b. Do you belong to Jesus?
Yes ___ No ___ Don't know ___

21c. Do you go to church?
Yes ___ No ___ Don't know ___

21d. Do you go to church each week?
Yes ___ No ___
If not, how often? ___

21e. With whom do you go to church?

Comments

INTERVIEW FORM

THE CHURCH

		Comments
21f.	Do you go to a church for hearing people or deaf people or both?	
21g.	If you attend a church for the deaf, is this church Catholic or non-Catholic?	
21h.	What does Mass mean to you?	
21i.	Why do hearing people go to church?	
21j.	Does anyone force you to go to church? Yes ___ No ___	
21k.	Does going to church help you? Yes ___ No ___	
21l.	What do you think about in church?	
21m.	Why do people genuflect in church?	

PRAYER

22.	Group Prayer	
22a.	To whom are these people talking? God ___ Other ___	
22b.	Why?	
22c.	Does God know what they are saying? Yes ___ No ___	
22d.	If yes, how does God know?	
22e.	Does God answer them? Always ___ Sometimes ___ Never ___	

INTERVIEW FORM

PRAYER

Comments

22f.   Can God help these people?
       Yes ____ No ____ Don't know ____

22g.   Does God answer with His voice?
       Yes ____ No ____

22h.   Does God talk only to hearing people?
       Yes ____ No ____

22i.   (If no) How does God talk to the deaf?

23.   Private Prayer

23a.   What is the boy doing?

23b.   Is he speaking to anyone?
       Yes ____ No ____

23c.   To whom? ____

23d.   Must he use his voice?
       Yes ____ No ____

23e.   Does God know sign language?
       Yes ____ No ____

23f.   Do you ever do this?

23g.   Did God answer you?
       Yes ____ No ____
       (If yes, how?)

INTERVIEW FORM

LOVE

	Yes	No	Sometimes	Comments
24.				
24a. Love for mother and father				
24b. Mother and father's love for you				
24c. God's love for mother and father				
24d. Love for house parents				

	Yes	No	Sometimes	Comments
25.				
25a. Love for the black man				
25b. Black man's love for you				
25c. God's love for the black man				

	Yes	No	Sometimes	Comments
26.				
26a. Forgiveness for the driver				
26b. Love for the hearing strangers				
26c. God's love for the hearing strangers				
26d. The boy and girl love for each other				

Overall Degree of Human Love	Overall Degree of Divine Love
Strong	
Mediocre	
Weak	

INTERVIEW FORM

LOVE

Comments

Yes | No | Sometimes

	Deaf	Hearing

26e. Does God love you like this?

26f. Does God love deaf or hearing people more?

Why?

COMPASSION

27a. Effort to help kitten. Yes ___ No ___
27b. Effort to help accident victim. Yes ___ No ___
27c. Effort to help with homework. Yes ___ No ___
27d. Effort to break up fight. Yes ___ No ___
27e. Effort to help old lady. Yes ___ No ___

Overall Degree of Compassion

Strong ____
Mediocre ____
Weak ____
None ____

Appendix VI
Interview Form Drawings

Questions 5, 5a, 5b

Most of the questions on the *Interview Form* were asked with the aid of a drawing. Original drawings were detached (9″ by 15″) and shown individually to each adolescent. In this appendix, however, several drawings are arranged on a single page and they are shown in reduced size. Question numbers which accompany the drawings are taken from the *Interview Form*.

Question 6

Questions 7, 7a, 7b

Questions 8, 8a, 8b

Questions 9, 9a, 9b

Question 10

Questions 11, 11a

Question 12a

Question 12b

Question 12c

Question 12d

Question 12e

Question 12f

Question 13a

Question 13b

Question 13c

Question 13d

Question 13e

Question 14b

Question 15a

Question 15b

Question 15c

Question 15d

Question 16a

Question 16b

Question 16c

Question 16d

Question 16e

Question 17a

Question 17a

Question 17a

Question 17a

Question 17a

Question 18

Question 19a

Question 19b

Question 19c

Question 19d

Question 19e

Question 19f

Question 20a

Question 20b

Question 20c

Question 20d

Question 21a

Question 21b

Questions 22a-c

Questions 23a-d, f

Questions 24a-c

Questions 25a-c

Question 26a

Questions 26a-c

Questions 26d, e

Question 27a

Question 27b

Question 27c

Question 27d

Question 27e

NOTES

CHAPTER I

1. H. P. Owen, *Concepts of Deity* (New York: Herder and Herder, 1971), p. 45.
2. *Ibid.*
3. See Appendix III.
4. "Morphological" here refers to the fundamental design of language construction.
5. Jean Mouroux, *I Believe* (New York: Sheed and Ward, 1959), p. 41.
6. Ben Seligman (ed.), *Molders of Modern Thought* (Chicago: Quadrangle Books, 1970), p. 149.
7. The one exception is St. Mary's in Buffalo where 20 adolescents were interviewed.
8. General Catechetical Directory (Washington D.C.: United States Catholic Conference, 1971), p. 45.
9. Ronald Goldman, *Religious Thinking from Childhood to Adolescence* (New York: The Seabury Press, 1964), p. 87.
10. Oliver E. Graebner, "God-Concepts of Deaf Children." Mimeographed (Valparaiso, Indiana: Valparaiso University, 1964), p. 4.

CHAPTER II

1. The Graebner Child Concept of God instrument approaches our purposes, but some variations, especially in administration procedure, would forbid its comparative use for "concurrent validity."
2. Cf. Quinn McNemar, *Psychological Statistics* (New York: John Wiley and Sons, 1969), pp. 245-275.
3. *Ibid.*, pp. 262-263.

CHAPTER III

1. John Macquarrie, *Principles of Christian Theology* (New York: Charles Scribner's Sons, 1966), p. 246. Also, confer St. Athanasius, *De Incarnatione*, VI, 7.
2. It must be remarked here that deaf people in general do not like to read. Very many of the adolescents interviewed candidly admitted that they never read the Bible. Rather than lack of interest in the Bible, many said the words are too difficult. Douglas 17WISC104V, acknowledging ignorance of the Bible, remarked: "I want to know how people know about God."
3. Paul S. Minear, *Eyes of Faith* (Philadelphia: The Westminster Press, 1946), p. 11.
4. *Timaeus*, 30-31.
5. In their zeal to offset this and convince the deaf of the reality of God, some religion teachers compare God with a ghost. This can make matters worse, as it did for Marie 18WAIS110A: "The priest told me that God is like a ghost. A ghost is not real. A ghost can blow like the wind. It is not true, like a fairy tale."
6. Macquarrie, *Principles of Christian Theology*, p. 139.
7. Anthony Padovano, *American Culture and the Quest for Christ* (New York: Sheed and Ward, 1970), p. 16.

8. Michael Schmaus, *The Essence of Christianity* (Dublin: Scepter Publishers, 1961), p. 34.

9. Pierre Babin, *Faith and the Adolescent* (New York: Herder and Herder, 1965), pp. 26, 36.

10. Paul Ramsey, *Christianity and Society*, Vol. VIII, 1943, p. 31.

11. For a listing of their writings, see the Cited and Consulted Works.

12. Carlos Cirne-Lima, *Personal Faith* (New York: Herder and Herder, 1965), pp. 26-29.

13. Wayne R. Rood, *The Art of Teaching Christianity* (Nashville: Abingdon Press, 1968), p. 21.

14. For a detailed account of how the Gospel content alters the teacher-pupil relationship, confer Rood, *The Art of Teaching Christianity*, pp. 18-26.

15. Joseph A. Jungmann, *Handing on the Faith* (New York: Herder and Herder, 1964), p. 195.

16. Conversion stories are personal and varied. Our explanation, therefore, has the force only of a guideline and is not to be construed as meaning that the experience is standard for everyone.

17. For a more detailed analysis of the personal act of faith, see the scholarly exposition of Cirne-Lima, *Personal Faith* (Herder and Herder, New York, 1965), especially pp. 193-203.

18. This presupposes a correct understanding of God, which is the subject of the forthcoming sections.

19. "Faith, Hope and Bigotry," *Psychology Today*, April 1970, and *Beliefs, Attitudes and Values* (San Francisco: Jossey-Bass, Inc. 1968).

20. Urban T. Holmes, *Young Children and the Eucharist* (New York: The Seabury Press, 1972), p. 36.

21. Earl Nightingale, "On Motivating the Disadvantaged Child," *Vital Speeches of the Day*, Vol. XXXIII, No. 1, October 1966, p. 23.

22. *Ibid.*

23. It is sometimes argued that procedures employed in mission countries are not applicable in the U.S., since we here deal with nominal Christians rather than non-believers. The criticism has merits and they will be elucidated shortly, and yet a nominal Christian stands in as much need of conversion as a non-believer.

24. Alfonso M. Nebreda, *Kerygma in Crisis?* (Chicago: Loyola University Press, 1965), pp. 104-108.

25. *Ibid.*

26. Urie Bronfenbrenner, *Two Worlds of Childhood* (New York: Russell Sage Foundation, 1970), p. 104.

27. Answers to some of these questions can fluctuate. Hence, the catechist can ill afford to be complacent, even though Quigley and Frisina in a recent study (1961) report that their data provide "no evidence that living in residential schools is detrimental to deaf children" in terms of educational achievement and psychosocial adjustment. Quoted by Schlesinger and Meadow in *Sound and Sign* (Berkeley: University of California Press, 1972), p. 120. For further information on the values and behavior of teenagers, see James S. Coleman, *The Adolescent Society* (Glencoe, Ill.: The Free Press, 1961). Also cf. Bronfenbrenner, *Two Worlds of Childhood*, pp. 95-120.

28. For a more detailed discussion of pre-evangelization today, see Nebreda, *Kerygma in Crisis?*, pp. 83-89.

29. Anita Röper, *Anonymous Christianity* (New York: Sheed and Ward, 1966), pp. 1-14, 147.

30. *Ibid.*, p. 12.

31. Before the arrival of printed and electronic media, the herald visited towns to announce the news of the day.

32. "East Asian Study Week on Mission Catechetics," *Lumen Vitae* XVII (1962), p. 725.

33. Jean Mouroux, *I Believe* (New York: Sheed and Ward, 1959), p. 91.

34. A criticism of the Baltimore Catechism is that its incorrect arrangement of material gives a wrong theological perspective: it tells man what he must do before he knows God.

35. In the early Church, only at the completion of catechesis proper was an adult considered ready for baptism.

36. Robert C. Dentan, *The Knowledge of God in Ancient Israel* (New York: The Seabury Press, 1968), p. 136. Also cf. Edmond Jacob, *Theology of the Old Testament* (New York: Harper and Row, 1958), p. 41.

37. Wolfhart Pannenberg, *Jesus—God and Man* (Philadelphia: The Westminster Press, copyright © 1968), p. 31. Used by permission.

38. For a study of this question and Christology in general, the catechist may refer to the landmark work of Wolfhart Pannenberg, *Jesus—God and Man, op. cit.* Also see Jacques Guillet, *The Consciousness of Jesus* (New York: Paulist/Newman Press, 1972).

39. Pannenberg, *Jesus—God and Man*, pp. 158, 159.

40. Cf. Appendix I.

41. William Friend and Eugene Hemrick, *Catholic Education in St. Louis: A Study of Religious Understandings, Attitudes, and Opinions of Catholic Youth in the Archdiocese of St. Louis* (Notre Dame, Indiana: University of Notre Dame Press, 1970), p. 107.

42. See Appendix II.

43. Joachim Jeremias, *The Central Message of the New Testament* (New York: Charles Scribner's Sons, 1965), pp. 36-38.

44. A question concerning Bible reading was asked of many of the deaf, although it was not asked uniformly and brought under statistical analysis. After studying the results, it is the subjective analysis of the investigator that the testees' knowledge of Jesus' life is inadequate.

45. Macquarrie, *Principles of Christian Theology*, p. 287.

46. St. Paul's explanation of spiritual bodies in 1 Corinthians 15:35-58 parallels this discussion.

47. Pannenberg, *Jesus—God and Man*, p. 397.

48. J. Navone, "Remembering and Worship", *Worship*, Vol. 43, No. 9 (November 1969), p. 545.

49. St. Augustine, *On The Trinity*, trans. by Rev. Arthur West Haddan, *Nicene and Post-Nicene Fathers of the Christian Church*, Vol. III (New York: Charles Scribner's Sons, 1900), p. 92.

50. Macquarrie, *Principles of Christian Theology*, p. 123.

51. *Ibid.*

52. When a person's dominant characteristic changed, his name changed along with it—e.g., Abram to Abraham (Gen. 17:5) and Jacob to Israel (Gen. 35:10).

53. Virgilius Ferm, *Forgotten Religions* (New York: The Philosophical Library, 1950), pp. 173-174.

54. St. Augustine, *Confessions*, Book 7, Chap. 10, trans. by Vernon J. Bourke, *The Fathers of the Church*, Vol. 21 (New York: The Fathers of the Church, Inc., 1953), p. 181.

55. Macquarrie, *Principles of Christian Theology*, p. 326.

56. Importantly, numerous deaf insisted upon reading the tombstone inscription, demanding to know the man's name.

57. H. Frankfort *et al.*, *The Intellectual Adventure of Ancient Man* (Chicago: The University of Chicago Press, 1946), p. 69.

58. E. A. Speiser (tr.), "Epic of Gilgamesh," X, iii., vv. 1-5, *Ancient Near East Texts*, J. Pritchard (ed.) (Princeton: Princeton University Press, 1950), p. 90.

59. Frankfort *et al.*, *The Intellectual Adventure of Ancient Man*, pp. 14-15.

60. Note the implications for the Eucharist.

61. Mary fingerspelled the word "spiritual."

62. *Enarr. in Ps 30*, quoted by A. Winklhofer, *The Coming of His Kingdom* (New York: Herder and Herder, 1963), p. 137.

63. Mircea Eliade, *Patterns in Comparative Religion* (New York: The World Publishing Company, 1970), p. 136.

64. Alois Winklhofer, *The Coming of His Kingdom* (New York: Herder and Herder, 1963), p. 81.

65. This is only meant as a pedagogical example. Its basis is God's revealing himself in human love and as specified in the Mosaic and Davidic covenants and perfected by Christ on the cross.

66. For a graphic account of the loneliness of the sinner, consider the plight of the younger son in the parable of the prodigal son (Lk. 15:11-32).

67. Frankfort *et al.*, *The Intellectual Adventure of Ancient Man*, pp. 160-161.

68. H. P. Owen, *Concepts of Deity* (New York: Herder and Herder, 1971), p. 37.

69. Eliade, *Patterns In Comparative Religion*, p. 109.

70. Cf. the *Mekilta de Rabbi Ishmael* (Vol. II), critical edition and translation by Jacob Lauterbach (Philadelphia: The Jewish Publication Society of America, 1933).

71. The Pentateuch.

72. *Mekilta*, pp. 280-281.

73. *Mekilta* (Vol. II), Tractate Bahodesh, p. 228.

74. *Ibid.*

75. *Mekilta*, pp. 275-276.

76. Eliade, *Patterns in Comparative Religion*, pp. 268-269.

77. Frankfort *et al.*, *The Intellectual Adventure of Ancient Man*, pp. 366-367.

78. Macquarrie, *Principles of Christian Theology*, p. 218.

79. Recall that only responses of believers were tested and brought under statistical analysis.

80. Schmaus, *The Essence of Christianity*, p. 18.

81. Joachim Jeremias, *The Central Message of the New Testament* (New York: Charles Scribner's Sons, 1965), p. 16.

82. Dentan, *The Knowledge of God in Ancient Israel*, p. 97.

83. Erich Fromm, *The Art of Loving* (New York: Harper Colophon Books, 1956), p. 8.

84. Fromm, *The Art of Loving*, p. 48; quoted from Simone Weil, *Gravity and Grace* (New York: G. P. Putnam's Sons, 1952), p. 117.

85. Louis F. Hartman, *Encyclopedic Dictionary of the Bible* (New York: McGraw-Hill Book Company, 1963), p. 90.

86. *Ibid.*, p. 766.

87. *New Catholic Encyclopedia*, Vol. IV, p. 196.

88. Denzinger 3001.

89. Macquarrie, *Principles of Christian Theology*, p. 189.

90. The interviews were completed before the onset of the Watergate investigations.

91. Eliade, *Patterns in Comparative Religion*, p. 43. Likewise, Kari and other deities; cf. pp. 46ff.

92. Cf. A. Cressy Morrison, *Man Does Not Stand Alone* (Westwood, New Jersey: Fleming H. Revell Co., 1944).

93. Owen, *Concepts of Deity*, p. 33.

94. Eliade, *Patterns in Comparative Religion*, p. 48.

95. *Ibid.*

96. E. L. Mascall, *Words and Images: A Study in Theological Discourse* (London: Libra Books, 1957), pp. 78-81.

97. Cf. Appendix I.

98. Frankfort *et al.*, *The Intellectual Adventure of Ancient Man*, p. 58.

99. *The New Catholic Encyclopedia*, Vol. 5, p. 563.

100. *The Summa Theologica of St. Thomas Aquinas*, Part I, Q. 10, A. 1.

101. *Second Apology*, 6; cf. W. A. Jurgens, *The Faith of the Early Fathers* (Collegeville, Minn.: The Liturgical Press, 1970), p. 57.

102. H. P. Owen, *Concepts of Deity*, p. 21.

103. *Ibid.*

104. Spirago-Clarke, *The Catechism Explained* (New York: Benziger Bros., 1921), p. 117.

105. Macquarrie, *Principles of Christian Theology*, p. 189.

106. Frankfort *et al.*, *The Intellectual Adventure of Ancient Man*, p. 231.

107. Dentan, *The Knowledge of God in Ancient Israel*, pp. 82, 86.

108. Eliade, *Patterns in Comparative Religion*, pp. 278, 338, 352.

109. Included in the 19% are some who seldom attend church. This accounts for the narrowing to 13% in Question 21d of those who literally *never* go to church.

110. Those pupils who remained at their residential schools on weekends attended

church with peers rather than family. During vacation, however, they did attend with their families.

111. Control group statistics on this question are significant beyond .01.

112. Macquarrie, *Principles of Christian Theology*, p. 348.

113. Henri de Lubac, *The Church: Paradox and Mystery* (Staten Island: Alba House, 1969), p. 16. This symbol was a favorite of ancient Christian writers, especially the Fathers of the Church. Christ, as the sun of justice, is the only source of light, and the Church like the moon, reflects his brilliance to a darkened world.

114. Walter Abbott (ed.), *The Documents of Vatican II* (New York: Herder and Herder, 1966), p. 18.

115. Paul S. Minear, *Eyes of Faith* (Philadelphia: The Westminster Press, 1947), pp. 31ff.

116. Joachim Jeremias, *The Central Message of the New Testament* (New York: Charles Scribner's Sons, 1965), p. 53.

117. Cf. Fromm, *The Art of Loving*, pp. 20ff. and Schmaus, *The Essence of Christianity*, pp. 24-25.

118. Cf. Macquarrie, *Principles of Christian Theology*, pp. 346-349. The eschatological dimension of the Church is obviously compatible with the anthropocentric emphasis of the Vatican II document, *The Constitution of the Church in the Modern World*.

119. Macquarrie, *Principles of Christian Theology*, p. 438.

120. E. L. Mascall, *Words and Images: A Study in Theological Discourse* (London: Libra Books, 1957), pp. 88-94.

121. Question 22g approaches .05 statistical significance.

122. Macquarrie, *Principles of Christian Theology*, p. 437.

123. Christian Duquoc, *The Concrete Christian Life* (New York: Herder and Herder, 1971), p. 48.

124. J. R. Sheets, "Personal and Liturgical Prayer," *Worship*, Volume 47, No. 7 (August-September 1973), pp. 405-416.

125. Recall the earlier mentioned notion of God's visits with Adam, etc. Also cf. Dt. 4:7; Is. 54:10; Jer. 31:31-34; Mt. 18:19; Lk. 24; Jn. 20—21; Acts 2; Rev. 21:3.

126. Cf. Question 22b and note the difference between the Catholic school and secular school deaf. Only 29% of the secular school deaf send up petitionary prayer, which corroborates their earlier weakness in recognizing God's omnipotence.

127. E.g., Question 26f was discussed in conjunction with Question 15.

CHAPTER IV

1. Cf. C. S. Lewis, *Miracles* (New York: The Macmillan Company, 1966), pp. 84, 89.

2. Johannes Weiss, *Earliest Christianity*, Vol. 2 (New York: Harper and Brothers, 1959), p. 697.

3. *Ibid.*, p. 699.

4. Jeremias, *The Central Message of The New Testament*, p. 21.

5. *The Summa Theologica of St. Thomas Aquinas*, Part 1, Q. 14, Art. 13.

6. For an excellent treatment of the symbolism of time, cf. E. Bevan, *Symbolism and Belief* (Port Washington: Kennikat Press, 1968), pp. 82-124.

7. Jeremias, *The Central Message of The New Testament*, p. 49.

8. Reginald H. Fuller, "Scripture Readings: Holy Week to Easter IV," *Worship* 46 (1972), p. 167.

9. Cf. Matthew 11:25ff and Luke 10:21ff and the footnote for Matthew 11:27 in *The New American Bible*.

10. Johannes Weiss, *Earliest Christianity*, Vol. 1 (New York: Harper and Brothers, 1959), p. 122.

11. *Ibid.*, p. 120.

12. Weiss, *Earliest Christianity*, Vol. 1, p. 123.

13. *Ibid.*

14. Pannenberg, *Jesus—God and Man*, p. 33.

15. *Ibid.*, p. 116.

16. In his *Cur Deus Homo*, St. Anselm elaborates a Christological theory of vicarious satisfaction. With minor adaptations, it can heighten deaf appreciation of the contemporary value of Jesus' life and death for them. Another approach sees the crucifixion as Christ's victory over demonic powers. It is elaborated by Gustaf Aulén in his *Christus Victor*.

17. Weiss presents the above summary in greater detail. Cf. his *Earliest Christianity*, Vol. 1, pp. 133-135.

18. Pannenberg, *Jesus—God and Man*, p. 107.

19. A detailed presentation of this is found in Macquarrie, *Principles of Christian Theology*, pp. 316ff.

20. For a closer examination of the primitive view of these ideas, cf. Weiss, *Earliest Christianity*, especially pp. 614-651.

21. Cf. Ronald Goldman, *Religious Thinking from Childhood to Adolescence* (New York: The Seabury Press, 1964); Hans Furth, *Piaget for Teachers* (Englewood Cliffs: Prentice-Hall, 1970); Carl G. Jung, *Symbols of Transformation* (Princeton: Princeton University Press, 1956—cf. p. 23).

22. Carl G. Jung, *Symbols of Transformation* (Princeton: Princeton University Press, 1956), p. 231.

23. *Ibid.*, p. 24.

24. *Ibid.*, p. 29.

25. This writer was recently asked to serve as an interpreter for Alonso, a deaf mental patient at Philadelphia General Hospital. Much of what Alonso signed was mythological material. For instance, Alonso repeatedly interrupted our conversation to look upward and nod affirmatively and affectionately at the god-man-king and the god-boy-king, both of whom comfort him in his hallucinations and shield him from the threats of ever-present monsters.

26. For a popular summary of Piaget's stages of thought, see Ben B. Seligman (ed.), *Molders of Modern Thought* (Chicago: Quadrangle Books), pp. 155-159. For a more technical summary, see Hans G. Furth, *Piaget for Teachers* (Englewood Cliffs: Prentice-Hall, 1970), pp. 30-42.

27. Cf. W. Dupre, "Myth and Reflective Thought," *The New Catholic Encyclopedia*, Vol. 10, p. 190. For further research into this area, see Ernst Cassirer, *Philosophy of Symbolic Forms*, 3 vols. (New York 1953-57), Vol. 2.

28. John Macquarrie, *Principles of Christian Theology*, p. 120.

29. John Knox, *Myth and Truth* (Charlottesville: The University Press of Virginia, 1964), p. 37.

30. *Ibid.*

31. *Ibid.*

32. *Ibid.*, pp. 23-29.

33. "The New Testament and Mythology," in H. W. Bartsch (ed.), *Kerygma and Myth*, trans. by R. H. Fuller (London: Society for the Promotion of Christian Knowledge, 1953), p. 10, footnote 2.

34. Knox, *Myth and Truth*, p. 3.

35. Frankfort *et al.*, *The Intellectual Adventure of Ancient Man*, p. 3.

36. *Ibid.*, p. 7.

37. *Ibid.*

38. *Ibid.*, p. 8.

39. Macquarrie, *Principles of Christian Theology*, p. 119.

40. Frankfort *et al.*, *The Intellectual Adventure of Ancient Man*, p. 7.

41. *Ibid.*, p. 6.

42. For a detailed study of the Semitic concept of mystery, cf. Raymond Brown, "The Pre-Christian Semitic Concept of 'Mystery,' " *Catholic Biblical Quarterly*, Vol. 20, No. 4 (1958), pp. 417-443. The article is continued in *Biblica*, Vols. 39 and 40.

43. Mircea Eliade, *Myth and Reality* (New York: Harper and Row, 1963), pp. 5-6.

44. *Ibid.* Also, for a treatment of myth in the contemporary world, cf. Andrew M. Greeley, "Myths, Symbols and Rituals in the Modern World," *The Critic*, Vol. 20, No. 3 (Dec. 1961—Jan. 1962).

45. Frankfort *et al.*, *The Intellectual Adventure of Ancient Man*, pp. 3-26.

46. Jung, *Symbols of Transformation*, pp. 171ff.

47. *Ibid.*, p. 232.

48. *Ibid.*, p. 233.

49. *Ibid.*

50. *Ibid.*

51. *Ibid.*

52. *Ibid.*, p. 225.

53. *Ibid.*

54. *Ibid.*, p. 226.

55. For greater detail, see Brevard S. Childs, *Myth and Reality in The Old Testament*, Vol. 27 of *Studies in Biblical Theology* (London: S.C.M. Press), and Ian Henderson, *Myth in the New Testament*, Vol. 7 of *Studies in Biblical Theology* (London: S.C.M. Press, 1952).

56. Cf. H. W. Bartsch (ed.) and R. H. Fuller (tr.), *Kerygma and Myth* (London: Society for the Promotion of Christian Knowledge, 1953), pp. 1-44.

57. Cf. Macquarrie, *Principles of Christian Theology*, pp. 122ff.

58. Cf. Susanne K. Langer, *Philosophy in a New Key* (Cambridge: Harvard University Press, 1971), pp. 139ff.

59. Roland DeVaux, *Studies in Old Testament Sacrifice* (Cardiff: University of Wales Press, 1964), p. 9.

60. *Ibid.*

61. *Ibid.* Cf. the similar texts of Psalm 34:21 and Psalm 31:11, Lamentations 3:4, and the vision of dry bones revivified in Ezekiel 37.

62. Carl G. Jung, *Psychology and Religion: West and East* (Princeton: Princeton University Press, 1958), p. 205.

63. *Ibid.*

64. DeVaux, *Studies in Old Testament Sacrifice*, p. 27.

65. In his *Symbolism and Belief* (Port Washington: Kennikat Press, 1968), Edwyn Bevan presents an extensive treatment of the symbol of light; cf. pp. 125-151.

66. *Ibid.*, p. 128.

67. Mircea Eliade, *Images and Symbols* (New York: Sheed and Ward, 1969), p. 110.

68. *Ibid.*, p. 113.

69. Bevan, *Symbolism and Belief*, p. 30.

70. Eugene McAlee, "Marriage in the New Testament," *A Theological Symposium on Christian Marriage* (unpublished) (Washington, D.C., 1966).

CITED AND CONSULTED WORKS

Aaron, Richard I. *Knowing and the Function of Reason*. London: Oxford University Press, 1971.

Abbott, Walter (ed.). *The Documents of Vatican II*. New York: Herder and Herder, 1966.

Anderson, Bernhard. *Rediscovering the Bible*. New York: Asociation Press, 1951.

_____. *The Unfolding Drama of the Bible*. New York: Association Press, 1953.

_____. *Understanding the Old Testament*. Englewood Clifs, N.J.: Prentice Hall, 1966.

Aulén, Gustaf. *Christus Victor*. New York: Macmillan Publishing Company, 1969.

Babin, Pierre. *Faith and the Adolescent*. New York: Herder and Herder, 1965.

Bartsch, H. W. (ed.) and Fuller, R. H. (tr.), *Kerygma and Myth*. London: Society for the Promotion of Christian Knowledge, 1953.

Berkovits, Eliezer. *God, Man and History, A Jewish Interpretation*. New York: Jonathan David Publishers, 1965.

Bevan, Edwyn. *Symbolism and Belief*. Port Washington: Kennikat Press, 1968.

Bittle, Celestine N. *The Whole Man*. Milwaukee: The Bruce Publishing Co., 1945.

Boman, Thorleif. *Hebrew Thought Compared with Greek*. Philadelphia: The Westminster Press, 1960.

Bronfenbrenner, Urie. *Two Worlds of Childhood*. New York: Russell Sage Foundation, 1970.

Brown, Raymond. "The Pre-Christian Semitic Concept of 'Mystery.' " *The Catholic Biblical Quarterly* 20 (1958), pp. 417-443.

Childs, Brevard S. *Myth and Reality in the Old Testament*. London: SCM Press, 1960.

Cirne-Lima, Carlos. *Personal Faith*. New York: Herder and Herder, 1965.

De Lubac, Henri. *The Church: Paradox and Mystery*. Staten Island: Alba House Publications, 1969.

Dentan, Robert C. *The Knowledge of God in Ancient Israel*. New York: The Seabury Press, 1968.

Denzinger, Bannwart. *Enchiridion Symbolorum*.

DeVaux, Roland. *Studies in Old Testament Sacrifice*. Cardiff: University of Wales Press, 1964

Duquoc, Christian. *The Concrete Christian Life*. New York: Herder and Herder, 1971.

Durrwell, F. X. *The Resurrection*. New York: Sheed and Ward, 1960.

Eliade, Mircea. *Patterns in Comparative Religion.* New York: The World Publishing Company, 1970.

————. *Myth and Reality.* New York and Evanston: Harper and Row Publishers, 1963.

————. *Images and Symbols.* New York: Sheed and Ward, 1969.

Frankfort, H. and H. A., John A. Wilson, Thorkild Jacobsen, and William A. Irwin. *The Intellectual Adventure of Ancient Man.* Chicago: The University of Chicago Press, 1946.

Frederick, Harriet E. *The Meaning of Abstract Concepts to Deaf and Hearing Children* (unpublished doctoral thesis): University of Illinois, 1965.

Friend, William and Eugene Hemrick. *Catholic Education in St. Louis: A Study of Religious Understandings, Archdiocese of St. Louis.* Notre Dame, Indiana: The University of Notre Dame Press, 1970.

Fries, Heinrich. *Faith Under Challenge.* New York: Herder and Herder, 1969.

Fromm, Erich. *The Art of Loving.* New York: Harper Colophon Books, 1956.

Furth, Hans. *Piaget for Teachers.* Englewood Cliffs, N.J.: Prentice-Hall, 1970.

General Catechetical Directory. Washington, D.C.: United States Catholic Conference, 1971.

Goldman, Ronald. *Religious Thinking from Childhood to Adolescence.* New York: The Seabury Press, 1964.

Goodenough, Erwin R. *Jewish Symbols in the Greco-Roman Period.* Vol 5. New York: Pantheon Books, 1956.

Graebner, Oliver E. "God-Concepts of Deaf Children." Mimeographed. Valparaiso, Indiana: Valparaiso University, 1965.

Greeley, Andrew M. "Myth, Symbols and Rituals in the Modern World," *The Critic,* Vol. 20, No. 3., Dec. 1961—Jan. 1962.

Gunderson, Arthur N. *A Linguistic Analysis of the Written Language of the Deaf* (Ph.D. dissertation). Northwestern University, 1965.

Hartman, Louis F. *Encyclopedic Dictionary of the Bible.* New York: McGraw-Hill Book Company, 1963.

Henderson, Ian. *Myth in the New Testament.* London: SCM Press, 1952.

Hofinger, Johannes and Theodore C. Stone. *Pastoral Catechetics.* Montreal: Palm Publishers, 1964.

Holmes, Urban T. *Young Children and the Eucharist.* New York: The Seabury Press, 1972.

Jeremias, Joachim. *The Central Message of the New Testament.* New York: Charles Scribner's Sons, 1965.

Jung, Carl G. *Symbols of Transformation.* Bollingen Series No. 5. Princeton: Princeton University Press, 1956.

————. *Psychology and Religion: West and East.* Bollingen Series No. 11. Princeton: Princeton University Press, 1958.

Jungmann, Joseph A. *Handing on the Faith*. New York: Herder and Herder, 1964.

Jurgens, W. A. (ed. and tr.). *The Faith of the Early Fathers*. Collegeville: The Liturgical Press, 1970.

Key 73 Congregational Resource Book. St. Louis: Concordia Publishing House, 1972.

Knox, John. *Myth and Truth*. Charlottesville: The University Press of Virginia, 1964.

Langer, Susanne K. *Philosophy in a New Key*. Cambridge: Harvard University Press, 1971.

Lauterbach, Jacob (crit. ed. and trans.). *Mekilta de Rabbi Ishmael*, Vol. 2. Philadelphia: The Jewish Publication Society of America, 1933.

Levine, Edna and Arthur Jillette, editors, "Interfaith Institute of Denominational Workers with the Deaf." *American Annals of the Deaf* 113 (1968), pp. 886-983.

Lewis, C. S. *Miracles*. New York: The Macmillan Company, 1966.

Liégé, P. A. *What Is Christian Life?* New York: Hawthorn Books, 1961.

Macquarrie, John. *Principles of Christian Theology*. New York: Charles Scribner's Sons, 1966.

Maritain, Jacques. *The Degrees of Knowledge*. New York: Charles Scribner's Sons, 1959.

Mascall, E. L. *Words and Images: A Study in Theological Discourse*. London: Libra Books, 1957.

McAlee, Eugene. "Marriage in the New Testament," *A Theological Symposium on Christian Marriage* (unpub.), Wash., D.C., 1966.

McNemar, Quinn. *Psychological Statistics*. New York: John Wiley and Sons, Inc., 1969.

Meadow, Kathryn P. and Hilde S. Schlesinger. *Sound and Sign*. Berkeley: The University of California Press, 1972.

Minear, Paul S. *Eyes of Faith, A Study in the Biblical Point of View*. Philadelphia: The Westminster Press, 1946.

Mouroux, Jean. *I Believe*. New York: Sheed and Ward, 1959.

Nebreda, Alfonso M. *Kerygma in Crisis?* Chicago: Loyola University Press, 1965.

Nightingale, Earl, "On Motivating the Disadvantaged Child," *Vital Speeches of the Day*, Vol. XXXIII, 1966.

O'Neill, Reginald F. *Readings in Epistemology*. Englewood Cliffs, N.J.: Prentice-Hall, 1962.

Oppenheim, A. Leo, *Ancient Mesopotamia, Portrait of a Dead Civilization*. Chicago: The University Press, 1964.

Owen, H. P. *Concepts of Deity*. New York: Herder and Herder, 1971.

Pannenberg, Wolfhart. *Basic Questions in Theology*, Vol. 2. Philadelphia: Fortress Press, 1971.

_____. *Jesus—God and Man*. Philadelphia: The Westminster Press, 1968.

Pritchard, James T. (ed.). *Ancient Near East Texts*. Princeton: Princeton University Press, 1950.

Rahner, Karl. *Do You Believe in God?* Paramus, N.J.: Newman Press, 1969.

_____. *Theological Investigations*, Vol. 1. Baltimore: Helicon Press, 1959.

Ramsey, Paul. "Christianity and Society," Volume VIII, 1943.

Reith, Herman. *An Introduction to Philosophical Psychology*. Englewood Cliffs, N.J.: Prentice-Hall, 1956.

Rood, Wayne R. *The Art of Teaching Christianity*. Nashville: Abingdon Press, 1968.

Röper, Anita. *The Anonymous Christian*. New York: Sheed ad Ward, 1966.

St. Augustine. *Confessions*, Book 7 Chapter 10, trans. by Vernon J. Bourke. *The Fathers of the Church*, Vol. 21. New York: The Fathers of the Church Incorporated, 1953.

_____. *On the Trinity*, trans. by Rev. Arthur West Haddan. *Nicene and Post-Nicene Fathers of the Christian Church*, Vol. III. New York: Charles Scribner's Sons, 1900.

Schmaus, Michael. *The Essence of Christianity*. Dublin: Scepter Publishers, 1966.

Seligman, Ben (ed.). *Molders of Modern Thought*. Chicago: Quadrangle Books, 1970.

Sheets, J. R. "Personal and Liturgical Prayer," *Worship* 47 (1973), pp. 405-416.

The "Summa Theologica" of St. Thomas Aquinas, trans. by the Fathers of the English Dominican Province. London: Burns, Oates and Washbourne, Ltd., 1920.

Tresmontant, Claude. *A Study of Hebrew Thought*. New York: Desclee Company, 1960.

U.S. Department of Health, Education and Welfare. *International Research Seminar on the Vocational Rehabilitation of Deaf Persons*, proceedings (May 25-June 14, 1968), edited by Glenn T. Lloyd. Washington, D.C.: Social and Rehabilitation Service, 1968.

Van Riet, Georges. *Thomistic Epistemology*, Vols. I and II. St. Louis and London, 1963.

Vernon, McCay. "Relationship of Language to the Thinking Process," *Archives of General Psychiatry*, Vol. 16, 1967.

Weiss, Johannes. *Earliest Christianity*, 2 vols. New York: Harper and Brothers, 1959.

Winklhofer, Alois. *The Coming of His Kingdom*. New York: Herder and Herder, 1963.

Index

Correct image of God, importance of, 31

Council of Chalcedon, 8, 210

Covenant, 174, 193, 208

Creation, and belief, 61-63; and knowledge, 144; as on-going, 213; and providence, 62

Creatureliness, 213

Crucifixion, effects of, 193-194; imputability for, 89-90, 194; as a killing, 90-91; and literalism, 87-89; psychological processes of, 215; related observations on, 91-92, 95, 101; testing for, 28; vicarious nature of, 91, 194

Curricula, need of, 13, 211, 214

Dante, 111

Darkness, 102, 207

Daydreams, 198

Deafisms, 225

Deafness, definition of, 5; effects of, 13, 218-224; kinds of, 5

Death, 105-106, 196, 203

De Brebeuf, Saint John, 216

de Chardin, Teilhard, 32

Deification of people, 83, 121, 125, 126

Devil, 71, 110-112

Diagnostic inventory, purposes of, 14-15; reliability of, 51; validity of, 52-53

Dionysius, 103

Directed thinking, 198

Divine activity, kinds of, 114; as observation and intervention, 114-117

Ecumenism, 66

Egocentrism and prayer, 185

Eliade, Mircea, 201

Enki, 107, 114-115

Ennead of Atum, 153

Eos, 200

Eschatology, and after-life, 105-106; and the Church, 174; definition of, 8; and resurrection, 93; and second coming, 196-197

Eternity of God, and analogous timelessness, 156; control group's understanding of, 155; deaf adolescents' understanding of, 154-155; description of, 153; and person, 155; testing for, 38

Eucharist, control group's understanding of, 100-101; deaf adolescents' understanding of, 97-100; and drama, 102-103; and Greek mystery religions, 103; importance of, 15; and physical health, 100; and prayer, 184; as real presence, 97-98, 100, 127; related observations on, 101; testing for, 29

Evangelization, description of, 8, 77

Experimental centers, 211

Existential, 8, 16, 101, 112, 119, 162, 173, 196, 214-215

Faith, act of, 73, 191, 210; and immaturity, 76, 128, 133; personal, 71-72, 191; and sight, 69

Fear and God, 134-135, 137-138, 140

Fingerspelling, description of, 6

Food offerings, 207

Forgiveness, and after-life, 112; and Eucharist, 98; and fear, 138; testing for, 47

Formal operational thinking, 31, 70, 199

Frankfort, Henri, 201-202

Fraternal love, and Church, 174; and community, 174; and Jesus, 127; testing for, 46

Fries, Heinrich, 71

Genuflections in church, 170-171

Gilgamesh, as hero, 202; and life, 107, 124

Ginott, Haim, 70

God, attributes of, see individual listings; as celestial being, 119, 130, 158-159, 175; control group's understanding of, 85 (see related listings); deaf adolescents' understanding of, 79-84 (see Anthropomorphism and related listings); and death, 154; as identified by control group, 85; as life-giver, 41; locale of 113; as person, 80, 155; and physical hearing, 143, 177; reality of, 32, 126-127; as a relational being, 165; sexuality of, 80; as spirit, 93, 126; understood as less than Trinity, 79

God the Father, deaf adolescents' understanding of, 79-80, 113; and Jesus, 80-81, 126; and Saint Joseph,

81, 84; and Judaism, 129, 194; and names, 155; prayer to, 176
Golding, William, 215
Goldman, Ronald, 198
Gospel, as criteria, 174; of John, 69; of Mark, 193

Heaven, 108-109, 122, 158
Hebrews and the deaf, 80, 121-123, 129, 143, 152, 161-162
Height, 208
Helios, 200
Hell, 110-112
Hellenism, 8

Idea formation, 217-219
Idols, 214-215
Immanence, 117-120, 132-133, 146-147, 156-157, 161, 163, 175, 185
Immortality and plants, 162
Immunized Christian, 76-77
Incarnation, 192
Intellect and psyche, 70-71
Interview Form, 51-54 (*see* Appendix)

Jeremias, Joachim, 173
Jesus, contemporary presence of, 39, 95-96; deaf adolescents' understanding of, 79-82, 92, 96; in Gospel of Mark, 193; and knowledge, 144; as "light," 206; manhood of, 210-211; and power, 150-151; as proof of God's love, 133; second coming of, 196-197; as Son of God, 82-83, 114, 126, 195-196
Joseph, Saint, *see* God the Father
Jung, Carl G., 198, 204-205
Jungmann, Joseph A., 72
Justice of God, description of, 136-137, 139, 141; testing for, 35
Justification, 173, 186, 193
Justin, Saint, 155

Killing of Jesus, 90
Knowledge of God, as causative, 146; control group's understanding of, 146; deaf adolescents' understanding of, 143-145; description of, 141-142; limitations of, 132, 142-146, 181; as personal, 145-146; and providence, 147; and sign language, 148, 181; testing for, 36; and transcendence, 146-147; as visual, 132, 143-145, 147, 169, 177

Language deficiency, 74, 91, 161, 183, 198, 225-226
Life after death, control group's understanding of, 107-108; deaf adolescents' understanding of, 106
Light, 102, 206-207
Literalism, 86-88, 91, 97, 101, 110, 122, 178-180, 199, 214
Loneliness, 156
Love of God, as basis of prayer, 177; control group's understanding of, 131-132; deaf adolescents' understanding of, 127-133, 191-192; for hearing people, 132; and related factors, 132-133; as universal, 175
Loyola, Saint Ignatius, 185

Macquarrie, John, 156, 199, 201
Marduk, 201
Mass, 101, 159, 166-167
Mekilta de Rabbi Ishmael, 121-122
Metaphors, of Church, 172
Miracles, contemporary, 67
Mishna, 121
Mother Teresa (of Calcutta), 174
Mouroux, Jean, 71
Mystery, 68, 153, 172, 202, 210
Myth, and anthropomorphism, 202; and communicating Christ, 202-203; and demythologizing, 204; description of, 200-201; and literalism, 199-200; literary form of, 153, 200-201; and objective reality, 200-201; in Old and New Testaments, 204; origin of, 198; and reflective thought, 199

Names and eternity, 155
Nativity, 27, 82
Natural theology, 70
Ndyambi, 153
Nebreda, Alfonso, 71
Nicodemus, 203-204
Non-directed thinking, 198

Pacific Islanders, beliefs of, 110
Pannenberg, Wolfhart, 81
Pantheism, 32, 124-126
Parables and the deaf, 86
Parental love, 130, 186
Peer models, 75-76, 212
Person and God, 80, 155, 161-162, 185, 192

Personal interview method, advantages of, 18; and deaf adults, 22; initial design of, 20-21; meaning of, 21
Pharisee and tax collector, 173
Physical body, 151
Piaget, Jean, 24, 31, 70, 198-199
Plants, 102, 107, 114, 159, 162
Polynesian beliefs, 110
Positivism, 67-68, 72, 96, 101-102, 210
Power of God, control group's understanding of, 149, 152; deaf adolescents' understanding of, 149, 152; description of, 148; and goodness, 152; importance of, 149, 152; as limited, 133, 149, 151-152; and mystery, 152; testing for, 37
Prayer, answers to, 44, 178-180; and clichés, 175, 184; as communication, 175, 184, 213; and divine power, 176; frequency of, 182; as outgrown, 182; reasons for, 176-177, 182; testing for, 44-45
Prayer of the deaf, God's knowledge of, 148, 177; prerequisites for, 173, 186; and strength, 152, 176
Pre-evangelization, description of, 9, 75-77; and schools, 76, 212
Presence of God, in churches, 158-162; in cities, 159-162; control group's understanding of, 160; deaf adolescents' understanding of, 157-159; description of, 156-157; on farms, 159-162; in man, 159-160, 163; and prayer, 184-185; in temple cult, 162, 164; testing for, 40
Pre-testing, 19
Proof, demand for, 26, 130-131; kinds desired, 66-67, 70, 99, 137-138, 160; and physical sight, see Sight, physical
Providence, deaf adolescents' understanding of, 115, 118-119, 147, 152; and eternity, 155; and Hebrews, 119, 148; and Jesus, 120; and prayer, 176
Psychology and conversion, 74-75
Puluga, 143
Punishment and God, control group's understanding of, 139-140; deaf adolescents' understanding of, 136-138; testing for, 35

Ramsey, Paul, 71
Rebirth, 203-204
Redemption and seeds, 162
Reincarnation, 106
Religious language, 87, 91, 101, 105, 107, 111, 121, 123, 153, 161, 172-173, 178, 184, 192-193, 213-214
Residential schools, and pre-evangelization, 75-76
Resurrection, deaf adolescents' understanding of, 92-95; in earliest Christianity, 194-195; percentages on, 92; related observations on, 92-93; testing for, 29
Revelation and divine visitations, 62
Röper, Anita, 77
Ruwa, 152

Sacraments in general, 97, 174, 203, 208-209, 215-216
Saints, role of, 191, 212
Sample, age level of, 24; size of, 16, 25
Seeing and believing, 69, 136
Sermon on Mount, 174
Sight, physical, 66-69, 95, 99, 106, 109-110, 114-117, 130-131, 136-138, 143-145, 147, 160, 169, 177, 183, 210 (see also Statistical Charts, Question 2c)
Siglish, 5, 192
Sign language, God's knowledge of, 148, 181, 183-184
Sin, 196
Sky gods, 119, 143, 146, 175, 191, 208
Smoke, 207
Soteriology, 9, 90, 196, 214-215
Spirit, deaf adolescents' understanding of, 93, 96, 106-107, 114, 151, 154, 176
Statistical significance, 53
Statistical tables, see Appendix
Statistical validity, 52-53
Stones, 102
Strict oralism, 6
Survey Form for School, 227-228
Survey Form for the Religion Teacher, 227
Symbol, and literalism, 206; meaning of, 206; amd metaphor, 206
Symbol, conventional, 102

Symbol, intrinsic, 102, 162; examples of, 206; importance of, 208
Symbolism, 98, 101-102, 104

Theoretical knowledge, insufficiency of, 71
Thought processes, *see* Directed thinking, Non-Directed thinking, Concrete operational thinking and Formal operational thinking
Time, 155-156, 194, 196
Total communication, 5, 17, 211
Transcendence, 117-119, 125, 132, 146-147, 156-157, 161-162, 181, 184
Trees, and the cross, 203; of life and death, 203; religious meaning of, 124; as symbol, 206

Trust in God, 30, 72, 152; *see also* Living faith

Unbelief and doubt, basis of, 65-66
Unmusical scientist, 68

Verbalism, 5, 104, 158
Virgin Mary, and God, 28, 32, 80-81, 83-84, 124
Visitations, divine, 62
Vultures, myth of, 203-204

Water, 203, 206, 208
Weak deities, 152-153
Weil, Simone, 133
Wine, 102-103

Yates Correction Factor, 54-57